CASH FLOW PRESCRIPTION

A BUSY PHYSICIAN'S GUIDE TO GENERATING PASSIVE INCOME

CASH FLOW PRESCRIPTION

DANNY BRAMER, M.D.

MERACK

Published and distributed by Merack Publishing

San Diego, USA
www.merackpublishing.com

Library of Congress Control Number: 2024909227
Bramer, Danny
Cash Flow Prescription

978-1-949635-71-3 eBook

978-1-949635-79-9 Hardcover

978-1-949635-32-4 Paperback

To God, my wife, and my kids. They stood by me, encouraged me, and lifted my arms when I couldn't do it myself.

CONTENTS

PREFACE 1

INTRODUCTION 5

PART ONE 17

CHAPTER ONE
The Five Pillars of Financial Freedom 19

CHAPTER TWO
Change Your Mind, Change Your Life 37

CHAPTER THREE
Debunking Your Mindset Myths 49

CHAPTER FOUR
Managing Other People's Mindsets 73

CHAPTER FIVE
Pillar Two: Learning 79

CHAPTER SIX
Use Your Network to Raise Your Average 99

CHAPTER SEVEN
Build Your Network and the Deals Will Come 107

CHAPTER EIGHT
Moving Forward and Getting in the Game 121

PART TWO 131

RESOURCE GUIDE 133

INVESTING SECTION OUTLINE 145

CONCLUSION 355

GLOSSARY OF KEY TERMS & CONCEPTS 359

ENDNOTES 371

ABOUT THE AUTHOR 383

PREFACE

It was a Sunday in 2013 when I called my business partner to tell him I didn't feel safe to work that day.

We ran a successful anesthesiology practice, but my vision was deteriorating to the point where I was now questioning my ability to safely perform the essentials of my job. I had no idea when I made that phone call that my last procedure had already taken place and I would never practice clinical anesthesia again.

Many months before that life-changing moment, I'd been at home balancing my checkbook when I noticed a "floater" in my left eye. I tried blinking it away several times, but it was persistent. The symptoms progressed rapidly over the next few days. Within twenty-four hours of symptom onset, I had completely lost vision in my left eye. I had nausea, dizziness, and vertigo. Something was seriously wrong.

The next several months were a blur of medical treatments and a search for a diagnosis. First, I thought I might have a brain tumor, then maybe multiple sclerosis. In fact, I ended up undergoing multiple sclerosis therapy for months, and still my vision continued to deteriorate—only now, it was affecting both eyes. This is an exceedingly unusual presentation for MS, so an ophthalmologist colleague of mine suggested I see her mentor, who dealt with very rare visual diseases. When the correct diagnosis finally came, it was a rare autoimmune disease. It was progressive, and it was incurable. Fortunately, it was only going to affect my vision—but in a profession that heavily relies on one's use of sight, that also spelled the end of my clinical medical career.

The diagnosis was a serious crisis for me and my family.

I had joined a successful anesthesiology practice in the beautiful state of Alaska where I had relocated my family from Kentucky. The move made it possible for my wife, Jeanne, to take a pause in her own career as a physician to stay home with our four young kids. After all the years and financial demands of getting two medical careers established, we were finally enjoying our life. Just as it seemed we were reaping the fruits of our labor, it all came crashing down. Jeanne and I were both terrified my condition would take away my ability to provide financially for our family. Although I had other investments, we were still dependent primarily on my physician income.

Long before anything happened with my vision and before we relocated to Alaska, Jeanne and I realized the way we were managing our lives in Kentucky was just not tenable. I was finishing up residency, and Jeanne was already a practicing OB/GYN. We were both working close to a hundred hours a week. We were really in a bind because we felt trapped by the lie we had bought into. We believed we "deserved" this or we "deserved" that because we had delayed gratification so much through medical school and residency. We bought *the* big house. We bought *the* nice cars.

On the side, I was making a go of it in the thoroughbred business with a second farm we'd bought, but I was spreading myself way too thin. I didn't have any free time at all. I would come home exhausted from being on call and miss my kids going to school. I kept telling myself, *That's just how residency is. It's only temporary.* But I knew unless we changed something dramatically, our life was on a trajectory that didn't prioritize our family. We had four awesome kids, but we had nannies and babysitters raising them. Now don't get me wrong, we considered our nannies part of our family. But we realized that's not why God gave us four kids. He gave them to us for *us* to raise.

Around that time, our church held a series on priorities and it sparked excellent discussions between Jeanne and me. One night, as we were talking about our life and our choices, and praying about what our next steps should be, I received an email about a job in Alaska. We both laughed it off, but there was a gnawing feeling the next day that prompted me to open the email and read it again. I called the lead partner and we talked for forty-five minutes. By the end of the conversation, I knew Jeanne and I needed to fly up there and see about this position.

Alaska was the beginning of the reset button in our life. We decided to change our lives, get out of the debt cycle, and let me work while Jeanne stayed home and prioritized the kids for a couple of years. We started aggressively paying down debt and, even though we owed a lot of money at the time, we made a decision to be generous first because God had been so generous to us. He gives us grace and mercy unending every day, and that was our motivation to be generous with our finances.

The position in Alaska was a great opportunity, and we were able to grow closer as a family. It felt like we were starting to make the important things important. Life was really, really good.

Then I started having issues with my vision.

INTRODUCTION

I've been where many of you are.

I was stuck in that busy physician role, in a two-earner household, with little autonomy. I was trading time for money, and still spiraling deeper and deeper into debt.

I constantly see young doctors graduating from medical school, and even more "seasoned" physicians, following the same patterns Jeanne and I did. So many physicians have hundreds of thousands of dollars of student loan debt. But being a physician comes with a certain level of prestige. Because you're a physician, you're expected to buy that first house—and it's supposed to be a big house—and you're supposed to get a nice car and you're "supposed to" do this and "supposed to" do that. You end up spending money you don't have and using any extra you do have to pay off debt, making it virtually impossible to get out of the debt spiral. It seems as though the only way out is to work more hours—to trade more of your time for money—and so it continues endlessly. No wonder physicians are burning out at record rates!

I want to see physicians stay in practice longer. None of us went into medicine for the money. Most of us went into medicine because we truly do have a calling to serve others. I've always loved the motto of Alpha Omega Alpha, "Worthy to serve the suffering," as I think it encapsulates how serving others is truly an honor. But let's be honest: the profession doesn't attract the same awe today that it did years ago.

After med school and residency, reality hits. The debt cycle pulls us in. Most of us become employees rather than entrepreneurs. Most of us are losing autonomy because medicine is being managed more and more like a business rather than a calling. Sure, many hospitals are non-profit, but so was the NFL until recently. "Non-profit" doesn't necessarily mean an organization is mission-oriented or patient-centered. We now carry record patient loads. If we have our own practices, we experience consistently declining reimbursements and relentlessly increasing bureaucracy, not to mention the pressures of treating patients in these unprecedented conditions. No amount of money can mitigate the risk of burnout and prevent physicians from leaving the practice of medicine—often forever. Burnout is as malignant as a catastrophic life event, maybe even worse. You're still walking, talking, doing all the things you did before, but you're a miserable human being to be around.

Given the chance to become financially independent, to free ourselves from the debt cycle, to stop trading our time for money, and to practice on our own terms, I think many of us would continue practicing for longer.

Maybe you are interested in investing to supplement your physician income, but throughout this book, I hope to convince you that investing in assets that cash flow can actually *replace* your income completely so you have true financial freedom and can choose to work versus needing to.

And it's not just replacing your income that pays the "regular" bills that I'm talking about. I will help you navigate and break free of the big life events that often keep us stuck in the trading time for money cycle, too. If you have a young adult going to college anytime soon, for example, let's assume it might cost you $35,000 per year. I'll show you how to invest in an asset that gives you $35,000 a year in cash to pay for their education and then will *still be a cash-flowing asset even after they graduate.* Compare this strategy for achieving financial freedom with putting aside money in a 529 plan that you suck dry until it's gone, and once it's gone, it's gone forever. It may come as a surprise to many people that an investment plan like this is doable, but it absolutely is. It's learnable. And if you're willing to learn, you'll eventually get back more time, make more money, and live a richer life than you ever thought possible.

When you generate reliable, steady income from your investments—which gives you the freedom to live life on your terms—you can decide how and when to pursue the practice of medicine. You can dedicate time to all of your other life goals like spending time with family, being generous, and pursuing your passions and your purpose.

MY STORY

Even before receiving an official diagnosis, my symptoms inspired me to research other career and business opportunities. I was desperate and looking for options. I went to a conference entitled "Non-Clinical Positions for Physicians," where I looked into becoming a Chief Medical Officer—among other things. At some point, though, I realized all these "jobs" could be taken away as well. As an employee, you're just one catastrophic life event away from financial devastation. So, being an employee wasn't the way I would achieve financial freedom for my family; I began to realize the only way to financial freedom was to be an owner. I decided that no job or circumstance was ever going to dictate my family's financial future again. But how would I accomplish this?

My first step was to research investments in various asset classes. I looked into oil and gas but decided that wasn't a path I wanted to pursue. I had seen some of my medical colleagues take a bath on an "investment" they were involved in. I looked into paper assets like stocks, bonds, mutual funds, and ETFs, but my dad—a homebuilder during the 1970s who lived a life of hard work and integrity—lost a large chunk of his savings in the stock market. *Twice.* That prospect wasn't appealing to me.

I started learning not just about how people truly create wealth for themselves and their families, but how people create *generational wealth.* I found that 90% or more of the wealthy—the top 1%—did it through real estate. They either got wealthy by investing in real estate or they used real estate to magnify their already-existing wealth.

I had a little experience in real estate on a small scale, and I came from a family of entrepreneurs. In addition to my dad (the contractor), one of my brothers has a successful landscaping company, another brother is a builder, and my sister has had successful business ventures ranging from sales publications to an ice cream distribution business. All my siblings and I have drive and a strong work ethic passed down to us by our parents. I helped pay for medical school by flipping a couple of houses and keeping some single-family rentals, so I knew firsthand how valuable cash-flowing real estate could be. The more I learned and the more I thought about it, the more real estate made sense.

"Economies of scale" is a term often used in multifamily real estate to describe the cost advantages that happen when you scale production and become more efficient, resulting in a decreased cost-per-unit. As I read real estate investing books and attended real estate conferences, I was trying to figure out how to scale my investments and create these economies of scale for myself and my family. I didn't want to be a landlord who was constantly hounded to fix the toilet and take out the trash; I wanted to make sure the properties were working *for me*, not the other way around.

On the way home from a mission trip in Nigeria, I stopped off in Kentucky to attend the wedding of a medical school buddy. Several guys from med school were groomsmen, one of whom was Matt. Matt was also a physician with an entrepreneurial background who already had a successful medical education company. I was jet-lagged and sleep-deprived, but somehow I was able to articulate what had been going on in my life with my vision issues and my quest for the perfect real estate play. Little did I know that Matt had already pieced together seventy-plus "doors" (real estate lingo for a single rental unit, but often used to describe apartment units), but he really wanted to jump into larger multifamily units. He was looking for a partner to combine forces and talent to take advantage of "economies of scale." There was that phrase again. We both understood the power behind that concept, and not long after the wedding, we decided to go into business together as real estate investors.

We recognized that we didn't know what we didn't know at that point, so Matt and I were determined to find someone who did know and have them teach us. Finding mentors was tough back then because there weren't a lot of well-structured programs. As physicians, we learned quite a bit in medical school, but residency is where we really honed our craft. We needed to find a real estate residency program.

We scoured the internet and found a group we were comfortable with after several conversations and interviews. We did our "real estate residency" with this group and learned everything they knew about multifamily investments and then took what we learned and developed our own business model buying multifamily properties.

Matt and I didn't have a lot of experience, but banks like to lend to physicians. Leveraging the background and the purchasing power we had, we got three different assets under contract with three different banks and closed them all within a very short time of each other. We went from owning nothing to buying 310 units practically overnight.

Fast forward fifteen months, and I had more than replaced my physician income with cash-flowing assets. We accelerated our five-year plan to the point that we achieved it in less than half the time.

It's hard to put into words the sense of relief, accomplishment, and excitement that surrounded that time in our lives. To seek the knowledge, make a plan, and execute it faster than I could have ever imagined? My wife and I were ecstatic and unbelievably excited about what this meant for the future of our family. I more than proved my concept that real estate was the way to true generational wealth—I was hooked! We quickly grew our multifamily holdings to over 800 units in the next two years.

Matt and I decided to expand our real estate holdings outside of multifamily, so we bought a boutique hotel, restaurant, and event center. Bringing that dead asset back to life was a heavy lift, but we learned a ton during the process. One thing I learned was diversification—even in real estate—made sense and could offer protection against different market cycles.

At this point, I decided to diversify into different subclasses of real estate and started with Single-Tenant Net Lease deals (Walgreens, Dollar General, dialysis centers) and then expanded into mobile home parks, single-family portfolios, vacation rentals and Airbnb's, real estate development, opportunity zones, RV parks, self-storage, mineral rights, land flipping, house flipping, shipping—the gamut. In more recent years, I've expanded into market instruments that provide a six-figure passive income: debt and equity investments I never dreamed I would have access to, and opportunities to purchase businesses that provide even further diversified, passive-revenue streams.

Once I replaced my physician income with investments that cash flowed, the change wasn't just financial. Our whole lives were transformed. It was an incredibly sweet time. Jeanne and I had already made the decision to be generous first, but now we could be *very* generous for the first time in our lives. We had the financial freedom to give our time, talents, and treasure to our church and to non-profits. We had time to really enjoy our kids. We were able to create a life centered around family and experiences, not obligations and work schedules. We were able to have super cool adventures together, and even explored all fifty states in the U.S. by the time our oldest went to college—traveling most of the states in an RV!

Once we committed to following the principles I will share throughout this book, we went from drowning in debt, working all the time, and having babysitters raise our kids, to living intentional lives of purpose and generosity.

You, too, can achieve this dream.

One of my hopes in writing this book is that the principles I share will enable physicians to continue practicing because there is a very real physician shortage. If I can help you unlock the Investable Universe, understand how to build a portfolio of assets that cash flow, and achieve financial freedom the way I did, you can keep practicing medicine because you *love it* and not because you *need* to trade your time for money.

THE CASH FLOW PRESCRIPTION

This book is split into two parts.

The first half (Part One) talks about the *why* and the *how* behind The Five Pillars of Financial Freedom. The rest of the book (Part Two) is a Resource Guide designed to provide valuable information that will help you decide *where* to invest your money.

In Part One, I will teach you about The Five Pillars of Financial Freedom that are the foundation of your investment practice:

- Mindset
- Learning
- Network
- Deal Flow
- Action

I will explain why mastering each of these pillars is key to mastering your financial destiny and why each of those components is critical to your success. I'll walk you through my journey to freedom, and then help you create a vision for your own.

One thing my loss of sight has taught me is that life is about more than packing my day with patients. I am more than my work. In the last few years, I have discovered that life is about family, fun, and generosity. In explaining my philosophy for how to live a good life, I will invite you to begin to imagine what your own ideal life looks like so you can create a powerful "Why" that will guide you as your own North Star throughout the journey.

Part Two is designed as a Resource Guide to explore the vast and exciting Investable Universe. My goal is to educate you on the myriad of investment options that can provide you with what I call "passively active" income. We'll look at a lot of different investment options, and I'll share what I love about each one, give you a few reasons why a person would invest in each vehicle, explore things to watch out for, show what a good deal looks like, and provide how-to's for taking action and moving forward. My goal in Part Two is to give you enough information to whet your appetite about a particular investment vehicle to determine if it feels like something you'd like to explore further. Seeing what piques your interest and which options resonate will help you narrow the playing field and give you a direction to head when taking action and getting into the practice of doing deals.

You can read this part like a "choose your own adventure" book, and it doesn't need to be read sequentially. For instance, when you learn of an interesting single-family home investment opportunity, turn to the pages that provide background information, tips, and suggestions on single-family homes. If you hear someone talking about mineral rights and need a CliffsNotes guide to get you started in understanding them, flip to that section.

While you could read the chapters of this book in any order, you'll get the most out of this book by reading the chapters in Part One first—in sequence. That's because the pillars are like a prescription, and the knowledge you'll gain will build on itself. After following this prescription, my hope is that you will have the confidence to change your relationship with money, achieve financial freedom, take your time back, and pursue a purpose-driven life.

You've been through this process before! (And you can do it again.)

As doctors, we've been highly educated. We earned undergraduate degrees, being mindful of the prereqs every medical student needs before they can take the MCAT. If we marry this process with the process of becoming an investor, your undergraduate degree is akin to all of the financial learning you've done thus far, and your life experience on wealth. Essentially, you've been gaining specific prereqs!

Everybody has some type of financial background (just like as physicians we all have an undergraduate degree), so we each have some frame of reference upon which we are building our financial knowledge. As we didn't stop with an undergrad degree and went on to med school, it involved elevating our education. Financial literacy is much the same: basics will get you to a general level of competence, but in order to achieve financial freedom and become an expert investor, you'll need to uplevel your education.

Learning is a foundational pillar, one which we—as doctors—are intimately familiar with. We know that learning needs to occur within a community of peers and with a knowledgeable mentor. This is your network. Trying to understand the Investable Universe is not unlike trying to tackle the MCATs for the first time: you need to work hard, be diligent, and cultivate a support team.

Just as we choose specialties when we apply for residency, you will eventually find your niche in investing, whether it be mobile home parks, multifamily, or something else. Your network here is crucial. In residency, you work closely with colleagues and attending physicians in order for the patient's condition to improve. In investing, you need mentors and a network of like-minded investors in order for your financial situation to improve.

Most physicians are self-motivated learners, or we wouldn't be where we are. While we were undoubtedly self-motivated during our education, it didn't preclude the deep need that still existed for sage physicians to direct us in our learning. For most of us, that was our residency director. He or she gave us the right books, invested time in us, and pointed us in the right educational direction. We were expected to work, but we were also there to learn. Throughout this book, you can think of me as your Investing Residency Director. I am here to provide you with the tools and the knowledge to succeed. I will help you gain knowledge in this space, obtain coveted access to resources, and give you tools to build out your team as you start this journey.

I wish I'd had these concepts at the beginning of my own investing career, but I didn't. The Five Pillars of Financial Freedom developed out of my personal journey and emerged as the result of my own learning. With this book, you're gaining access to my experience. You're learning from the years I've spent in the weeds and mud, so I can save you from making the mistakes I've made and the struggles I've had to overcome. I'll share insights into the sophisticated network I've developed, along with the deal flow that comes with it. I am unique in the fact I am a physician who went out and sought, acquired, hired, fired, operated, and exited in a lot of different deals. I have an unusual combination of real-world experience across a vast landscape of different investment vehicles—an encyclopedia *set* as opposed to just one volume. With this book, you are gaining the ability to fast-track your education and put your money to work smarter so you can be free sooner.

How soon?

When I meet people at conferences and share my story, I'm often asked how long it will take to achieve financial freedom. It's different for everybody. Just as we actively practice our skills in residency, we need to take action in investing and get in the game to put our education to work in the real world. "Practicing" medicine is a verb. By definition, practicing doesn't mean that you're stagnant. It means you are always growing, always learning, always continuing forward. The most important thing is to take a step. We tell our kids all the time, "When you're afraid, just take a step." Take one step, and then take another step, and then take another step. Before you know it, you're walking toward financial freedom! It may not be in fifteen months like it was for me, as it depends on how much time you put into it. But if you choose to follow The Five Pillars, I feel confident I can drastically compress time in your journey to financial freedom.

Speaking of time, if you're wondering where you'll find the time to do all of this inside your already busy schedule, later in the book I will share a tool that will help you examine where you're spending your time and how to reprioritize your financial autonomy. Additionally, I will give you actionable guidance on taking the next steps to generate steady, reliable, passively active income that can replace and exceed your physician income. I want you to stop trading time for money, achieve financial freedom, and live a life of purpose on your terms.

If you take one thing away from this book, I hope it is this:

You can (and should) start investing now.

Thank you for choosing me to be your guide on this adventure. It really is an honor and a privilege to be able to pay forward my experience to help you break free of the trading time for money cycle and achieve true financial freedom.

Danny Bramer

PART ONE

THE FIVE PILLARS OF FINANCIAL FREEDOM

CHAPTER ONE

THE FIVE PILLARS OF FINANCIAL FREEDOM

As physicians, we've absorbed the Hippocratic Oath. It's woven into our belief system. We learn to analyze a situation over and over and over again before we make a decision because, above all else, we must not do harm. When we're working outside of medicine, that habit can lead to inertia and frustration. If we don't overcome this tendency, then we'll learn and learn and learn and do nothing with that knowledge. It's no wonder that, as physicians when beginning to invest, we often fall into frustration; logically we understand we need to act, but we just don't have the margin to actually go out and do it, and we end up right back where we started.

Outside of medicine, we need to become people with a bias toward action. While education and a certain level of caution are necessary, the bigger emphasis must be on taking steps forward. When I started investing many years ago, I went out and sought advisors and mentors in the space, and I learned what they did. I equate that stage of my education to residency: in medical school we learn a lot, but we don't really have any operational expertise. Residency is where we learn to hone our craft. Once we know our craft, we're able to go out and confidently treat patients. It's the same with investing: once you gain the skills, you're able to go out and do well.

Outside the medical field, most entrepreneurs aim to prove a concept before they start a new venture. Once they prove the concept, they know enough to jump in. In real estate investing, there are a lot of nice-to-knows, and there are also a lot of don't-need-to-knows out there. The main thing is to figure out the core things that you must know and then get in the game. As you learned in the introduction, I call the need-to-know concepts "The Five Pillars of Financial Freedom" (Mindset, Learning, Network, Deal Flow, and Action). By following the cash flow prescription contained in these concepts, I could more than replace my income as a physician and gain the financial independence I never thought possible. And I can't wait to teach them to you now, too!

In my coaching practice, I've worked with a sixty-seven-year-old, soon-to-be-retired physician. I've worked with a thirty-three-year-old who had just finished up a cardiac fellowship. People from every background—all different age groups, all different nationalities, men and women—are learning how to achieve the financial freedom to live life on their terms. These pillars are intended to get you thinking about your priorities and setting goals to get you where you want to be.

The Five Pillars of Financial Freedom were distilled from a list of about twenty-five different characteristics of powerful pathways to financial freedom. Through time, as well as trial and error, I have honed in on the most crucially important ones and synthesized it into only five pillars.

I have seen The Five Pillars work in my life and the lives of many others. It's a formula with a track record of proven success in my world. This is not an overnight success prescription, but a different way of thinking, learning, and living. This isn't the fad diet where you rebound and gain more weight than you lost. This is adopting an absolutely different lifestyle and keeping the weight, old baggage, or faulty ways of thinking off!

Each of The Five Pillars is equally important, however each one may become most important at a different time. For example, when you are just starting out, examining your mindset is crucial. Without a significant mindset change, you won't be able to break the cycle you currently find yourself in. You have to adopt a proper mindset in order to take the first step and set yourself up for success. Otherwise, the whole house of cards will come crashing down. As you get further along, once you are really honing your network and getting access to deal flow, then these pillars become more load-bearing.

The Five Pillars are not a checklist, per se. The process is much more cyclical. You might be months (or years) into your investments and then come across a deal in an asset class that seems lucrative but makes you nervous. At that point, you need to re-engage the learning pillar and become a student of this new opportunity. There is a constant ebb and flow between The Five Pillars, depending on the situations that arise.

Let's begin by taking a high-level overview of The Five Pillars. Then, we'll spend the rest of Part One diving into the details and essential learning of each individual pillar.

THE FIVE PILLARS

- Mindset
- Learning
- Network
- Deal Flow
- Action

PILLAR ONE: MINDSET

I grew up thinking you had to "work" for a living. There was value placed upon working with your hands. You had to have tangible products to show for your work. I couldn't understand how anyone could simply make transactions to earn money. Exploring this belief was the beginning of my mindset shift, that I could actually make money while I wasn't at "work."

Adopting the right mindset is so crucial it needs three full chapters in Part One—and I believe it's the most important of The Five Pillars to get right for long-term success without limits.

First, we'll explore the inherited and ingrown beliefs you have about money. Where do these beliefs come from? Are they true? Can you rewrite the script you have been telling yourself? Then, we'll take some action to reorient your mindset. By revealing the "mindset myths" that masquerade as common wisdom, I will deprogram you away from the myths that can keep us all trapped in the debt cycle and toward action that creates a virtuous cycle. Next, we will discuss the mindset of those around you. It has been said that we are influenced most by the five people we spend the most time with. But, what if your spouse, your family, your business partners don't share your financial views? How can you overcome this hurdle? Cultivating powerful relationships will definitely lead you down the right path—and we'll discuss this topic in depth.

Examining your mindset when it comes to money, debt, and wealth creation is crucial on the road to financial freedom. We have all inherited a belief system from our families and our lived experience. Some of these core beliefs are simply not true. Before you can find financial freedom, you need to debunk some of this limited thinking and explore your relationship with money, how you view possibilities in life, and how you approach the hurdles that will make or break you.

PILLAR TWO: LEARNING

I make it my goal to learn something from every conversation I have. No matter how far along you are in your journey in life, you always have something to learn from someone.

Investing is a high-stakes game. If you don't know the rules, you are setting yourself up for epic failure. With knowledge, however, comes power and opportunity. This book will point you in the right direction toward invaluable resources and people who will help you grow in competency and confidence.

PILLAR THREE: NETWORK

I've heard that our lives are ultimately about the dash between two dates: the date we're born and the date we die. Your net worth is all about the dash, about what you did in between. And your net worth isn't necessarily just financial; it is all you encompass.

Robert G. Allen is most often credited with the quote, "Your network is your net worth." Knowing the right people will help you elevate the potential that lingers in the dash. Knowing the right people will accelerate your trajectory toward financial freedom and personal fulfillment.

This book will define who you need to know and help you learn how to develop an empowering network of experts to supercharge your real estate investing results.

PILLAR FOUR: DEAL FLOW

The more deals you do, the more your network increases, and the more access you get to increased deal flow. It's a virtuous cycle. Doing a deal gets you on the radar of brokers, wholesalers, bankers, and other sellers. The wheel of fortune keeps spinning.

Money makes more money. Connections give birth to more connections.

This book will provide insight into the most lucrative deals and teach you how to create your own cycle of virtue.

PILLAR FIVE: ACTION

Achieving goals requires time, energy, and motivation—and the rewards of your effort can last for generations. Not unlike medical school, there needs to be a method to your action, and a thoughtful plan is required. You can't just jump in and figure it out later or you could get absolutely clobbered.

When you have a baseline of knowledge and business sophistication, the training wheels come off much faster.

This book will give you insight and confidence to take action. It will show you where to start and how to assess the risk involved so you can set yourself up for success, get in the game, let the "real" learning begin, and achieve your desired vision.

Before we dive into the Five Pillars of Financial Freedom individually, however, it is critically important for you to understand WHY you personally want to be financially free. What will it give you? Why does it matter? What life will it allow you to live?

FINDING YOUR "WHY"

Have you ever Googled the reasons people want to earn financial freedom? Try it.

I recently typed in "Why do people want to be rich?" and found two interesting op-eds.

One, written by an investor by the name of Daniel Ally, was titled *7 Reasons to Become a Millionaire:*

1. To make an impact
2. To inspire others
3. To gain control
4. For enjoyment
5. To find confidence
6. To engage in philanthropy
7. To enjoy the journey[1]

The other article, titled "Why You Should be Rich," was posted on Healthpreneur.com and listed only three reasons, but they definitely overlapped with Ally's seven.

1. You can help more people
2. It comes as a result of your personal growth
3. You can live a better life[2]

To me, the reasons stated above equate to living a purpose-driven life, which encompasses many things: enjoying time with family and friends; having the time, energy, and resources to give back to my community; engaging in hobbies; and traveling. While it's nice to have ample free time, I can become as bored as the next guy, so having a purpose-driven life also requires intention. From the moment I get up to the moment I go to sleep, I need to feel that my time and money are well spent.

MY PURPOSE-DRIVEN LIFE

FREEDOM

Noun

The power or right to act, speak, or think as one wants without hindrance.

The state of not being imprisoned or enslaved.

My own personal priorities—the filter my worldview is derived from—are *Faith*, *Family*, and *Freedom*. Applying The Five Pillars of Financial Freedom through the lens of these three priorities has afforded me the ability to really pursue my passions. Every investment I make needs to further these priorities in my life. It needs to allow me to be generous in my Faith. It needs to support my priority of Family, and allow me to intentionally curate our lives so we have experiences together. And it needs to provide Freedom—financial independence—which is what allows us to fulfill our individual and family dreams.

Over time I've realized that in order to feel like I'm living a life of purpose, some fundamentals must be in place within each of my three priorities of Faith, Family, and Freedom at a more concrete and tactical level. For me personally, these are: Generosity, Routine, Reflection, Leadership, and Vacation.

Let's take a look at each one.

GENEROSITY

Jeanne and I prioritize generosity. God has blessed us with good fortune and showers us every day with His grace and mercy. We are grateful and feel called to be generous with what we've been given to steward. Sure, we could buy a lot of nice stuff, but we choose experiences with family and generosity instead. My goal is to give away 90% of what I make. To do that and still keep the lights on, I need to generate quite a bit of income. So, each year, I make a percentage goal for giving and work to increase that percentage with each passing year. I've not yet hit my 90% goal, but I have increased my giving percentage every year since making the goal. We have been blessed to be a part of several organizations worthy of our funding. We regularly donate to missions that are working to reach the lost, the widowed, the orphaned, and the poor. We give to organizations that work with teenage moms, single parents, and people experiencing homelessness. We give generously to our church and are very involved in medical missions as well.

Being generous goes well beyond just stroking a check. We have all been given gifts and talents to share. We are each a tool, a vessel, and we should use our gifts to lift others up. We are not necessarily born as giving creatures. In fact, we are horribly selfish. Just refer to your average two-year-old when asked to share if you don't believe me. Being generous is modeled to us and we assimilate it by practice. The more we practice, the better we are at it.

I want my generosity to continue long after I am gone. For that reason, I make it a priority to model it for my kids so they can carry on what my father and mother instilled in me: be generous first.

ROUTINE

Time is precious, so I want to fill my time with things that matter. In this season of my life, that means focusing on being available for my family. If my kids have basketball or an art or drama event, those take priority. Balance is the most important thing, and I have intentionally built it into my daily routine.

Routines help me a lot. My mornings generally consist of devotion time and exercise. Then around 8 a.m., I begin my work day. I work on my active investments, respond to emails, and have investor meetings until early afternoon. The rest of the afternoon is spent cultivating investment opportunities and addressing outliers that are pressing. By early evening, I have the margin to spend time with my wife and kids doing what we want to do. Sometimes, things pop up that alter the routine, but having a routine is my attempt to ensure I maximize my most productive time windows and family time as well.

Because I value my time and know what it is worth, I want to maximize my hours in my zone of genius—which is finding great deals. This can be very time-consuming as I receive dozens of emails every day regarding potential investment opportunities. So, I created a triage system using a virtual assistant. My virtual assistant looks through my inbox and flags potential deals for me to check out based on my acquisition criteria. Out of approximately every hundred deals, my VA whittles it down to maybe twenty, and out of those I'll do a deep dive on three or four. Due to the many passions in my life and work, this system allows me to triage what needs my attention so I can be efficient and actively create more cash flow, all the while finding time to spend with my family.

In the exercise that follows, you'll learn how to calculate what your own time is worth to help you prioritize your life and activities in the most efficient way. Let it be a guide as you establish your own routine that works for you.

EXERCISE

What is your time worth?

Time is your most valuable asset. As you navigate all of the different pulls on your time—family, career, hobbies—it becomes important to triage where you put your focus and your energy.

Investing is no different. We know we need to invest money to make money. That's certain. But the questions become: Where do we invest actual dollars, and where do we invest our time to maximize return? How do we strike that balance? Where do the time and effort reap the biggest rewards?

I encourage you to spend some time reflecting on what your time is worth. When you know how much money your investments are making in relation to the time it takes from your busy schedule, you can use this basic information to determine the return on investment (ROI).

If you are in a season of your life where you have more money than time, maybe a more passive investment makes the most sense. You can utilize vetted sponsors for syndication investments or hire management companies and keep yourself at the 30,000-foot view level for personal investments. You have the luxury of not becoming involved in the day-to-day operations and simply collecting what I like to call "mailbox money"—returns that show up as checks in your mailbox without much hassle or headache.

If you have more time than money, however, maybe being more of an active investor can accelerate your path best to financial freedom. Youth and time are huge assets. If you don't have much money, a better investment might be one that you need to be fairly involved in—like flipping mobile homes, flipping houses, running Airbnbs, etc. These businesses can create wealth, but take more effort. When you hire someone to run them for you, you might make 10%-15% cash-on-cash. But if you choose to do it yourself, you can increase your return exponentially. It just depends on your current situation.

What will grow your wealth quicker?

Try this. Take the amount of gross income you brought in last year from your investments (we want to look at the number before taxes because your ultimate goal is to pay zero taxes). If you were working on investing two days a week, then use those numbers to determine what you made per hour over those two days.

This is a very powerful exercise because you might realize that for the time you worked on your investments, you actually made $500 per hour. This can be a huge reframing moment where you now think, Why am I wasting my time cutting my grass? My time is worth $500 per hour! I can pay someone else $40 an hour to mow my lawn and instead free up my time to find more investments.

This number will help you answer the question, Should I be doing this, or should I hire someone else to do this? In real estate and investing, your mindset eventually shifts from HOW can I get this done? to WHO can help me get this done?

If you aren't investing yet, do the same exercise with your W-2 income. Figure out what your time is worth and start paying others to take low-level activities off your plate so you can then focus on creating wealth through investing. Your time is valuable. Use it wisely!

> When you realize the exponential returns on your time investment and you can utilize your vast network of people to support your growth, you will understand that the life you truly want to lead is within your reach.

REFLECTION

In full disclosure, one thing that is not built into my routine is time to relax. I don't like to be idle. Relaxing is not my thing. (Maybe that's the Catholic guilt from childhood creeping up in me.) However, if I don't build in time for relaxation, opportunities for reflection are virtually impossible. I'm really trying to work on this aspect in my life.

How do I do this? First, I make myself put my phone away for one hour a day. This helps to give me the margin to relax and reflect daily. On Sundays, I try to put it away for the majority of the day and focus on spending time with my family.

One week a year, I sneak away into the wilderness with no phone or internet access. This helps me to center. I'm able to pray, reflect, and let my mind be flooded with thoughts of gratitude.

When I incorporate these practices, I find myself much more productive, creative, and generally a nicer person to be around.

Even though living out reflection as a value is still a work in progress for me, focusing on it and making it a priority in the small ways I'm doing now helps me keep it front and center and creates momentum that leads to more opportunities for me to grow personally, professionally, and spiritually.

LEADERSHIP

I want to make an impact and give back to others. I think the best way to lead is to serve others. Being a leader to me is equipping, empowering, and enabling others to achieve their goals and be better humans.

I wear a lot of leadership hats, but one of my favorites is facilitating a men's ministry group for my church. Having time with the men from my church and sharing life struggles and successes is an amazing bonding experience. It's mutually transforming, and it makes me a better leader. I always tell the groups I am with, "You might be ahead of me, beside me, or behind me on this walk, but we are all going to move forward together."

No matter what leadership position I'm in, my goal is to elevate those I'm working with. The best way I've found to do this is to understand what their needs are and what roadblocks stand in the way to success. Together, we systematically meet the needs and remove the roadblocks. I've found this to be a great recipe for becoming an effective servant leader. It's a pretty simple recipe for producing amazing humans. By serving and adding value to those around you, you generally see value come back around to you as well.

Looking for ways to become a better leader, both of others and in my own life, is an important practice I'm committed to living daily.

VACATION

Oddly enough, vacation throws me off. It hurls me out of one of my other fundamentals: routine. But it's also necessary and good for me, because routines can become monotonous and confining.

To me, vacations are what I like to call "productive expenses." I need them. My family needs them. My wife needs them. And, as an added bonus, we've found ways for even our vacations to produce cash flow!

When we wanted an RV to travel around the country, I knew it was going to cost me a couple hundred thousand dollars, which was a little hard for me to swallow. So, I told Jeanne that if she could find a way to cash flow it, I'd totally be behind buying an RV. She found a website that allowed you to rent your RV, which allowed her to make our RV available for rental. She rented it for about a year, and ended up getting three years' worth of cash flow built up. It made total financial sense and allowed us to be better stewards of our money elsewhere.

We made amazing memories in the RV, giving us some of the best vacations of our lives!

YOUR PURPOSE-DRIVEN LIFE

Now that I've shared what brings my life purpose and joy, I think it would be a useful exercise for you to consider your own. Please spend some time thinking about and writing out your answers to the four questions below.

1. Why do you want to have financial freedom?

2. If you had **absolute** financial freedom, what might your purpose-driven life look like?

3. Considering your "why" and knowing the vision for the life you want to lead above, what are your main priorities in life?

4. What are some tactical and practical ways you could live out this purpose on a regular basis?

The "why" from question number one above is your driving force. Use it as a North Star to keep you anchored in meaning as you progress along the journey to financial freedom and creating the life you outlined in question number two.

Your "why" is what is the most true form of inspiration to help you weather the storms when things get difficult along the way, and it is your "why" that creates texture and meaning in your existence. You can be rich and live your ultimate life as you designed it in question two, but without knowing your "why," it will likely be empty and meaningless. It's living with the answer to question one in the foreground of all you do on a regular basis that will make you truly wealthy at the end of your life.

Now that you have some clarity on exactly what you are striving for, it's time to dive into Mindset.

The importance of this pillar simply cannot be stated enough.

When you allowed yourself to dream big above, was there any part of you that believed you could never really have what you described? Did you even truly allow yourself to dream as big as you could have? Or was there a part of you that only felt safe putting down a vision for a life you know on some level you might actually be able to achieve? Can you allow yourself to believe that **absolute** financial freedom is achievable for you and your family? Your answers to these questions reveal important insights into your Mindset and some of the obstacles that may be blocking you from living the life of your dreams.

Once you've read through the remainder of Part One, I invite you to come back to the questions above and answer them again. Push yourself to dream bigger than you've ever allowed yourself to dream, and continue to fortify and refine your "why" until it becomes a burning desire.

Financial freedom CAN be yours.

Let's go!

CHAPTER TWO

CHANGE YOUR MIND, CHANGE YOUR LIFE

PILLAR ONE: MINDSET

American psychologist Dr. Carol Dweck is widely considered to be the leading researcher on mindset. Dweck famously coined the terms "fixed mindset" and "growth mindset" to describe people's beliefs about intelligence and how their brains learn. People who have a fixed mindset believe that intelligence is innate, that we are born with certain talents and a fixed capacity for knowledge. People with a growth mindset believe that our brains are malleable, capable of growth through learning and effort.

Scientifically speaking, neuroscience researchers describe our brains as having plasticity. "Connectivity between neurons can change with experience. With practice, neural networks grow new connections, strengthen existing ones, and build insulation that speeds transmission of impulses. These neuroscientific discoveries have shown us that we can increase our neural growth by the actions we take, such as using good strategies, asking questions, [and] practicing...."[3]

Many of us developed either a growth or fixed mindset based on our personal experiences in the home and at school as children. We listened to and digested messaging we received from parents, family members, neighbors, and teachers. We also received explicit and implicit messaging about money from a very early age. From the media, to overhearing adult discussions, to watching our parents manage their own finances, we developed a relationship with money almost by osmosis. Perhaps you remember hearing some of the following phrases as a kid:

> *"Money doesn't grow on trees!"*
>
> *"We can't afford that."*
>
> *"You only live once."*
>
> *"You can't take it with you."*

Without awareness or intention, we cultivated a mindset based on scarcity or instant gratification during crucial cognitive developmental stages by default rather than by design. And sadly, many people carry this same mindset into adulthood.

THE MINDSET YOU INHERIT

I lived in the same house my entire childhood. We never moved. Maybe that's the reason I move every four years now.

My dad was a builder, and we lived in a typical builder's home: Everything needed to be repaired, but nothing actually *got* repaired. Our house was small for such a large family—roughly 1,000 square feet—and for many years, we had one bathroom for nine people. The guys stayed upstairs in an attic-like space, an extension at the top of the house. There were two super-small rooms with bunk beds. It had a triangulated roof, and when I was on the top bunk of the bed, my nose would hit the ceiling. The girls got their own bedrooms. Not that I'm bitter or anything.

As the youngest child, I remember always having to share my bedroom. It wasn't until high school, when most of my older siblings had moved out, that I finally ended up having my own room in the attic.

Our house had leaks and a bit of mold. We were on an ancient septic system. My dad worked all the time, and by the time he got home from working on *other people's* houses, he was generally not too interested in working on ours. It was the 1970s, and interest rates were crazy. I remember him getting a loan from the bank, which he used to feed us and build the next home. My dad was not a guy who ever cut corners. He would build the best house you've ever seen and would do it on a shoestring budget.

I remember childhood Christmases being great. We didn't get a lot, but there was always a surprise gift that was something you were hoping for. One year, I really wanted roller skates. Roller skates came in different shapes and sizes, but there were these certain boots that people had, with amazing wheels and special bearings. If you had those, you were just the coolest. They were the Maserati of roller skates. I ended up getting the Kia-level version that Christmas. I modified them to look better and was pretty happy in the end. My parents did the best they could with what we had. My dad worked really hard to make sure everybody had something.

My dad had a scarcity mindset. He was born in 1933, so he grew up in the shadow of The Great Depression. His dad was an alcoholic who couldn't hold down work. His mom had mental health issues. When we cleaned out her house after she died, we noticed her mattress was a bit lumpy. We cut it open, and it was stuffed with $5 bills. There were tons of cardboard boxes in her closet—also stuffed with $5 bills. She wasn't a saver; she was a hoarder of money because she grew up without it. My grandparents lost everything during The Depression, and I think that shaped my dad as he carried that mindset throughout his entire life.

He had tons of character and integrity. He always did the best job possible for those he worked for. He was a bit quirky, though…especially when it came to money. An example: He refused to drive a car that cost more than $4,000, which meant our cars were often "fixer uppers." His ninja move was to buy hail-damaged vehicles that had been totaled and had a salvage title. The whole car would look like a golf ball, but they ran great!

My mom worked at a bank for over twenty years. She and my dad loved and honored each other, and I'm grateful for the example they set for all those years, but I'm not sure they were ever super congruent when it came to managing money or having an equal say in how it was spent. I remember a lot of conversations where it was clear that my dad held the finances pretty tightly, and I think my mom may have struggled a bit with that. Dad didn't believe financial matters were a team sport.

MY FATHER'S INVESTMENT MINDSET

A visionary and builder named Al Schneider reinvigorated the Galt House in Louisville, Kentucky, in 1972. It had a difficult history, but he restored it to its former glory. It's now an iconic 1300-room hotel that overlooks the Ohio River and houses numerous conventions and conferences. Back when Mr. Schneider was considering this massive lift to bring the Galt House back to its former glory, he asked my dad to partner with him to build it. Instead of seeing the vision, Dad saw every potential roadblock. He had some previous dealings with partners that didn't go well, so this informed his decision-making for the rest of his life. Dad decided to rely on himself and his family rather than taking a chance on others. He turned him down, and Mr. Schneider went on to expand into another tower and many other projects from there as well.

When he got older, my dad regretted not saying yes to that offer. He called it "the worst business decision I ever made." Recently, there was a large dispute over Mr. Schneider's estate as well as the fate of the Galt House Hotel. In the balance was $280 million in inheritance, as well as a very public and nasty fight for the hotel. Looking on the bright side, I guess my dad saved our family from fighting over a bunch of money after he was gone. But, more seriously, it was a lesson to me to live life with no regrets, take calculated risks, and not be afraid to say yes when opportunity presents itself.

Investing takes time. It takes effort. It takes intention. It takes knowledge. It takes trusting those mentoring you. It takes a willingness to learn. My dad had tons of positive traits but was known to be a bit proud and headstrong on occasion. There were times in his life when he thought he was investing, but he was really just speculating. His principal wasn't safe. In truth, any investment can be a speculation if you don't do your due diligence. He was trying to do it alone, and that is a dangerous proposition when it comes to investing.

For example, one time my dad bought a mobile home park. For the record, I love investing in mobile home parks, but only in those that fit very specific criteria. When he bought his park, the infrastructure was horrible and he wasn't aware of it. He didn't do the necessary due diligence. The septic was terrible, and there were literally too many issues to name. He hired one of my uncles to run it, trusting him because he was family. He had zero experience in this asset class and, unfortunately, had a lot of substance abuse issues as well. He ended up stealing quite a bit of money and peace of mind from my dad, and this "investment" nearly bankrupted our family.

I actually think my dad had too high of a risk tolerance when it came to his belief in himself and too low when it came to trusting others. He thought he could do things better than anybody else, and often could. However, rather than seeking partners, a network, a mentor, or education, he would just do it himself. Mr. Schneider could have been the perfect mentor for my dad. He was a great developer, a visionary, and a successful businessman. But my dad had a mindset that included a winner and a loser, rather than believing a rising tide can raise ALL ships. As a result, he missed out on a life-changing opportunity to partner with an expert and change the trajectory of his financial future.

Dad was an amazing operator, but to be a successful investor, I've come to realize you either need to tap into networks and mentors who have had success or you end up taking unnecessary risks. Dad believed in the mindset myth that high risk equals high reward, and it almost bankrupted the family. You know the phrase, "you have to risk big to win big"? This is a myth because the more you educate yourself, the more you actually mitigate the risk. So, the mantra should be "low-risk, high-reward." That's the true formula. When I realized this, it was a huge shift in mindset for me.

WE VALUED HARD WORK

When I was younger, my whole ecosystem revolved around my small town and what my brothers were doing with their businesses. People worked, collected their paychecks, and went home. If you didn't work with your hands, there was an implication that you really didn't "work." Hard work was good. It was biblical, and it encapsulated your identity.

When I told my dad I was going to med school, he half-jokingly said, "You'll do anything to get outta work, won't you?" He didn't think that doctors worked. Doctors write prescriptions and play golf. I can see now that this was coming from his upbringing and the mindset his parents instilled in him.

Over the years, I've learned work is *not* why you live. It's *not* why you were put on this earth. It's definitely a means, but it doesn't dictate who you are, like it did for so many in my small town growing up. My dad used to say, "You have to be the hardest worker out there. If you aren't outworking those around you, then it's going to be tough to be successful." While there is tons of value in hard work, it was still faulty thinking. You are not what you do, and you can find much more success and fulfillment with a team than you can as an individual. I know this *now*, but back then, it was a mindset hurdle I had not jumped yet.

The mindset shift was understanding what truly gives fulfillment. It's not necessarily about what we *do* for work, but if that work aligns with our purpose, passion, and calling in our lives. Beautiful things can happen when these forces meet in our vocation, and the result can be contentment that's evident to all those around us.

SEEING THROUGH A NEW LENS

I never knew anybody who was rich when I was growing up. I didn't see a really nice house until I was in high school, when I would work with my brother landscaping in the places where all the wealthy people lived. I couldn't believe the size of the houses we would work on. I simply didn't know they existed.

In my family, my uncle was probably one of the wealthiest people I knew. He was in the healthcare field and was also an entrepreneur.

The first hundred-dollar bill I ever received was at my eighth-grade graduation. Most had given me a nice card with a few dollars in it, so I was blown away at my uncle's generosity. However, I remember thinking, *How much money does this guy have, that he can just float me a hundred?* It seemed unreal to me that people had that much money. He also had time. Sure, he worked a lot, but he seemed to *enjoy* what he was doing. He was one of the first people I saw who really loved what he did, and it manifested in quite a bit of financial success as well.

My best friend had a very nice place growing up. They had stuff. They had space. They had margin. His family had a pool where we would all swim. His mom would cook amazing quesadillas and apple crumbles and other food that was generally not available at my house. She didn't have to work, and I thought, *Man! His dad must be working all the time to be able to have his wife stay at home!*

His house was fun. It was comfortable. It wasn't stressful and harried, and his dad seemed to enjoy what he did for a living. He owned a small business and was a CPA. Even during tax season, his busiest time of the year, he worked more, but he also had employees who helped him manage everything pretty well. I remember his dad swimming in the pool with us, having summer drinks, and taking us to football games. He didn't have to go out and work with his hands every day to make a living. It struck me that this person owned a business that gave him fulfillment and financial success without having to be there all the time. This railed against my worldview at the time.

Even still, I have to fight off the mindset myths about work that pop into my head on occasion—especially with my own kids. They may tell you I'm not great at keeping my opinions to myself, but when I think about my mindset surrounding work from when I was a child to now, I've come a long way!

INSTITUTIONALIZED MINDSET

There is a lot to be admired about my father. His character, integrity, and work ethic were unmatched. He instilled a lot of these positive traits in his kids. I don't think it's my dad's fault that he had a scarcity mindset about money and found his value in working long hours. He learned from his parents and the environment in which he was raised. I was raised in a blue-collar community. Aside from a few smart entrepreneurs—like my uncle and my friend's dad—everyone else we knew lived a life just like ours. The mindset was a product of the culture we grew up in.

Fast forward to today, we are still indoctrinating our youth with faulty thinking about money. Think about what high schools teach kids about money: When you study hard, you get a good job. When you get a good job, you get money. When you get money, you buy stuff. The more stuff you have, the more successful you are. The only problem is, the more stuff you have, the more you have to trade time for money to keep said stuff!

Universities are no better. The foundational curriculum was developed by titans of industry, such as Rockefellers and Carnegies, who wanted to create a workforce needed for their businesses and factories. They didn't develop colleges to nurture entrepreneurs. They developed college so we'd go out and get jobs at their companies. Obviously, universities have evolved, but the basis of their roots cannot be disputed. Additionally, plenty of worthy professions come out of universities, medicine being one of them! What I'm saying is that we should also be taught about mindset, true financial literacy, taxes, and investments, and we should receive education not only in topics that will help us earn money but also keep it and grow it outside of the traditional methods as part of higher education.

LIFE LESSONS

The last fifteen years of my dad's life were so sweet. He completely mellowed and became very introspective. He realized there was a lot he could have done differently. In those years, I could talk to him about anything and he was super encouraging.

There are many things I can take from my father: his work ethic, his character, his ability to persist and pursue. There was nothing he couldn't do because he would outwork anybody, and he gave it all to us. He never felt like the task was too big.

I get my generosity from both my parents. They were generous to the end of themselves when it came to other people. With us kids, they weren't always generous with money simply because it wasn't there, but they gave us their time and love.

I remember the day I saw my dad put a hundred-dollar bill in the offering at church. I was very young but can definitely recall feeling mad about it. I was like, *We're at home eating eggs for the tenth night in a row, and you just gave the church $100?!* In retrospect, it was a very impactful moment on me that helped shape my faith and belief system. Later in life, it still speaks to me how much my dad valued his beliefs.

I also see a lot of his flaws in myself, especially when my stressors kick in. I try to do it all myself, and I want to control the situation. I buckle down and work harder, work more hours. That was my default for many years—just work through it.

In the past fifteen years, I like to think I've evolved a bit. When things get tough now, I know to look at myself in the mirror and try to figure out if I'm part of the problem or the solution. I ask myself who I can lean on for advice or next steps. When it comes to hiring people, I know I have a certain zone I need to stay in and find people to help me fill in my talent gaps. I find smart people and let them be smart by equipping, empowering, and enabling them.

For better or worse, I'm grateful for everything I learned from my parents. I've learned to be a hard worker and a generous person. They definitely made mistakes, but because of them, I had the drive to find a better pathway when it came to finances.

Despite what you were born into, it is your responsibility to examine core beliefs you may have inherited about money—be it from school, from your community, or from your parents. Keep the traits that serve you and change the traits that don't. Introspection with a critical eye is what gives us the power to change our own trajectory.

My dad came around in the final years of his life, learning to relax and connect to the more meaningful things in life. Thankfully, I learned this lesson earlier than he did, and I hope my kids will never have to work through that hurdle at all. Just because you inherit a mindset doesn't mean you are stuck with it for the rest of your life. You can learn more and do better.

Let's spend some time exploring some of the money mindset myths *you* may have inherited during your formative years. The following chapter unpacks some of these myths and offers a healthier perspective on some of the beliefs you may need to let go of in order to find financial freedom.

CHAPTER THREE

DEBUNKING YOUR MINDSET MYTHS

PILLAR ONE: MINDSET

Your mindset will make or break you. It is the source of your wisdom, your strength, your resilience, and your drive. It's not a one-and-done action item. In the last chapter, I encouraged you to examine your inherited beliefs about work and wealth closely. That was an imperative place to start, but it's certainly not the end of the journey. You need to keep a constant check on your mindset. When times get tough, it's really easy to slip back into unhealthy and habitual ways of thinking.

How will you handle mass media saturation about market climbs and dives?

How will you respond to a deal that has taken an unexpected turn?

How are you going to keep your mindset strong during trying times?

We know that the real estate market is ever moving and changing. I have had the benefit of experience, living through several cycles. It can be hard not to get caught up in the highs and lows. One of the things that keeps me steady is a quote famously attributed to all-time great Wayne Gretzky, "Don't skate to where the puck is. Skate to where the puck is going."

When the real estate market is unstable, you need to lean into a learning mindset. This is the time to understand financial markets, debt and equity, and the economy. You need to understand how real estate cycles work. Rising interest rates don't rise forever. (The average is 1.9 years.)

All of this is to say, when the going gets tough, your mindset needs to be tougher. Not only can you ride out the storm, but you may be able to come out the other side in a better situation than you anticipated. But remember, in these moments, it can be very easy to let the media sway you, to let fear and scarcity influence your choices, and to make impulsive decisions. When we find ourselves overwhelmed by stress, we are all at risk of falling back onto our unhealthy beliefs about money. In order for you to recognize when this is happening, you need to develop an awareness of your unhealthy beliefs.

American psychologist Albert Ellis coined the brilliant term "stinking thinking" to describe our tendency as fallible humans to ruminate in thoughts and beliefs that don't serve us. In the previous chapter, I shared some of the stinking thinking I inherited from my father. In this chapter, in an effort to encapsulate our entire menu of thoughts, we'll take a look at some common misconceptions or "mindset myths" surrounding money. Let's see if we can debunk some of the stinking thinking you may have engaged in. We'll discuss the limiting mindset myths that have prevented clients I've worked with from moving forward toward creating financial freedom. I'll also share some personal stories about how I overcame some of my own mindset hurdles.

If a certain myth resonates with you, I encourage you to ask where it originated. Do you actually know it to be true? Or are you open to a new way of thinking? If a myth does not strike a chord with you, feel free to move on.

MINDSET MYTH #1:

I have to trade my time for money.

THE TRUTH:

When you're an owner, you can regain your time and autonomy.

As I mentioned before, I was raised to believe that the harder one worked for their salary, the wealthier they would become. Not only that, but there was massive value and self-worth attached to the amount of labor one performed.

I now believe in working *smarter,* not working harder. One of the experiences that taught me this lesson was our first hotel purchase. When we bought this really unique asset, we didn't know a lot about hospitality, events, restaurants, or running a spa. However, we did have a ton of experience with heavy-lift capital improvement projects, and we had a strong vision of what this hotel and event center could be one day. We started the project doing what we did best: renovations. The only issue was, we didn't know what we didn't know about the other aspects of the business. The "old" me would have put my head down, figured it out, probably taken a lot of years off my life, and likely would not have had a great outcome. The "new" me knew this was outside my zone of expertise, and I didn't want another job; I wanted a business. So what to do?

An excellent book about helping businesses thrive is *Good to Great*, written by Jim Collins. In this book, one of his concepts is "getting the right people on the bus" and then "in the right seats" so it moves to its destination seamlessly. Using this concept, we sought out people for the right seats to help with the hotel, restaurant, event space, and spa. We knew where our strengths were, and we then surrounded ourselves with expert employees on our bus that complemented those, as well as sought out mentors with operational expertise.

After compiling inside and outside expertise alongside our vision for building a destination hotel and event center, systems quickly started to come into place that streamlined operations and allowed this dream to become a reality! We were able to turn a lifeless oddity in the middle of Central Kentucky into a world-class hotel, restaurant, event venue, and spa because of leaning on the practice of hiring smart people and equipping, empowering, and enabling them to be brilliant.

We put key people and systems in place so that we could work *on* the business rather than *in* the business (a concept outlined in the book *The E-Myth Revisited* by Michael E. Gerber). We hired a COO and general manager and were able to back out of operations altogether, giving us the autonomy to spend more time with our families, travel, do mission work, or enjoy whatever filled us with purpose and passion.

We were no longer trading time for money in this business, we had a nice passive source of income, and we had the satisfaction of bringing a local iconic venue to life!

I believe the endeavor was successful because we started with the right mindset. We had the desire, but lacked the expertise. Therefore, we built a team that filled all the right seats so we could stop trading our time for money and have another diversified passive income stream.

This example illustrates how we took a very "active" business and implemented people and systems to transform it into a passive investment. I understand this isn't an example that will resonate with everyone. But I included it to illustrate if we can do this with a business with so many facets to it, imagine how much easier investing passively in real estate can make the process!

MINDSET MYTH #2:

I can achieve financial freedom through employee-based income if I just work hard and save enough.

THE TRUTH:

It's extremely difficult to achieve generational wealth through employee earnings alone.

In Louisville, Kentucky, where I grew up, we have massive neighborhoods with beautifully landscaped medians. One of my brothers owns a landscaping company. He would get very lucrative contracts during the Kentucky Derby because every neighborhood wanted to look beautiful by adding flowers to every median strip. When I was in college, he asked me if I'd like to help and offered to pay me by the flower planted rather than hourly. He was offering ten cents per flower.

I was used to being paid by the hour and was a bit apprehensive until I did the math. I usually put about 4,000 flowers in the ground daily. That's $400 per day—which was a LOT more than I made by the hour. In order for me to hit that 4,000 daily plant total, I needed two guys, one to go ahead tilling all of the flower beds and the other would be with me, handing me flowers to speed up the process. I asked my brother for two guys and he agreed. Before I knew it, we were putting 4,000 flowers in the ground every day!

It was the first time I realized the 10x power of the entrepreneur. Instead of merely acting as my brother's employee, I saw the power of running my own mini-business, which brought in way more cash. Unfortunately, I was still an employee and still subject to the biggest thief of generational wealth: W-2 income taxes.

It may be instructive here to take a look at how self-employed entrepreneurs make money and compare it to how employees make money. Business owners bring in revenue, deduct all of their expenses, and THEN get taxed on the residual. If you're a W-2 employee, though, your pay is taxed FIRST. You are then left with the rest to pay your expenses and live on. Some physicians may be in a tax bracket as high as 40%, so they are starting with 60% of their pay before they have even paid the first bill. Additionally, there are usually state and local taxes taken out of the paycheck as well. Now can you see why I say income taxes are the biggest thief of generational wealth?

Physicians in private practice used to be business owners, not employees. In the past, tax law allowed for other sources of income and tax advantages to supplement and shelter their physician income, respectively. Now, most physicians are employees of large healthcare corporations rather than business owners. This new reality limits the ability of most physicians as W-2 employees to realize any deductions or to build wealth of any kind, let alone generational wealth. Consider the average physician graduates with over $250,000 of debt, and most have a home and car payment. They spend residual income on debt payments, leaving very little for investing.

Making matters worse is the fact that the government has taken away a lot of the levers that doctors could once pull to generate wealth. Even if physicians didn't have their own practice, they used to be able to write off passive losses against active income. That meant one could generate passive losses from real estate investments, and offset the tax burden of their W-2 physician income. So physicians would buy cash-flowing real estate, take legal losses on it via depreciation, and then offset their active physician income with those losses, thereby reducing their tax liability. They can't do that anymore.

We live in a new world where physicians need to learn how to build tax-advantaged income streams and shelter as much of their revenue as humanly possible from the great thief: income tax. If they can't do it in their medical practices, they need to find creative solutions to find profitable investments that can still offset their active income. One example is short-term vacation rentals.

Right now, if you have a short-term vacation rental, like a condo, that you list on Airbnb or Vrbo, and you spend at least 100 hours per year on your short-term vacation rentals, you are considered to be materially participating in a business. This makes this income and depreciation active, so it can offset active W-2 income. Some criteria must be met to meet the "material participation" standard, but the point is that physicians can use this asset class to create cash flow while using the depreciation to offset their tax burden. Learning how to keep your hard-earned income from being lost to income taxes is a massive start toward creating generational wealth.

Taking this approach is a really good way to generate active losses from real estate, keep more of your income, and then put it to work investing in other cash-flowing, tax-advantaged assets. No matter how hard you work or how much you save, it's difficult to create true wealth if you start with 60% or less of what you earn. This is just one strategy physicians can employ to potentially save hundreds of thousands of dollars in taxes, and—the more you save, the more you can reinvest.

MINDSET MYTH #3:

Paper assets are the best investments for individuals.

THE TRUTH:

Investing in paper assets is speculating.

My dad put all his savings aside in the stock market because that's what he had learned was the "right way" to secure his retirement. He lost his retirement savings *twice* when he needed it the most and was not able to retire comfortably. I watched that happen and decided I never wanted to be in that position.

The so-called experts advise to never try to time the market. They tell us to leave our money in the market even if the value of our portfolio is falling. But what if you need the money and the market is not doing well? It's great to say, "Don't time the market," but do you really have a choice when it's time to retire? My dad didn't.

When the market plunges like it did in early 2022, it's not a good time to retire. Financial planners will tell you, "Just keep your money in the market. Let it ride. The market always comes back." But what if you need your money now? It's not going to come back in time to meet your needs. And if you attempt to take distributions anyway when the investments aren't generating gains or dividends, then you're drawing out principal.

That's not a solid investment in my mind. To me, there's investing and there's speculating. Investing is where my principal is relatively safe, and there is an opportunity to make a profit. Speculating is where my principal is not safe, and there is an opportunity to make a profit. Hard assets such as real estate can definitely have down years, but I've never seen a situation where all principal was lost. I've definitely seen too many stocks to count go to absolute zero in my time as an investor. If I bet on the Kentucky Derby, no matter how educated I am in horse racing, my principal is not safe. Are paper assets really any different?

The number one rule of Warren Buffet, the long-time chairman of Berkshire Hathaway who is known as the "Sage of Omaha," is: *Don't lose principal.* And rule number two is: *Remember rule number one*—because when you lose principal, you lose the velocity of money.

Most financial planners will report on "average returns," and average returns are not what you need to look at. You need to look at *actual returns.* If you look at actual returns, they will tell you exactly how your paper investments have been doing. Most people are shocked. I'd rather invest my money in cash-flowing assets rather than hope and pray that I'll have enough to retire someday—if the market's in an upcycle.

This mindset myth seems to be the birthplace of a whole host of sub-myths. Have you ever found yourself saying (or thinking) one of these gems?

- 401(k)s, IRAs, mutual funds, stocks, bonds, etc., are the safest/most appropriate/most advisable investments for "regular" people.
- Since I'm a physician, I should hire a financial professional to manage my investments.
- Only sophisticated, full-time investors should put their money in hard assets.
- Other investments are too risky for me.

Let me assure you, none of the above is true. My hunch is that you simply have some unlearning and relearning to do. In this book, we'll discuss different kinds of hard assets you may acquire so you can be an investor, not a speculator!

MINDSET MYTH #4:

I can "save" my way to retirement.

THE TRUTH:

In the wise words of author Robert Kiyosaki, "Savers are losers."

One of the most difficult aspects of a person's mindset to conquer is the belief that they need to earn a steady paycheck and save for the future.

I am a cautionary tale of why saving your paycheck is not a reliable security blanket.

When my vision caused me to lose my steady income, I was completely unprepared. We had some short-term disability insurance that helped bridge a few gaps, but as far as a long-term solution? I didn't have one. When I talk to people about why they need to focus on investments rather than saving, one of the primary reasons I provide is that we simply cannot predict a catastrophic, life-changing event.

What will happen if you, as the breadwinner of your family, have to stay home indefinitely? What if, God forbid, you die? You probably have life insurance, but if you are thirty-five years old, the likelihood of having enough money to last your spouse the rest of their life isn't very high. Gaining financial education and taking control *will* create a legacy that outlasts you because—for the rest of your spouse's life—they will have access to continued cash flow.

I'm a big proponent of keeping six months of cash in a reserve account that pays high interest, but after that, any excess cash I have goes into acquiring cash-flowing assets. When you leave money in a savings account, over time you are actually losing money as the interest you are earning in a savings account rarely keeps up with inflation. So, as that money sits in an account, you are actually losing value and not taking advantage of the time value of money. There are high-interest savings accounts that require much higher minimum balances, but I consider these investment vehicles, not necessarily savings accounts.

Rather than squirreling their income in a savings account, I advise people to do something different with their take-home: Pay yourself first. This means buying assets that will spin off equity for years, maybe even generations to come.

Real estate can give you the possibility of being financially free much faster than any other asset class. I'd much rather invest in a passive asset that is going to give me 20% annually and has the potential to double my money every five years over sticking it in a savings account and letting the bank make money off lending against my hard-earned capital.

Additionally, if you take your cash flow from investments and put it right back into other cash-flowing assets, you will experience the velocity of money. Before you know it, you could be living off passive income and practicing because you want to, not because you have to! Then you can decide exactly how you want to spend your time. Do you want to practice twenty hours per week? Do you want to stop practicing altogether? Financial freedom changes the way you look at life.

I urge you to move away from scarcity thinking. We've all been conditioned to believe saving is always good. It definitely makes sense to keep enough cash in an account for peace of mind in case there is a need for it. For the most part, though, savers end up being losers.

MINDSET MYTH #5:

My house and car are assets.

THE TRUTH:

Unless it cash flows, it's not an asset.

As investors, we need to have principles that we live by and stick to. One of my key investor principles is to only buy assets. That may sound simple, because it is.

If something puts money in your pocket, it's an asset.

If it takes money out of your pocket, it's a liability.

As I referenced earlier, it's important to understand the difference because many people think their house, car, boat, and/or their shiny new golf carts are assets. They aren't, even if they are paid off, unless you are using them to create cash flow. Renting your car on Turo or your house as an Airbnb can turn liabilities into assets. But if that thing you bought doesn't put money in your pocket every month, it's a liability. Don't fool yourself.

After my wife and I purchased an RV, for instance, we cash flowed it for a year by renting it to other people when we weren't using it. The money we made paid for the next three years. We then sold it for a profit when there was an extreme shortage of RVs during the pandemic.

At first you might feel some anxiety about letting other people use your house or your car or your RV. Release your emotional attachment to your possessions. Possessions are not important; it's the memories made with them that are the true treasures. When we accomplished our goal of seeing all fifty states and paying for it with cash flow from the RV, we got rid of it. At that point it would soon be a liability, and we didn't want to be in the RV rental business forever.

For every liability you owe, you will want to have an asset that cash flows to cover it. It's okay to have a house. We have a house and we use it as a gathering place for lots of family and friend events. We love our home, but I don't purport that it's an asset. I like to call it a "productive expense." This way, it's characterized correctly, and I don't erroneously log it in the asset column on my balance sheet. Instead of deceiving myself into thinking it's an asset, I allocate some of my income from investing and purchase assets that pay for my mortgage.

You don't have to rent your house, your car, or even your RV. Just understand they are liabilities and don't lie to yourself that they are assets. It's a major mindset shift for most, but it will simplify the way you look at investing going forward.

MINDSET MYTH #6:

It takes money to make money.

THE TRUTH:

You can get started without a lot of cash on hand.

There are ways to get started with investing that don't require a lot of money down on your part.

In my late twenties, I decided I wanted to go back to medical school after completing my first mission trip. My grades were good and I had a strong CV, but not a lot of money saved to pay for it. I also didn't want to take out a bunch of student loans again, as I'd just finished paying off my loans from my first round of college.I had my own home at the time and had some equity in the property. I didn't have a ton of cash, but I talked to the bank about getting a home equity line of credit I could draw on when needed.

I started searching for a business to start that could potentially help me pay for med school. As I mentioned before, I came from a family of builders and landscapers, so I had a working knowledge in these areas. I decided I would drive around neighborhoods and look for houses that were distressed. Little did I know this practice had a name: "driving for dollars." Basically, I would look for tall grass, boarded-up windows, and houses with lots of deferred maintenance. I would simply walk up to the front door and knock. Looking back, this was probably a bit dangerous, but it turned out to be pretty effective! I would introduce myself as an investor who was looking for property in their neighborhood and ask if they would entertain a sale. I would also look up homes going to foreclosure auctions and contact those owners as well.

For those homeowners who were interested in selling their home, I would look up the comparables to get a good idea of what the house was worth. I would then investigate to find out exactly how much the owner owed on the loan. I would offer to pay off the loan as well as give the owner some amount over that to get a fresh start and out from under the burden of the home. Remember, I was pretty cash-poor at this time, but I did have a home equity line to draw on. There were also many lenders who were eager to lend to "flippers," so I used their funds to secure the loan to purchase the home and used my home equity credit line to access the cash I needed to close as well as complete renovations. Effectively, it was zero cash out of my pocket.

I had a system where it took me roughly fifteen days to complete renovations and an average of nineteen days on the market to sell the home. In under thirty-five days, I could close, renovate, and sell the property without spending a dime of my own cash reserves. I used the bank's money for the entire process. This system helped me pay for a large portion of my medical school expenses.

This was obviously an active endeavor, but I was able to do this with literally no cash out of my pocket. I usually advise people that if they have more money than time, be a passive investor. If you have more time than money, be an active investor. Regardless, don't let the lie of "it takes money to make money" hold you back from achieving financial freedom.

MINDSET MYTH #7:

All debt is bad.

THE TRUTH:

There is a difference between debt and leverage.

I'll agree that *debt* is generally bad, but if you'll indulge me—*leverage* can actually be a good thing.

What's the difference?

Leverage is when you use OPM, or "other people's money," like a bank to buy an asset that cash flows. Leverage plus excellent due diligence equals an opportunity for profit. Debt is bringing on a liability to pay for an expense that takes money out of your pocket every month. For example, getting a second mortgage (liability) to buy a car (expense) is considered debt. However, if you use that second mortgage to buy an apartment complex, you are employing the concept of leverage because you are using the bank's money to purchase an asset that is cash flowing and can create wealth for you and your family.

If you subscribe to this mindset, you'll start accumulating assets that cash flow as a priority and understand the nuance between debt and leverage. As long as the arbitrage you are making on the asset makes sense, acquire as many assets as you can using leverage. In times of a great economy, you can push the leverage a little higher and likely still be safe. In times of uncertainty, maybe ratchet the leverage down a bit to where you have more room for economic shocks and still maintain cash flow.

If you borrow money at 4% interest and you're making a 10%+ return on your investment, for example, you are getting a nice arbitrage between what you bring in and what you have to pay monthly. Additionally, you're driving appreciation on the asset, having the loans paid down by tenants, and realizing tax-advantaged income. As you accumulate assets, you can use this arbitrage to pay off your other debts, go on a vacation, or continue to buy more assets!

So yes, debt is not a good thing. Used wisely, however, it can be transformed into leverage, allowing you to build wealth through acquiring cash-flowing assets.

MINDSET MYTH #8:

Working to reduce my tax liability is tax evasion.

THE TRUTH:

The government incentivizes you to do what it doesn't want to do.

The IRS explains that tax *avoidance* is "an action taken to lessen tax liability and maximize after-tax income," while tax *evasion* is the "failure to pay or a deliberate underpayment of taxes."[4]

It is perfectly legal and legitimate to maximize available tax incentives to reduce your tax liability and maximize after-tax income. Most of the tax code actually deals with incentives meant to decrease taxes and promote growth. Tax incentives in the tax code exist for a reason: When you employ available tax deductions in the tax code, you're helping do what the government needs to do and doesn't want to do itself. The government doesn't want to explore for oil and gas, so it greatly incentivizes this activity in the private sector. They don't want to be in the housing business, so there are massive tax advantages to investing in real estate. Clean energy is expensive and time-consuming, so the government established tax breaks to incentivize ingenuity in this area. I love showing investors how to maximize their net income through utilizing perfectly legal tax reduction strategies that the government has put in place to reward productivity in the private sector.

I understand these tax laws can be complex and are subject to change, so having a team you trust in your corner is well worth the investment. There is a world of incentives that are available to you if you have the right network to tap into.

MINDSET MYTH #9:

Investing in hard assets is a win-lose proposition.

THE TRUTH:

With the right mindset, investing can and should be a win-win.

The problem with a win-lose mindset is that in order for you to win, someone else has to lose. I simply don't believe this to be true.

An accumulation mindset (win-lose) says, "I'm going to work 7,200 days, and I'm going to accumulate money, and I'm going to put it all away in a 401(k), stocks, bonds, mutual funds, and ETFs and hope it doesn't run out before I die." The accumulation mindset assumes that there's a finite piece of pie, that there is a limited amount available to everyone. So the more one person gets, the more someone else has to lose.

An abundance mindset (win-win), on the other hand, understands that a rising tide raises all ships. It's about adding value to other people's lives. An abundance mindset knows that as you add value, your life will be enhanced as well. It's really about how you can help the human race, not about how much money you can make. The more you add value to people's lives, the more you're going to see that value come back to you.

An abundance mindset is about being a resource to others and an asset to the world, rather than just hoping "I can squirrel away enough money so I don't run out before I die." This concept isn't new or crazy or high-minded. It's just a fact that the more you are a resource to others, the more you will prosper not only financially, but from a purpose, values, and "what am I here for" standpoint. And 99% of the time, you will also benefit financially from it as well.

All real estate deals should be a win-win. Investing is based on an abundance mindset because people are actually able to create mutually beneficial relationships. With real estate loans on rental properties, for example, the bank wins a profit from the loan, the seller wins income from the sale of their property in a liquid market, the buyer wins an asset that pays for itself over time, and the tenant wins a better place to live, and so on.

With an abundance mindset, you don't have to wait 7,200 days to retire. You can retire as soon as your income outpaces your expenses. This idea of waiting until you're sixty-five to retire? Not for me, thanks! I emptied my retirement account, put it all in real estate that produced cash flow, and was retired within fifteen months. I'm not saying this should be your path, but it could. It starts with rewiring your thoughts and beliefs to create an abundance mindset.

Here's how the abundance mindset works in practice: We bought an apartment complex on the East Coast that was 68% occupied. The owner was a physician from the West Coast who had little time or desire to manage the complex. The ratings were well below three stars because he had no active management in place. He did not have any debt on the property, so he really had no incentive to fix anything up. We offered him a very fair price based on net operating income (NOI), and he was thrilled (win for seller). The bank was super eager to lend to us, as we had proven our ability to turn around apartment complexes (win for bank). We took over, renovated all the unoccupied units first, and raised occupancy to 95% within three months while cash flowing the entire time (win for us). We then proceeded to renovate every unit that came vacant until almost 70% of the units were renovated. We also held community events for the tenants, started a scholarship fund for the complex, and built storage units in the basement of several of the buildings so the tenants in the studios could have extra storage (win for tenants).

That's the power of the abundance versus accumulation mindset—it can be a win-win-win-win where *everybody* wins...not just the investors in the deal.

MINDSET MYTH #10:

There's no way out of the debt cycle.

THE TRUTH:

With the right mindset, you can generate a virtuous cycle.

You might be thinking that debt is a normal part of modern life. Everyone is in debt, especially physicians with enormous student loans. If you are an optimist, you might think that you'll be in a position to get out of debt in X number of years by staying focused and paying down what you owe over time. While this is a common mindset, this thinking can be destructive.

When you are in debt with too many liabilities and expenses, it keeps you in an elevated underlying stress level, a fight-or-flight response you are always living in. It forces you into a myopic outlook and can rob you of joy. Instead of attributing it to the burden of your student loans and other debts, you can slip into an *everything is bad* way of thinking. You then start to view life in a negative way, and you feel trapped. It is exceedingly hard to change your mindset when you are constantly in survival mode. Your mind focuses on thoughts such as, *I've got to work more. I have to get rid of these loans.*

I was talking to a client recently whose student loan payment is $4,800 a month. I shared one of my investment principles with him: *Let every investment stand for something.* Investments need to be motivating and encouraging. If you understand that your student loan can be covered with passive investments, that gives you room to breathe and can start a virtuous cycle. As mentioned before, the virtuous cycle is where you invest in assets that cash flow. This cash flow eventually covers your liabilities and expenses, and you can eventually produce enough capital to purchase more assets, and the virtuous cycle begins again!

This all can be overwhelming and a bit scary—kind of like medical school and residency was at one time. My advice is to just take a single step. Take one small step toward controlling your finances, then another, then another. A great mentor along the way can really compress time here as well. Having a mentor gave me a ton of confidence, spun me out of the debt cycle, and greatly accelerated my entry into the virtuous cycle.

CHANGING YOUR MINDSET IS AN INTENTIONAL CHOICE

Every mindset shifts over your lifetime. These shifts are usually not massive tectonic movements. It's usually small course corrections, sometimes prompted by necessity, that lead you to seeing things differently.

As physicians, we grow and learn every day. We do this for the benefit of our patients and to be better physicians. If the data changes, we adjust our practices. Why should our life outside medicine be any different? My hope for this book is to open your mind to new possibilities and alternative ways to achieve the freedom of time we all covet. Go over these myths again and see which one is holding you back the most, and be intentional about debunking it in your own life. It was a game changer for me, and I'm confident it can be for you as well.

So now you're starting to think a little differently. But the fact of life is that most of us don't exist in a vacuum. We exist in community with others who influence our lives and our thoughts. Who we work with, live with, and share our dreams with often can accelerate or completely derail the abundance mindset we are trying to cultivate. The next chapter explores how to navigate your changing mindset with the mindsets of those you are close to so that you can work toward your goals together.

CHAPTER FOUR

MANAGING OTHER PEOPLE'S MINDSETS

PILLAR ONE: MINDSET

Most of us are not going through this life alone. We have families, friends, parents, and spouses who depend on us. Those we create life with most likely have their own ideas (and inherited beliefs) about money and wealth. Even if you have done the hard work of debunking your own mindset myths, what do you do when your spouse doesn't share your new, enlightened mindset and financial vision for the future?

Jeanne and I never really talked about finances at all. In the early days of our relationship, finances really never came up in conversation. I was still pre-med, and she was already a practicing physician. We knew where we were on the financial food chain, and the rest remained relatively unsaid.

In my family, we never talked about money. It was completely taboo. On the other hand, Jeanne's family—especially her mom—was very open about how much things cost and how much they earned, but they never really received any financial education. Jeanne's family understood that they had a little more than others and knew how important it was to be good stewards of what they had. There was also a sense of fairness in the family. For example, if Jeanne's sister got a chunk of money when she graduated from college, then everyone could expect the same. Nobody got more. Nobody got less.

My family was a little bit different—not worse or better, just different. If my dad said, "Don't worry about it," you didn't ask questions. He was at the top of the hierarchy and was less open about our financial situation. Like Jeanne, I wasn't given a lot of financial education growing up, either.

Our financial plan initially was to get a job, make money, hopefully get a better job, and make more money, then put that money into some type of ethereal financial retirement plan that no one ever told me about. Then, we would have enough money to retire when we finished working (whenever that might be). Back then, Jeanne really didn't even balance her checkbook. She just knew that she made more than she spent. I was a good bookkeeper, but still worlds away from having a true vision for our future wealth.

After Jeanne and I got married, we lived the life we thought we deserved because we had been working so hard and had delayed gratification for so long while I was in med school. We were sucking money out of our pockets every single month. We were house-poor like most others in 2010-2011. Jeanne and I were becoming much more intentional in raising our kids and developing our careers, but we were far from intentional with our finances. It wasn't until we were in Alaska that we realized we needed to dig ourselves out of debt.

HOW TO BUILD TRUST

When I first suggested that real estate was the way to generational wealth, it took a lot of trust on Jeanne's part that I was making the right decision. The reason we were able to succeed was because we had such a good and open relationship about our finances. I told her everything. She saw all of our loans, all of our balances. We celebrated paying off high-interest-rate debt, and we did it all together because there were no secrets.

Secrets will get you into trouble. If you are talking to your spouse about an investment and you are not upfront with them from the very beginning, it's going to be super difficult to build trust. It's going to be really hard to convince your significant other to get on board with your vision if you hold back on the hard conversations, your fears, and the risks.

Jeanne knew that I was a very thorough investigator, that I always did my due diligence. So when we sat down and I explained what I was going to do, I made sure I was transparent with my plan. I was going to invest a lot of money, and I was going to find the best operators in the space who did what I wanted to do. I would pay them to teach me everything they knew, and I think that resonated with her. I wasn't just going to go out there and do this on my own. I was investing in my education. She respected that.

If she had been uncomfortable with my proposal, we probably wouldn't have done it. I think she knew how exciting the possibilities would be and trusted that if I failed, it wouldn't be from lack of preparation and knowledge.

THE POWER OF TRANSPARENCY

Full transparency is the easiest way to build trust. Have your spouse jump on calls with you when interviewing sponsors and potential partners, or even go on a due diligence trip with you. Have them with you when you speak to the property management company, or even your coach. The more involved they are in the process, the better. Share what you are learning. Take them to meetings. If they feel you are hiding things, especially if (when) deals don't go well, it is toxic and dangerous—not only to your relationship, but also to your family's future and your own peace of mind.

I found it really easy to talk to Jeanne about deals that were succeeding, but the ones we were struggling with or, heaven forbid, almost lost—those were hard to talk about. If you stay in real estate long enough, you are going to stumble from time to time. Having great mentors is the easiest way to minimize the impact of your mistakes. If your spouse sees you being intentional about who you hitch your wagon to, it brings a level of reassurance, even during the times when things aren't going as well as you might both like.

TALKING ABOUT STUDENT LOANS

It can be difficult when your spouse feels the heavy burden of your student loan debt. The stress of it can even lead to sleepless nights, marital issues, and poor decision-making based on fear rather than facts.

High student loan debt is correlated with low job satisfaction and professional burnout. Couple that with the ever-changing healthcare climate where hospitals are buying out physician groups and making them see more patients, and it's no surprise that marriages and other relationships are affected by the strain of it all.

Most couples fight about finances and kids. If you start a marriage with your finances upside down, that stress bleeds into everything else. It becomes difficult to talk about your dreams when you are weighed down by your reality. Then you forget how to dream. You forget how to imagine. And you may even forget why you became a physician in the first place.

Partnership and transparency will save you. Sharing your fears with your spouse creates a sense of honesty. Taking time for you and your partner to dream together, *despite* your debt, allows you both to imagine an alternate reality where you are not drowning. Then, involving them in the creation of an action plan to bring that dream to fruition will feel like something you are overcoming together, saving you from a battleground of resentment. Mindsets tend to merge rather than diverge this way.

BUSINESS PARTNERS

Every successful partnership has a Visionary and an Integrator—terms coined by Gino Wickman in his insightful book *Rocket Fuel*.

In my early years, my business partner and I were both Visionaries. I am a trailblazer by nature, but I often found myself relegated to the role of Integrator whenever we were working together. In our partnership, he became "the wow guy" and I was "the how guy." I wasn't happy, but it was necessary at the time.

The management of the people and processes fell largely to me, and it quite honestly sucked the life out of me. Most days, I was a reluctant participant because I simply didn't like what I was doing. My partner was having meetings, negotiating, and sharing our vision—and these tasks were filling him up because he was playing to his Visionary strengths. I was dealing with the reporting, financials, underwriting, legalities, and behind-the-scenes operational stuff. While I was really good at it, I simply did not like it at all. It mentally drained me because it wasn't playing to my own Visionary strengths.

Partnerships are great, if they are yoked correctly. You have to be complementary to each other. If you are competitive in your talents versus synergistic, everyone sees it. That's what happened to us. We realized we were great friends, but that we probably shouldn't be working together. If we did want to continue our business relationship, we had to find a way for it to be on a larger scale where we both were able to utilize our Visionary strengths (for example, me dealing with investor education and him dealing with acquisitions). We both needed to be filled up in order for this partnership to succeed.

At the end of the day, we engaged in a series of really hard, really honest conversations about who we were and what we each needed from our partnership. When I was dishonest with him (and with myself) and just continued to do what I felt I needed to do instead of what I *wanted* to do that would serve the business best, it bred a resentment that almost cost us our relationship.

Even if you and your business partner share similar mindsets, other factors come into play that determine the success of the partnership. No matter who you are working with—a spouse or a business partner—it's imperative that you lead with honesty, integrity, and transparency. Understand who you are and what fills you up. Then, make sure whatever role you assume complements your skillset and gifts.

CHAPTER FIVE

PILLAR TWO: LEARNING

"BE QUICK TO LISTEN, SLOW TO SPEAK."

JAMES 1:19

I strongly believe that you cannot learn simply by reading. While you might develop a base level of understanding by reading, in order to become an authority on any subject matter, you have to do it. That is why two of The Five Pillars of Financial Freedom are Learning and Action. But when done right, learning does begin with knowledge and education first—especially with something as technical as investing.

As doctors, we have followed three distinct hierarchical ways to climb the ladder of education: there's medical school, there's residency, and there's fellowship. In the realm of investing, we can also follow an educational ladder. First, we read books and gain technical knowledge. Then we join an investor club, find a mentor, subscribe to paid subscriptions, and/or join a master class to gain shared experience and wisdom from others. Lastly, we arm ourselves with the right team to invest wisely, and we learn by doing. Similar to our journey to becoming physicians, there can be variations in the pathway. This chapter is designed to provide you with multiple, valuable options that are intended to increase your knowledge base and confidence in taking control of your financial future.

I believe there are multiple layers to deep and rich learning—layers that must be explored sequentially in order to be successful.

My own personal framework for the four-step process of learning:

- Equip
- Educate
- Engage
- Empower

1. EQUIP yourself with the proper mindset and make a commitment to be always learning

As we discussed in the initial few chapters, I firmly believe that mindset will set you up for success or doom you to failure. As physicians, we are generally lifelong learners who actively question, collaborate, and seek knowledge. Investing is no different. You need to be curious, be patient, and become a student of the game. You need to know the rules before you play. One of the easiest ways to nurture this mindset is to be constantly open-minded and inquisitive as you move through this new world. Ask questions and listen! Quick to listen…slow to speak.

Every day is a learning experience for me. I'm not trying to patronize people when I tell them that I learn something from every single person I talk to. I think that is a learned ability, an ability to ask questions. And even when some people don't think they can add value, when I ask the right questions, they can offer a new perspective, making me think, *Oh, I never thought of it that way.* There is enormous value in asking questions, for both parties involved. I see something in a new light, and they become empowered to think, *You know what? I do know some things.* It surprises me the amount of people who believe they don't know anything. It paralyzes them, and they don't even know where to start. Adopting a learning lifestyle—a constant hunger for knowledge—opens doors you never even knew were there.

Recently, I was talking to a buddy of mine who was interested in investing in a deal I'm working on. He was asking me, "Man, how do I work with you? How do I start?" My best advice was for him to find something he was interested in and that he wanted to get involved with, and then learn as much as he could. The more we learn, the more questions we have. One piece of knowledge leads to the next great question. You don't have to know a lot to get started. You just need to start by asking a question.

That's how I learn. For example, when I first started purchasing car washes, I didn't just run out and start buying them. I started by asking the questions, *Who can I partner with? What resources do I need? What data will best serve me in this subclass? What are my specific acquisition criteria?* Sometimes it meant calling a person who has an active deal and having a discussion. Sometimes it was me reaching out to my network saying, "Hey, I'm interested in car washes. Anybody out there currently in this space?" Sometimes it was utilizing platforms to research car washes and making site visits for best practices. It often takes a deep dive, but you can usually uncover data this way, which enables you to further your journey and figure out if this is the asset for you.

I'm always looking to learn more, no matter the circumstance. I recently returned from an annual trip with some childhood friends. We have done this every year for the past several years, and it's a great way to stay connected with some of my dearest friends. However, we usually end up looking at different properties while we are on our trip, and as a result, I now own several short term vacation rentals in Gulf Shores, Alabama. It doesn't hurt that this vacation has now become a valid company expense because I meet with my property management, work on the assets, and investigate new opportunities every year. I'm constantly thinking about investing because I love it. It's my passion and hobby, and it gives me a ton of fulfillment, especially when I can share what I know with others. So, I don't really look at it as work. Truthfully, some days I go down a rabbit hole and it leads nowhere, but I don't think that's a waste of time. I may not have unearthed an amazing lead, but at least I still learned something new that day…even on vacation.

2. EDUCATE yourself

Before diving into the world of investing, It's imperative to get the correct training. There are tons of programs out there that spend more on marketing than they do on developing the actual content of what they teach. It's crucial to find subject matter experts you know, like, and trust. Once you find them, learn from their experiences and expertise. We can do this in a number of ways: by subscribing to online resources and newsletters, by reading books on investing and listening to podcasts, by actively seeking a knowledgeable mentor, or by joining learning groups and masterminds. There are a myriad of options!

My advice to you is to make learning part of your everyday life. Listen to a podcast or an audiobook when you're in the car. Ask questions of everyone you meet who is a few steps further along the path than you. Spend time online researching what interests you. Read amazing books. In residency, we were immersed in a culture of learning, and we were ravenous to master our skills. Tap into that med student mentality and carry it into your daily routine.

Because my eyesight isn't what it used to be, I'm a big fan of Audible and podcasts. I spend hours exploring informational websites and participating in Slack and Circle channels as well as several discords. Google can be a great resource if you want to find some peer-reviewed information and credible data as well when you're starting out.

Here's a list of resources I use regularly:

- LinkedIn
- Mastermind and Facebook groups
- Slack and Circle channels of like-minded investors
- The Morning Brew
- globest.com
- *Harvard Business Review*
- Trusted thought leader websites and courses
- Newsletters (both paid and free)
- ibisworld.com
- bizbuysell.com
- neighborhoodscout.com
- rentometer.com
- airdna.co
- irr.com
- mobilehomeparkuniversity.com
- bestplaces.net
- costar.com

- crexi.com
- propstream.com
- My blog, free ebooks, and other information about ways to start your investing journey on my website at cashflowmd.com.

MENTORS

A relationship with a mentor is the bridge between book education and doing it yourself. Through reading, going to conferences, and listening to podcasts, you will have learned enough to know which questions to ask a mentor that will draw out their experience and expertise. Mentorship takes the learning out of the abstract and allows you to have a shared experience. With guidance and support, you will be able to discover where the landmines are and learn from your mentor's experience of what didn't work and what did work in his or her career so that you are in a better position to take action.

A good mentor is somebody who is currently where you want to be. Keep in mind, though, that just because someone is a little further down the road doesn't mean they are qualified to be your mentor. I've made that mistake a few times. Ideally, you want to find someone who has gone to the mountain top, maybe had a tumble or two, but recovered in a better position with lots of wisdom to share. There are so-called "experts" out there who have been in business for just about a minute who "teach" but have limited firsthand experience—some have never actually actively done any deals themselves! From the beginning, I made it a point to learn from people who have put in the time. I want to know they've lived through a few market cycles and came out stronger on the other side so they can better equip me with what they learned from their experience. I want mentors who are tried, tested, and true.

A good mentor will help you uncover your own superpower. For example, mine helped me discover I'm a problem-solver and skilled at correcting inefficiencies. From medicine to real estate—solving problems is the common denominator in everything I've done. I've become adept at finding inefficiencies and figuring out how to build a better mousetrap. That's essentially what I do with the Investable Universe: I spot opportunities and figure out how to leverage them. In order to be able to offer people true solutions to a problem, however, I need to have breadth and depth of knowledge that comes both from education *and* experience. Having one or two things in my tool belt isn't enough—If you're a hammer, everything is a nail. I'm more of a Swiss army knife: A versatile lifelong learner who constantly searches for new experiences, ideas, strategies, tools, and solutions.

MY VERY FIRST MENTOR

Although I didn't come from a classic academic family, I was pretty gifted in that realm. I knew I wanted to be in a profession where I served people, as that was my passion. I didn't know any doctors or really anyone in healthcare except my sister-in-law. She was an occupational therapist at the time, and I shadowed her where she worked in a major rehab hospital. I was fascinated after spending time in the spinal cord unit by how she was able to impact her patients' lives. It seemed like a good fit for me, so I decided to become an occupational therapist.

I was fortunate in that a rehabilitation hospital in town paid for a large part of my education. In turn, I agreed to work for them for as many years as it took until my salary equaled what they had paid for my education.

When I had been working for them for less than a year, the government made drastic healthcare changes, which hit rehab hospitals hard.

Employers panicked because overnight the government drastically cut reimbursement for things like physical therapy, occupational therapy, and speech therapy. They were caught completely off guard and implemented patchwork cost-saving strategies that were doomed to fail. We used to be able to take an hour to evaluate our patients and be involved in their treatment plans. Now, we had fifteen minutes for evaluation and had to pass along the treatment plan to an OT or PT aide. Even then, the revenue shock was just too much for a large rehab hospital to absorb. They let over thirty therapists go, and the newest ones were let go first...like me.

Because they did not have a position for me, they forgave my indebtedness. That was a huge blessing. The not-so-good part, however, was that I was now out of a job. I ended up doing some *locum tenens*—going around and doing spot therapy here and there—but I quickly realized that wasn't something I was very interested in doing for the rest of my life.

My uncle I mentioned before (remember my first $100 bill?) was a pharmacist, but he was also a very successful entrepreneur. I wasn't sure about everything he did—I just knew he did a lot. I came to find out that he had started generic pharmaceutical manufacturing companies where he would manufacture off-label brands. He also started a very successful durable medical equipment company. My uncle was involved in lots of entrepreneurial pursuits, so I called him and asked if he had any ideas. He told me something that struck me as odd at the time: if I learned to sell, I would always have money.

It felt kind of smarmy. What did I know about sales? I had worked as a landscaper all through school. We dug ditches and we made beautiful landscapes, and by the end of the day, I could see what I produced. It was tangible. Sales just seemed like something people who couldn't (or wouldn't) work hard did. I didn't realize initially that what my uncle really meant was **I needed to learn how to add value to people's lives**.

However, I took his advice quite literally, and I jumped into pharmaceutical sales. I learned quickly that sales isn't just about selling. I needed to figure out where the pain points were with the physicians and the patients, and how those could be solved with the medicines that I could potentially offer. It wasn't necessarily, *I've got this medicine, and I have to make this doctor believe that it's a good medicine.* It was more along the lines of, *Let's solve this problem together.* I liked being a problem-solver.

I knew that if my pharmaceuticals would help that physician's population, it would be a win for both of us. My job became about seeing the gaps in patient care, and then just seeing if what I had would fill some of those gaps. It was a really eye-opening experience for sure, and it taught me exactly what my uncle wanted me to learn: to find a way to add the most value I could to the lives of patients, physicians, and the staff.

Being a pharmaceutical rep was the beginning of my love of medicine. I had to learn a lot about the human body, anatomy, and physiology. I liked that aspect of OT as well, but I was enthralled with learning pharmacokinetics, pharmacologics, pharmacodynamics, and all of the different ways that medicines act on the body.

It was the message behind the sales job that arose from my very first mentor, my uncle, that helped me uncover my true and lasting passion and one of the greatest secrets of business and life success: learning how to add value to people's lives. It's *everything*.

I still make it a priority to ensure I have quality mentors around me. Having experts in my corner who are further along in the journey than me has been one of the greatest force multipliers of my ability to have success.

LEARNING GROUPS AND MASTERMINDS

One of the most profitable investments I've made (and continue to make today) is in my own education. I've already talked about learning from books, experience, and mentors—now I want to discuss putting your actual money to work by investing in yourself. It is crucial to your success. In fact, I suggest you take 10% to 20% of the money you plan to invest and first set it aside for education. The best asset you can invest in is what's between your ears: the more you know, the more value you're going to add. The more value you add, the more value you attract to yourself.

One of the ways I choose to up-level my education is to join learning groups. As the entrepreneur Jim Rohn said (and I've said a hundred times since), "You are the average of the five people you spend the most time with." The scripture 1 Corinthians 15:33 says it this way: "Bad company corrupts good character." When talking with my kids about this Bible passage, I couldn't help but say, "Yes! Exactly! Show me your friends, and I'll show you your future. It *matters* who you are hanging out with! You become most like those you spend the most time with." It's the same reason why people seek out great residencies and medical schools: they want to learn from the best. And so do I.

When I realized that I was losing my vision and wasn't going to be able to practice anesthesia, I spent a huge amount of time and money on self-improvement. I needed to take stock of my skill sets and see what was going to bring the most fulfillment, purpose, and happiness. I could potentially become a Chief Medical Officer or get involved in academic medicine, but those options didn't really appeal to me. They just seemed like another job I could potentially lose. Reading *Rich Dad, Poor Dad* by Robert Kiyosaki really changed my life, because it showed me that financial prosperity is about the assets, and shifted my paradigms around money and investing. I began having conversations with my wife, and talking about the possibility of leaning into real estate as a sustainable financial future.

I realized that in order to be successful, I'd have to learn and then take action with somebody who had done it before. I would start with multifamily real estate, and then I would rinse and repeat with every new asset class I wanted to learn. When my business partner and I decided we wanted to focus on multifamily, as I've mentioned previously, we read *Rich Dad, Poor Dad*, and it made total sense to me. But then, we went out and sought mentors in the space who walked alongside us for almost nine months. They taught us everything they knew about multifamily.

But it wasn't easy. There I was, losing my ability to practice medicine, and the learning group was wanting me to pay $20,000 to join. I mean, $20,000 was (and still is!) a lot of money. I was the sole breadwinner in the family, and because it felt as though my future wasn't totally known, spending this felt like a huge leap. I did enough research to be confident about the program, and then—despite a few reservations—I decided to do the program. It was scary. I couldn't help but wonder, *Am I making the right decision with this?*

At some point, though, I had to trust myself. I'm a fairly smart person, and it's not like I was just throwing $20,000 in a slot machine. I'd done a lot of research into this space, and it wasn't like I was skimming the internet looking for ideas and ran across this group by chance. I believed in the concept of cash-flowing assets. I believed in the economies of scale offered by multifamily. Then I started to really narrow down and search for the people who were very good at what they did and who would be willing to teach me.

My confidence didn't erase my fear, though, which is not necessarily a bad thing. Some fear and anxiety can keep you motivated, and keep you interested. Just as in med school, you always needed to have something keeping you focused and pushing you a little bit. That fear of the unknown can be a motivating tool, but I understand that for a lot of people it can be paralyzing, too. If I had been randomly searching the internet and came across a learning group who advertised, "Hey, come learn from us for $20,000," I would have been paralyzed. But it was a deliberate process of going down a path that culminated in me discovering my first learning group. It was much more of a deliberate search than it was just throwing spaghetti at a wall to see what strand sticks.

I understand that there are hurdles when it comes to investing in yourself. And a lot of it goes back to mindset. Whether it's a real financial or a psychological/perceived hurdle, you might have to overcome a lot to invest in yourself at this level. Let's use a $50,000 mastermind fee as an example. That's a lot of money! It's daunting and scary. But what if the group could change the way you think, invest, grow your circle, and have huge implications for your life? As far back as 1937 when Napoleon Hill wrote the runaway classic *Think and Grow Rich*, he devoted an entire chapter to "The Power of the Mastermind." To summarize, power is required to achieve success. You acquire that power from a group of people who have come together for the realization of a definite purpose. A harmonious Mastermind alliance amplifies power exponentially.[5]

You have to take responsibility and ownership of your future, and you have to view the cost as an INVESTMENT versus an expense. Learning groups and mastermind groups are an amazing way to surround yourself with people who think differently, who think in ways of abundance, who think of ways of investing rather than speculating about how not to run out of money before you die. The age of the internet has really kind of ignited this type of learning. Social media has provided a powerful platform for leveraging knowledge, and it has really awakened a lot of folks.

Learning groups introduce you to a network of people who are open to having meaningful conversations. But let's be clear: I'm not talking about just throwing money at something and hoping you learn. I'm talking about finding out where your passion and/or your interests lie, and then educating yourself and investing in yourself fully by joining a group where both the peers and the leadership team will be powerful multipliers to your learning journey.

3. ENGAGE in your learning

The term "passive" investing is thrown around a lot. I think it's very possible to be a passive investor from a time requirement standpoint eventually, but it's virtually impossible to be passive from a knowledge or learning perspective. Even if you aren't doing the deals actively, you need to be able to hold the sponsor to the highest accountability, so understanding each step is vital. Each step requires education, experience, and a reassessment to see what needs to be done differently the next time you do a deal. This requires engagement.

We didn't become excellent physicians overnight. It took dedication and effort over time. We shouldn't expect to become expert investors without dedication and effort, either.

The way we have honed our skills in medicine is a similar methodology you will undertake to master your craft as an investor. It takes money, time, and effort to learn how to:

- Find the deals
- Underwrite the deals
- Negotiate the deals
- Do due diligence
- Acquire the assets
- Complete the value-add
- Exit the deal
- Rinse and repeat

Think of the great mentors and attendings who guided us along the way to becoming physicians. The ones we remember stretched us. Their methods were probably not "I tell you, and then you do"—it was more about getting us to trust ourselves and developing our expertise. They instilled new ideas and techniques while skillfully melding them with the already-existing knowledge we had. We couldn't simply be passive observers. We had to engage. I think engaging is how most physicians learn best. We get stretched and are made to be a little uncomfortable, while simultaneously thinking through tough problems and questions. We then assess our performance and adjust accordingly. Lots of similarities to investing.

When you actively engage in your education, you tend to learn things on a different level. Now is the time to take ownership of what you want your future to look like. It's not up to some financial planner… it's up to YOU.

And this isn't just about engaging with your learning at the macro level: it is equally relevant and important at the micro level, too. If I'm going to take the time to read a book, for example, it needs to be something that moves the needle for me. I like to read the book with at least one other person and share takeaways. Sometimes it's a peer, but one of the most powerful multipliers in my educational quest has been having my mentor walk me through some of the key principles in the book and how they can apply to my situation. I guess what I'm suggesting is not being a *let's just read a book and put it down* type of person. My time is valuable, and so is yours. Ask your mentor for books that can compress time for you and have them highlight life applications they have drawn from it. If I'm going to spend my time on a particular subject, it has to be applicable to my life, and I want to walk along the path with a person who knows the way. I think this separates an investor from a spectator.

It's not just reading or listening to a podcast or going to conferences—it's all of those things put together and ENGAGING with the content through dialogue and conversations with a strong mentor that catapults you toward financial freedom. Find a strong mentor to guide you, engage in active learning, and find the investment vehicles that will give you the cash flow and ultimately the lifestyle you desire that trading time for money as a doc just can't give you.

4. EMPOWER those who come behind you

Once you have developed a foundational competency in investing and have experienced some success, one of the most rewarding ways to deepen your learning is to share your knowledge with someone else. When we teach, we need to think about *why* we make the decisions we do so that we can explain our reasoning to others. We are forced to evaluate the quality of our track record, and analyze successes and failures. It is through teaching that we reflect and improve our own skill set.

A MINDSET OF GENEROSITY

We've been taught by society that it's survival of the fittest, that there is a limited amount of pie, and everybody has to fight for their slice before it's gone. That's faulty thinking—one of those mindset myths we discussed earlier.

It's of the utmost importance to me that I'm involved in assets and deals where everybody wins. When we start talking about being generous with our time and knowledge, the mindset of being a "giver" really needs to be a part of who you become. The more you give of yourself to other people and the more value you add to others, the more personal satisfaction and purpose you will receive. Contentment and peace come from being able to lift others up with you. Isn't this why most of us went into medicine in the first place?

If you are a person who has a scarcity mindset, who is out for yourself, or who thinks there's only so much to go around, you may make money, but you will never be truly wealthy. Being rich is one thing, but being wealthy is about so much more than finances. What's more important—to have a ton of money, or to have contentment and peace along with the money? For the record, I strongly believe you can have both when you're operating in abundance.

BECOMING A MENTOR YOURSELF

As I began to find success in real estate and other investments, a lot of other physicians approached me, asking to have coffee, lunch, or dinner with them in exchange for some advice. After gaining forty pounds from all of these coffees and food, I realized that this wasn't the best way for my health to give back to my colleagues.

In my mid-40s, I had a series of really good financial exits and began to think, *Okay, what's next?* I felt like I had a certain skill set that could help solve many of the financial issues physicians often brought up when we met. My colleagues were suffering, but I could help them. I put out as much free content as possible and let people consume as much as they wanted on their own. But there are a lot of people who don't want to do it on their own. So, I began to focus on how I could support physicians in a more tangible way. That was when I became a mentor to others.

Time and time again, I heard from physician friends and colleagues how miserable and overworked they were. They were burnt out and afraid that they wouldn't have enough money set aside to retire. A lot of these folks had forgotten why they went to med school. Some had even forgotten why they became physicians in the first place.

My driving passion behind mentorship was my firm belief that having your financial house in order enables you to practice medicine because you *want to,* not because you have to. There is freedom that comes with having financial security. My mentorship involved much more than just investing and real estate. It revolved around fundamental mindset shifts like finding the "why" behind our actions.

The older I get, the more I understand Maslow's hierarchy of needs. When you are in survival mode and doing what you have to do to get by, you can't possibly serve others well. There are many layers between survival and self-actualization that are never explored, and your purpose gets buried beneath the daily grind. My goal as a mentor is to help take people from surviving to thriving, to then open up their minds so they are free to reconnect with their deeper purpose. There is a direct alignment between a person's spiritual path of purpose and the work they do. This begins with *why* you do what you do.

What does "finding your why" really mean? It's discovering your purpose, passion, or the deeper reason behind what you do. My *why* is Faith, Family, and Freedom, as I mentioned earlier. It's up to you to identify the core motivations that drive your actions, choices, and goals. Finding your *why* involves introspection to understand what truly matters to you, what brings meaning to your life, and what gives you a sense of fulfillment. It's a guiding principle that helps you stay focused, motivated, and aligned with your values as you navigate your life. Finding your *why* is super important, because you're going to need it. When times get tough, it's the *why* that you will lean on for purpose, joy, and fulfillment.

That's why the phrase "practice because you want to, not because you have to" resonates so deeply with me. I strive to reconnect people to their original purpose and why they are in medicine in the first place. We can wander pretty far away from the true north on our life's compass if we engage in actions contrary to our *why*. We get busy with things that don't matter, indebted to possessions we don't need, and stuck in a rat race with no margin for error. But what if you *had* margin?

I help people find their way back to margin. Once you are able to create some margin, you can breathe again, dream, and engage in life! Your *why* becomes your driving force—not billing more relative value units (RVUs). Since that first coffee with a beleaguered colleague many years ago, I knew it was my passion to share my secrets with as many physicians as possible so they can practice for as long as they want… *because they WANT to.*

WE LEARN IN COMMUNITY

There is no doubt that real estate investing is a team sport. Whether you are a mentor, mentee, or peer, it pays to create a network of like-minded people. These are trusted partners who are willing to have conversations on a regular basis, sharing successes and failures, knowledge about the economy, and other factors that influence the value of your investments and potential opportunities. The greater your network, the more ability you have to make your own educated, informed decisions about how you would like to invest your money. Your network will, in large part, decide your net worth, so build your community wisely! Let's dive into the next chapter and learn how to do just that.

CHAPTER SIX

USE YOUR NETWORK TO RAISE YOUR AVERAGE

PILLAR 3: NETWORK

"Your network is your net worth. How do you value your network? Well, if you don't value it, cultivate it, and nurture it, it becomes worthless. If you do value it, it becomes priceless."
Robert G. Allen

ONE RELATIONSHIP CAN TRULY CHANGE EVERYTHING

One of my colleagues uses a fantastic tagline: "You are one relationship away." I really think that's true. The more quality people we engage with, the more we learn. You never know where the next great deal will come from, or who has that insight. So, it's important that you remain open, form strong relationships, and ask a lot of questions. Work with those you know, like, and trust. Make sure you evaluate the relationships you have and the mentors you choose to learn under as you will likely emulate their path.

And—you've done this before. When you were going into residency, you looked at the residency director, the attendings you would be working with, and the reputation of the program. When finding a group to invest with, you need to be asking similar questions...Have they done this before? How long have they been doing this? What are their results? Instead of asking if you are going to become a better physician at this residency program, you are reframing to ask: *Is my financial picture going to get better by investing with this group?*

You truly may be only one relationship away from exponential growth.

WHO'S IN YOUR NETWORK?

Your network is not simply about the number of people you know, but the *quality* of connections you make.

Ideally, you want to make connections with people and service providers—with a variety of expertise—that fall into five main categories:

- Structural Support
- Financial Support
- Subject Matter Experts
- Operational Service Providers
- Advisors

Some specific examples of these are as follows:

QUALIFYING YOUR NETWORK

Here are some questions I like to ask people I'm considering bringing into my circle in an effort to gauge their level of expertise and general outlook on investing. By including these in my initial conversations with them, I am able to assess how they may help accelerate my circle's financial and/or time freedom. Thinking about how they can add value to MY CIRCLE rather than MYSELF broadens my perspective and takes the focus off of me personally. It's of the utmost importance to me to determine not just if someone will contribute in a meaningful way to my life but also—perhaps even more importantly—if they are someone I would risk my reputation on by referring others to them. That's the power of a great network: it shortens the learning curve by having a pre-vetted group of amazing humans who, by association, have accelerated trust. As such, it's critically important to figure out if someone in your network aligns with your vision, has invaluable knowledge, can offer mentorship, and/or is an innovative thinker.

Tactical Questions

- What do you currently do with your income?
- Have you ever run a balance sheet on your finances?
- Have you ever had any side-gigs or entrepreneurial pursuits?

- Do you log your time? How much time do you spend on what activities?
- How does your calendar reflect your priorities?
- What is your biggest pain point?
- How does this affect your ability to engage in new pursuits?
- What are your abilities and superpowers?
- Do you use a financial planner?
- Are you an accredited investor?
- What three things can I help *you* the most with?
- Have you been in a mastermind program?
- Do you have a mentor(s)?
- Are you a mentor yourself?

Philosophical Questions

- What is your relationship with money?
- What was your retirement strategy five years ago, and what is it now?
- What is "a lot of money" to you?
- Do you have investment rules?
- How do you spend your time?
- What does the picture of your perfect life look like?
- If you had true financial freedom, what would your life look like?
- Why do you want to embark on this journey?
- Is all debt bad?
- Who influences your financial decisions the most?
- What books do you love?
- How do you learn from mistakes?

I find these questions to be excellent conversation starters, because each one naturally leads to follow-up questions. For example, when I ask what someone's relationship with investing and money is, I usually follow up with:

- What are you investing in now?
- How much are you currently investing?
- What have you invested in in the past?
- What are your investment goals?
- Do you invest inside or outside of the stock market?

These questions often help me quickly realize if I'm speaking with someone who I'd like to work with (or not). For instance, I was on a call with a neurologist who "had it all figured out." He told me he had maxed out his 401(k), his 457, and his 403(b) plans. When I asked him if any of these created cash flow for him currently, he simply said he didn't need cash flow right now because he had a great job. My next question was, "What would happen if that job was taken away?" He became defensive immediately rather than thoughtfully considering the question. He wasn't the least bit interested in exploring alternative investment strategies, he only wanted me to validate what he was already doing. I knew right away to put a red light on the relationship. He was so closed-minded and stuck in his beliefs about the "right way" of doing things that I couldn't even pry the door open a little bit. I don't want to work with people who don't want to be collaborative or open to alternative strategies.

Personally, I want people in my circle who are humble, hungry to learn, and generous with their knowledge. I like people who think a little bit differently, and even if they don't agree with me, they are still excited about having a conversation and hearing new ideas. I learn a lot from these relationships. I've had people respectfully disagree with me and say, "Well, I used to own rental property, and it was horrible." Instead of responding with "I'm sorry to hear that," and steering away from the conversation, I want to know more. So I'll say, "Tell me about it. I'm interested because that has not been my experience. I'd love to hear what happened." Then it becomes a conversation we can both benefit from.

A CASE STUDY IN THE POWER OF NETWORKING

In 2021, I was researching hot real estate areas within five hours of where I live. Often when I invest, I want to have the option for operational input, so I like to have direct flight access or at least a reasonable drive to the location.

I found an Airbnb two hours away that was rated an A+ (the strongest rating for short-term vacation rentals). I started to get more granular in my exploration and found that this property checked all of my boxes. So, I reached out to my commercial broker, asking if he knew anyone in the area. He mentioned some names of brokers who might have some off-market deals (I always prefer off-market first).

In 2021 it was almost impossible to find a house. Everyone was overbidding, and you just couldn't find a deal. Yes, it was competitive—but I was still a firm believer that the deals were out there if you were willing to do the work and utilize your network.

My broker put me in touch with his contacts and put some feelers out. I ended up talking to a local broker who mentioned three Airbnbs not yet on the market. It just so happened that the sellers needed a fast close on one of them due to a messy divorce. I was able to offer a cash deal with a quick close at 20% less than the appraised value. They took it.

I would never have found this deal without curating a robust network years before this.

CHAPTER SEVEN

BUILD YOUR NETWORK AND THE DEALS WILL COME

PILLAR 4: DEAL FLOW

There's a reason Deal Flow is further down the continuum of The Five Pillars. Without a proper mindset, knowledge of what constitutes a good asset, and a network in place, you don't have the fundamentals needed to be considering deals. These pillars build on each other, so skipping out of sequence will weaken your foundation and can bring your whole investment structure crumbling down.

The deals will come. And when they do, you'll be equipped with the proper mindset, knowledge, and network to maximize the opportunity. The more deal flow you get, the more your network and knowledge grows, and your mindset continues to evolve. It's a virtuous cycle.

Building a strong network on your own in order to get access to more individual deals for yourself will take time and effort and has a steep learning curve. No question about it, there IS an easier way to get vetted deals if you're willing to leverage the power of trusted partners (see the section on Fellowship in the next chapter on Pillar Five: Action). For now, though, let's continue down this path and assume you want to actively engage in finding deal flow on your own. How do you go about getting access to deals? Where do you start?

While there is no exact "how-to guide" or road map to getting deals on your own since there are a LOT of variables in terms of time, experience, and expertise, here are a few tips and tricks to at least get you started:

1. Define your investment criteria: Clearly articulate the type of investment you are interested in and what parameters the deal must have to work for you. Most call this their "Acquisition Criteria." The more narrow and specific your criteria are, the quicker you will be able to notice the right deals when they cross your path and the easier it is for brokers and sellers to know what you're looking for.

2. Leverage your contacts by reaching out to your existing network and letting them know about your investment criteria. They may provide referrals or introductions to others that can bring you a potential investment opportunity and grow your network at the same time!

3. Grow your circle using targeted outreach. Proactively contact brokers, owners, lenders, or entrepreneurs in the space you want to be. This can be done through referral from a colleague, cold calling, email introductions, attending industry conferences, or leveraging your mentor.

4. Develop a strong online presence. Consider creating a professional website or online profile across different channels that highlight your investment focus, value you add, and expertise. If you have past successes, include these as well so those with deals can see you have the ability to perform. Social media platforms such as LinkedIn are great for sharing insights, networking, and having conversations with people in the investment community you're trying to gain traction.

5. Go to local investor clubs, meet-ups, and conferences, or consider joining a mastermind group. There's no better way to meet other investors and owners than to go where they are and show you are for real. These interactions provide opportunities for networking, new partnerships, and discovering potential deals while also learning from others in the process. And don't forget…YOU KNOW THINGS TOO! Do not sell yourself short. Everyone has value to add.

6. It's a good idea to prioritize potential deals. Maintaining a deal tracking system using specific software, spreadsheets, or even a dedicated deal flow management tool can help keep you organized and rank deals against your acquisition criteria. Regularly review, adjust, and follow up on the opportunities that best fit your criteria to ensure you're spending time on the correct types of deals.

7. Have your house in order and don't "kick tires." Nothing will turn off a seller or broker faster than someone who has a million questions but no ability to close. Get qualified and funded, and be ready to move forward. Respond quickly to communications, and get ready to be decisive. Deals can often move faster than you think, so being proactive and equipped is super important.

Remember that creating deal flow requires consistent effort, patience, and persistence. Continuously refine and adapt your strategies based on your goals and market dynamics. Once you get the first deal under your belt, you'll be shocked at how the deals then start to *find you*. Beginning is hard and tedious, but if you set up your systems correctly from the onset, it will pay dividends for many years to come.

ANALYZING AN INVESTMENT

There are different ways to analyze a deal's return on investment (ROI), or how much profit the investment stands to generate.

Here's a short glossary, in layman's terms, that will be helpful to know in advance (and for a full glossary, please refer to the back of this book at the end of the Resource Guide):

ROI - return on investment - ROI tells you how much money you've made (or lost) on an investment or project after accounting for its cost.[6]

MOIC - money on invested capital - Also known as *equity multiple,* MOIC is a measurement of your return based on capital invested: if you invest $10,000 and return $100,000, the MOIC of your investment is 10x.[7]

CoC (Cash-on-Cash) return - This refers to the calculation of cash income earned on the cash invested in a property.[8]

IRR - internal rate of return - This is the annual rate of growth an investment is expected to generate, taking into account the amount of time the money is invested.[9]

There are an inordinate number of ways to quantify the idea of returns, but to me where the rubber meets the road is Cash-on-Cash—the money I'm getting, based on my invested capital. This is important because it tells me how quickly I will get my principal back. The faster I get my principal back, the faster I can reinvest it into my next deal.

I also lean heavily on MOIC or Equity Multiple (EM) return parameters in deals that don't necessarily have a large cash flow component. If I am invested in a development deal that has a three- to five-year time horizon on the investment, for example, I may see very little cash flow for years during the construction phase. As a result, my CoC during those five years may be minimal to nothing because it's not generating cash flow. However, upon the sale of the asset, the EM may be 3-5x—meaning I have tripled or quintupled my initial investment over those years it was invested. In this instance, it's the EM I'm interested in, not necessarily the cash flow.

CREATIVE FUNDING STRATEGIES

When the deals start to flow, you're going to need access to funds.

Oftentimes, the people in your network are the key players in getting you what you need, but for learning purposes we need to talk about the *how* and the *what* before we talk about the *who*. Having an education in creative funding strategies is an important fundamental to master so you have a strong sense of which tool may come into play and be most applicable for each different type of investment deal that rolls in once your momentum gets going.

Let's start by exploring some well-known and lesser-known various funding options available. It's difficult to say which is my "favorite," as every asset I purchase has a different underlying situation.

Seller Carrybacks/Seller Financing

If I *did* have to pick a favorite strategy, this is probably it. This is when you negotiate with the seller of the asset to carry a portion (or all) of the note to where the owner provides some or all of the financing.

It's great for the seller because they don't realize the entirety of the sale upfront and can be taxed on the proceeds incrementally. If they're selling a $10 million property but they have a $5 million note, for example, they only pay capital gains on $5 million immediately. It can be a powerful tax strategy for them.

This financing option offers both parties a lot of flexibility. The note can be set up to amortize, have no payments, have just one balloon payment, or pay interest only for a set amount of years. Let's say you are taking over a mobile home park that has really low occupancy, thus low immediate cash flow. You know you can raise it to 85% occupancy in a year or two, but you don't want to carry a heavy monthly loan payment for all that time. You could ask for a 50% seller carryback, which has a balloon payment in three years. The seller would get 50% of the sales price upfront, and they would carry the other 50%. The "other" 50% is where you can get creative. You may work it out to where you'll refinance in two years and pay the seller off in one balloon payment, or you could just make interest-only payments on the seller note portion to help with cash flow. It's super flexible and offers lots of creativity for both buyer and seller.

A seller willing to hold part of the note is generally a good sign to me. It shows me they believe in what they have built, and the success they expect us to have with the asset. If the deal is completely seller-financed, the seller effectively acts as the bank and is in a first position on the mortgage on the property. If a bank is involved and the seller is offering partial financing, the seller will have to take a second position on the mortgage behind the bank.

Repair Credits

This is a great way to decrease the out-of-pocket costs in purchasing an asset. It usually results after due diligence uncovers deferred maintenance that definitely needs to be addressed, but wouldn't be a deal breaker (and the repairs could be completed over time). Instead of retrading the entire deal at a lower price and having to reengineer bank loan docs, sales agreements, etc., the seller agrees to pay for some of the necessary repairs to the property by crediting the buyer the amount it would take for the repairs on the settlement (closing) statement. Any credit to the purchaser on the settlement statement decreases the out-of-pocket equity required to close and can be a great lever to use if you are trying to minimize the cash needed to close.

Leverage

I like to call leverage "OPM," which stands for "Other People's Money." This can be creative depending on the lender's appetite for the asset, but this is basically going the traditional route and getting a loan through a bank.

Remember, as we discussed in the mindset chapter, there *is* a difference between leverage and debt. Debt is when you take on a liability to buy an *expense* (like a mortgage on a home you're going to live in). Leverage is when you take on a liability to purchase an asset *that cash flows.*

Creativity with traditional loans can look like periods of interest only, pushing leverage to a higher loan to value (LTV), lengthening the amortization schedule, making the loan assumable, or carving out a nonrecourse pathway, to name a few. Using leverage is a powerful and necessary tool in my investment toolbelt.

Dual-interest Banking

What if you could invest your money into a product that is earning interest and creating equity, and at the same time use the same money and put it to work in other investments as well? Can you imagine being your own bank? That's what dual-interest banking allows you to do.

Using the chassis of permanent life insurance, you are able to borrow money from yourself, pay interest to yourself, and put the borrowed funds to work in other investments, as well.

To utilize this strategy, you invest in either Index Universal or Whole Life policies. Most policies make 3-9% annually, so your principal in the life insurance investment grows. You then borrow against the funds in the policy and put them to work in another investment, so you're effectively growing your wealth two different ways.

As the policies season, you can begin to borrow from them for retirement as well. The super attractive aspect of this is these funds are tax-free because they are a "loan" from your policy, not a distribution. It's a very nice way to lend money to yourself for investments now and loan money to yourself later for tax-free retirement!

A word of warning: only work with fiduciaries in this space. There are a lot of bad actors out there, so I encourage you to do your full due diligence to find the right partner. You want to find an independent broker who has access to any policy on the market so you can choose the best investment for your situation and not what the broker is beholden to because they work for a big box insurer. Some of these policies offered by company agents have 80% commissions or higher the first year, and are loaded with fund fees as well. Additionally, they encourage you to leave your funds in the policy to "season" before borrowing out to invest in other assets (because the first year is so laden with fees and commissions—there is rarely money available to borrow against!). Fiduciaries generally take MUCH less in commissions and fees, and give you access to borrow your funds within hours…not years.

If this option sounds too good to be true, you can find out more at cashflowmd.com/our-affiliates/ and decide for yourself.

Self-directed Retirement Account (SDIRA)

SDIRA's are a great way to fund your investments. Whether you're using a Traditional or Roth IRA, I generally recommend using these tax-*advantaged* vehicles to invest in tax-*dis*advantaged assets. For example, if you want to use your SDIRA to purchase a rental property, it's still likely going to outperform the stock market, but you aren't realizing the full potential of the tax advantages available to you. If you use your SDIRA to invest in a tax-disadvantaged asset like a debt fund or a house flipping partnership, the proceeds you make from these endeavors *will* realize the tax benefits of using the SDIRA as that profit comes back into your SDIRA tax-free.

Broker Dealers

This is a bit of an advanced strategy, as you'll have to have a legal structure in place that will allow for this type of capital. With this type of funding, broker dealers (licensed professionals who keep their accreditation through continuing education and training) essentially act as paid capital raisers and bring investors to your deal for a fee. They are hired to drum up interest in your deal through their vast network of investors. You pay them a percentage, generally 3-6%, of the capital they raise for your deal, and—in turn—they bring you accredited investor capital for your deal. You must be *absolutely sure* they are registered as a broker dealer, because there are strict SEC requirements they must meet in order to be considered a broker dealer, so be sure to do your homework.

If you are just starting out capital raising and don't have a robust investor network yet, this can definitely be a viable option.

Small Business Administration (SBA) loans

An SBA loan does a great job of providing capital to folks who might otherwise not be able to get it. SBA loans generally have a lower interest rate, longer amortization periods, and kinder terms than traditional loans. However, they also come with a lot of red tape. The reporting requirements can be onerous, and many times people need to hire a third party to help (which can be expensive). Regardless, this is a viable option for people wanting to buy, sell, and operate businesses. These loans also often take a long time to originate, so if the deal is time-sensitive, this may not be the funding vehicle to consider.

Private Equity Lenders

Private equity is a pooled source of funds that lend to specific types of operators. These "pooled sources" are generally high net-worth individuals and institutions such as endowments, family offices, and pension funds.

This type of financing is generally very expensive. Many times, the private equity lenders require partial ownership in the venture. Other times, they negotiate a preferred debt position, equity kickers, or warrant coverage (a piece of equity in the deal or some type of "sweetener" on the back end that lowers your returns and "sweetens" the deal for them)—*in addition to* seeking returns through capital appreciation. Additionally, the private equity lender will likely ask you for a personal guarantee.

These investors are at a higher risk because their success is based on the performance of the business they become involved in. If it fails, they have nothing (unlike a hard asset lender). For this reason, private equity lenders tend to take on an active interest in the deal: providing strategic guidance, or negotiating a board seat.

This type of investment is usually less liquid. The exit strategy generally involves selling the equity stake through the sale of the company, or taking it public through an initial public offering (IPO).

Hard Money Lenders

A hard money loan is a type of loan that is secured by real property, and is usually a short-term bridge loan. These loans are primarily used in real estate transactions and are often called "asset-based" loans. These lenders are generally individuals or companies and not banks. The primary advantage of a hard money loan is *speed.* Hard money loans can be arranged much more quickly than a loan through a traditional bank. In some cases, hard money lenders can issue funds in as little as a day, while traditional banks have a wait time of thirty to sixty days for funding. Most hard money lenders can offer flexibility on lending limits as well, and loan terms are generally short (six to eighteen months).[10] Not only are the returns typically very healthy for the hard money lender, but they also have the right to retain the asset should the borrower default on payments. And even though the loan is secured by real property (i.e., real estate, machinery or equipment, accounts receivable inventory, etc.), don't be surprised if hard money lenders also require some type of personal collateral during uncertain economic times to de-risk their investment. The value of the collateral becomes a critical factor in the lending decision, and if the value isn't appealing, lenders may look elsewhere in your portfolio for additional collateral.

Asset-based loans are a strong option for people looking for short-term loan periods. These funds allow you to stabilize or improve your assets. For a physician who wants to start flipping houses, for example, a traditional bank loan may not work (they'll want to see your experience, and they may want your own house as collateral as well), so a hard money loan is potentially ideal. This funding option tends to be very expensive (as the lenders charge upfront points, prepayment penalties, and generally have very high interest rates), but if you're doing a short-term investment or a flip, that might not matter because you'll be planning to pay the loan back quickly regardless.

(High-limit) Credit Cards

I know several people who started by getting a credit card with a $25,000 limit and used it to make a down payment on their first property flip (BEWARE: this strategy depends entirely on how quickly you can flip your project!).

My average flip is forty-one days in rehab and nineteen days on the market, which puts me right at the sixty-day mark. If you purchased with a credit card, the strategy would be to make the minimum payments each month, then pay off the balance upon sale of the property. Then you can use the profit made from that deal as your equity for the next.

To be clear, I am not encouraging you to go out and get $300,000 worth of credit cards and buy a bunch of houses. It's much cheaper and less risky to use other sources of capital. This may, however, be a viable way to at least get started. You need to do your homework: check out the average days on the market on the MSA (more on this in the Real

Estate sections in the Resource Guide in Part Two of this book), know the neighborhood, and have a good idea of how much you can sell for.

There are a number of factors that are beyond your control timing-wise with a flip, so be cautious when utilizing this strategy and make sure you have a Plan B in case things go sideways so you don't end up paying 29.99% APR if you get stuck holding the property for longer than you'd hoped or expected.

Other Creative Financing Strategies

There are a number of other strategies I've successfully used for different deals, depending on the underlying situation at play for each one. They are:

- Negotiating with banks to push leverage
- Using HELOC or equity from other assets
- Bringing on strategic partners (general partners)
- Seller Equity (seller stays in on the deal and injects cash from sale into deal)
- Syndication (limited partners)
- Funding via a 1031 exchange
- Funding via capital gains from the sale of a business
- Loans from friends and family

For you to jump in and take action (the fifth and final pillar we'll dive into in the next chapter), you're going to need funding.

Whichever funding route you choose to take, it's highly likely that your network will be an integral part of finding the right type of capital you need to close the deal.

By building your network as you read about in the last chapter, you'll be starting to gain momentum for deal flow while also building the relationships you'll need to execute the deals when it's time to take action (which is now!).

Read on to get equipped to move forward and officially get in the game with your first deal.

CHAPTER EIGHT

MOVING FORWARD AND GETTING IN THE GAME

PILLAR FIVE: ACTION

We've discussed earlier about physicians' propensity toward analysis paralysis. This is where we overanalyze to the point we paralyze ourselves and take no action. This is why Action is the last pillar. I agree, jumping into "action" without the other four pillars firmly in hand is a recipe for disaster. However, if the other pillars are in place, it's time for action. You can research for weeks and weeks. But eventually, you have to take action to realize the fruits of your labor. To truly understand something and to gain mastery, you have to move forward and "get in the game."

THE QUESTION IS WHEN, NOT IF

I believe wholeheartedly in investing in real estate despite the economic cycles. I don't wait to buy real estate, I buy real estate and wait. Not all real estate is created equal, however. It is important to carefully choose the type of real estate you want to invest in rather than purchasing the first deal that comes along.

At the writing of this book, I'm very bullish on development because we are in a huge supply hole and the economy is stalling a bit. There are not going to be a lot of people building for the next two to three years. By focusing on development, we deliver our bright, shiny new asset in three to four years when the economy will be recovering and the interest rates lowering. There will be huge demand for our supply.

Investment success is really about reading the tea leaves—seeing a problem or inefficiency and deciding where to invest in the solution. This involves informed decision-making and de-risking the investment with your knowledge and expertise.

DON'T LET FEAR HOLD YOU BACK

While I believe real estate investments are amongst the safest ways to create cash flow, it's not a foolproof plan. If you stay focused on the possibility of failure, however—on the slight chance you might lose your money—you might never take the leap. That's why I started this book by talking about mindset. If you're doing it the way we've spoken about throughout every section of this book, you aren't throwing your money into the wind: you're taking smart, calculated risks by doing thorough due diligence.

If you are still struggling with a few nerves, here is some advice I can offer:

1. Take the time to identify what you're afraid of and try to understand where it's coming from. Sometimes recognizing, acknowledging, and naming your fears can help you take steps to overcome them.

2. Once you've identified your fears, challenge them by questioning their validity. Are your fears based in reality, or are they exaggerated in your mind? Are they born from past trauma or mistakes, versus the true current situation at hand? If you've done your homework and partnered with good people, reminding yourself of this will instill confidence and alleviate concerns.

3. Instead of diving headfirst into a fear-inducing situation, take small, gradual steps. Your first deal isn't going to be the one that sets you up for life. Start with an investment that won't break the bank, and slowly push yourself outside your comfort zone. Each small victory will build your confidence, and remember: we're playing the long game.

4. Remember that we all fail once in a while. The key is to learn from your mistakes. Or, even better, learn from mine and those of the other mentors in your life (it's a lot cheaper that way!). There will inevitably be a few speed bumps along the way, but instead of letting the fear of failure paralyze you, view failure as an opportunity to learn and improve.

5. Visualize success and let this vision inspire you. Imagine what is possible once you have passive cash flow coming in that exceeds your expenses. Think about how your life could change for the better. This can help reprogram your mind to focus on success rather than fear.

Remember, everyone experiences fear at some point, but it's how we respond to it that makes a difference. By facing your fears head-on, you can break free from their limitations and open yourself up to a world of possibilities.

INVESTING VS. SPECULATING— THE IMPORTANCE OF DUE DILIGENCE

We've discussed this earlier, but it's so important it's worth revisiting the difference between speculating and investing again. Speculating is where your principal is NOT safe and you have some expectation of a return. Investing is where your principal is much safer and you have some expectation of return. Remember Warren Buffett's two rules of investing? Rule #1 and #2? Speculating is the easiest way to break these rules! It's important to take action, but it's even more important to take the *correct* action. We are investors, not speculators.

The best way to discern between the two is through your due diligence process. We will cover the details of the process in Part Two, but understand this ***must*** be done before action is taken. In the Mindset Myths section earlier on, I referenced my dad and the times in his life when he thought he was investing, but he was really just speculating. His principal wasn't safe. In truth, any investment can be a speculation if you don't do your due diligence (and it must be done properly and thoroughly—not just on the surface level).

When I become interested in an investment or asset class, I will immerse myself in it, learn as much as I can, and surround myself with the best possibilities for success. The more and more I practice this approach, the more intuitive the preparation process becomes, and—in truth— the easier it is to take action. Taking action on a deal that is outside your realm of knowledge IS speculating. It's risky, and it's gambling. The more you learn about a specific investment vehicle, the more you start to understand the red flags, what a good deal does (and doesn't) look like, and your confidence grows. That confidence makes it easier to take action in a way that is safe and is truly *investing*—not speculating.

The first time I got into multifamily real estate, it took my partner and me three months of searching to find the right area we wanted to be in. *Only then* did we start having conversations with brokers. Fast forward to the present, and in my most recent ventures into car washes, we were able to put together a general partnership in about forty-five minutes—with several million dollars of equity generated by a series of a few texts. The difference in the amount of time it takes and the speed in which you can take action depends a lot on your level of expertise and experience in a particular investment vehicle as well as the size, depth, experience, and expertise of your network. It will (and should) take time early on, especially if you're doing the deal on your own. This amount of time will reduce as your mastery increases, as will your speed when you partner with seasoned veterans who have ample deal flow and deep experience in your chosen investment vehicles.

FELLOWSHIP

As a physician, you are undoubtedly an expert student. You have dedicated years of your life to mastering your craft. You are constantly seeking new and innovative information that helps you become better, smarter, and more efficient. Investing is no different. We live in a world that offers a plethora of information, often at our fingertips. Now you need to reach out and grab it, and focus in on the key elements that have the ability to really move the needle in getting you results.

But doing so alone can be scary.

That's why I believe in the power of synergy, and working together toward a common goal.

I love the symbolism of the word "fellowship." By definition, it refers to a friendly association, especially with people who share your interests.

By the time you are in a surgical fellowship, for example, you already know surgery. You know your craft pretty well, but you're really getting zeroed in and specialized in your training. A lot of that comes with just doing more and more of what you've already been doing while expanding your horizons. In this stage of learning and practicing, your network becomes a crucial part of your team. You are joining up with others who are laser-focused—a bunch of like-minded surgeons who are learning alongside you, a company of equals with whom you can brainstorm, problem-solve, ask questions, share resources, and have inspiring conversations. This group is guided by a fellowship director who has more experience but still learns alongside the fellows as well.

This book dives into sophisticated topics and concepts, so it is definitely an advanced course in and of itself. However, before fellowship comes residency, so—as we spoke about in the introduction—you can consider this book your *investing residency.*

If by this point in the book you're ignited with the desire to delve further into forging a life of financial independence for you and your family, I also have designed the "Cash Flow Prescription " course tailored just for this purpose. It's more of a real estate fellowship where you can access a wealth of resources to embark on this journey alongside me. Within this course, my role extends beyond just presenting concepts; it's about diving deeper into the realm of smart investing and providing you with nuanced insights and hands-on strategies to enhance your prowess as an investor, all while guiding you step by step toward achieving your financial goals. You can find a direct link to the course using the QR code located at the back of this book.

Why go further into fellowship with me?

I have spent multiple six figures on my education through mentors, masterminds, courses, conferences, modules, and various other forms of education. I have over two decades of invaluable breadth and depth of experience that others do not. It's one thing to talk with someone who has invested $100,000 as a limited partner for nuggets of wisdom but quite another to collaborate with someone like me who has actually been in the trenches doing the necessary work like finding deals, getting land entitlements, working through zoning approvals, negotiating contracts, going through construction or capital improvements, taking the project to a certificate of occupancy or implementing the value-add, doing the cost seg, harvesting equity in the form of a strategic finance or exit, navigating tax issues, being on that side of it—that's a whole different level of education and experience that you need. I've built teams and systems to operate ubiquitously, no matter the asset purchased. I've purchased self-storage facilities and understand the pitfalls and how to underwrite and manage them. I own RV parks, mineral rights, short-term rentals, NNN properties, hotels, and mobile home parks. Whoever I choose to speak to and learn from—whoever becomes a part of my network—is a practical expert, not just a theoretical one. They make me a better fellowship director, and my tribe benefits from the increased exposure, network, and knowledge as well.

Whether you enter fellowship or camp out at the residency level for a while, my goal for this book is to be the trusted resource for you to use on your journey.

No matter what you end up investing in, make sure it's a deal you are comfortable with. I care deeply about placing other investors into deals I believe in and feel like they are the right fit for their goals. It really is about doing what's best for the investor. If someone is asking to invest in a deal with me and the deal is outside their financial parameters or doesn't get them closer to their goals, I will always be honest and transparent right from the get-go.

For instance, if I have a development deal and I get a call from someone who is looking for cash flow, I will let them know this likely is not the deal for them. Sure, we believe in the deal and need to raise the capital, but I'll only do so if it's in the investor's best interest. Long-term relationships with my investors are established when I find win-win investments.

A lot of this mentality comes back to my faith and to the Golden Rule: "Do unto others as you would have them do unto you" (Matt. 7:12). Even though taking action and getting into the game is important, it's also important to remember that this won't be the only deal ever, and that holding out for the *right* deal that meets your goals and needs is paramount. I hope this helps you understand a little about my mindset toward helping others and if you are eager to craft a financial future that resonates with your aspirations and goals, now is the time to delve into our "Cash Flow Prescription" course. It is designed to offer engaging material that empowers you to navigate the complexities of investing with confidence. By the end of this self-directed journey, you'll emerge with a Customized Cash Flow Prescription guide, your personal blueprint for financial freedom, meticulously tailored to support and guide your investment decisions. Go scan the QR code at the back of the book to take the first step toward mastering your financial destiny.

THE TIME IS NOW

Now that you have digested The Five Pillars of Financial Freedom, the time has come to move away from theory and into practice. We all know that merely reading about medicine is vastly different from learning how to diagnose and treat the patient in your office.

The next section of the book (Part Two) is meant to act as a practical Resource Guide, offering background information, tips, tricks, and actionable advice when it comes to making real-life investment decisions.

I want to preface this section of the book with a heads-up that we're about to get granular. There are a lot of details, which may bog you down without an understanding of how this section works. Unlike the previous sections of this book, the Resource Guide does not need to be read sequentially (other than starting with the introduction to it). If something doesn't feel relevant in the moment, skip it and dive in later. But if you hear someone talking about car washes or opportunity zones as an investment vehicle, for example, then coming back to Part Two repeatedly and flipping to the specific section(s) of the Resource Guide to learn more about these particular investment vehicles to see if they might be right for you is exactly the purpose of this portion of the book. Additionally, I have gathered all of these resources on the Resources page of my website, cashflowmd.com, which can be quickly accessed using the QR code at the end of this book.

Let's go!

PART TWO

INVESTABLE UNIVERSE RESOURCE GUIDE

RESOURCE GUIDE

THE INVESTABLE UNIVERSE

The Investable Universe: All vehicles available in which you place capital with an expectation of a return

This Resource Guide is meant to be an efficient tool to increase your knowledge and comfort level in many investment areas, and act as an initial tool for exploration. It is designed to help you start to decide which vehicles and asset classes speak to you and give you an overview of the investment vehicles I love most. Read it, dog-ear the pages, highlight and underline them…but the bottom line is, USE it!

DISCLAIMER: This Resource Guide is granular, technical, and very detailed at times. Feel free to skip investment vehicles that don't resonate, and/or use it as a tool to learn on an ad-hoc basis as you go along your journey. If you hear about mineral rights at a cocktail party and want to learn more about it, for example, flip to that section when you're ready. You can read this part like a "choose your own adventure" book, and it doesn't need to be read sequentially other than this opening introduction to it in order to gain the greatest benefit.

BEFORE WE BEGIN

As physicians, we have dedicated our lives to education and training. Most of us have built successful careers as a result. In medical school, we were taught to focus on medicine and hire someone to take care of the money. I think we've been sold on flawed logic with that idea: your future is simply too important a topic to be left to someone else as the primary decision-maker. Our work doesn't end when we leave the office or hospital—you must become the CAPTAIN of your future to ensure you have a solid investment strategy in place to secure your financial stability *outside of medicine.*

One way to do this is to invest in assets that aren't correlated with the stock market. This is a decision you must take personal responsibility for, as most financial advisors will point you straight to the stock market as your financial "savior." It's no secret that I'm not a fan of the stock market, and I am always looking for opportunities outside of Wall Street. You will notice this section doesn't mention stocks, bonds, mutual funds, or ETFs. The truth is, you won't find that information anywhere in this entire book. I think the stock market is closer to speculating than investing. Personal opinions aside, however, the main message I hope you glean from Part Two of this book is that **the true pathway to financial freedom is diversified passive income streams in various asset classes**. In that vein, I fully intend to explore and expand on a variety of viable investment options available in the investable universe—options I know personally and have firsthand experience with, ones that have proven themselves to me to be valuable and provide return on investment based on my CAPTAIN discernment tool (which we'll go through in detail momentarily).

Before we dive into the nitty-gritty, though, let's review a few key ideas.

ASSETS AND LIABILITIES

One of my key investment principles is only to buy assets. The basic definition of an asset, as defined by Robert Kiyosaki in *Rich Dad, Poor Dad,* is something that puts money *in* your pocket. A liability, on the other hand, is something that takes money *out* of your pocket. Ready for some hard truth? Your house, your boat, your car, your second vacation home, and that shiny new golf cart you tour through your neighborhood…those aren't assets, even if they are paid off. (That is, *UNLESS* you create an income stream from them.) While they may be nice to have, the way most people utilize these items is for their sole personal use and enjoyment, and as such they do not produce cash flow and therefore aren't assets by the definition above. Don't try to fool yourself into thinking liabilities are assets. Join me in becoming an asset hunter!

HARD ASSETS

This book focuses on hard assets: tangible, physical resources or assets you can own that possess value. If I can touch, feel, or hold it, I want to see if I can make it cash flow. Consider these hard assets long-term investments that continue to perform when "soft" assets take a downturn (i.e., the stock market).

SCALING DIVERSIFICATION

It's worth repeating: if you take anything away from this part of the book, I hope it is **whatever you choose to invest in, resist the temptation to put all of your eggs in one basket.** Diversification is a scaling strategy that mitigates risk by "spreading out" or allocating investments across different vehicles to reduce your exposure.

Scaling not only in assets but income streams as well has become a core principle of mine. I diversify both within real estate investments and those outside of real estate. The real secret sauce is to develop as many passive income streams as possible, from as many sources as possible. I'm a big proponent of investing in hard assets that are inflation-resistant, but even within hard assets, it's important to be sure to diversify. Whether it be a shipping business, an Airbnb, land, minerals, oil, or real estate, I intentionally choose investments that will not only survive but *thrive* in any type of economic environment. Diversification can put you on the path to becoming financially bulletproof.

A DISCERNMENT TOOL: CAPTAIN

When it comes to deciding on a potential opportunity, it is often helpful to follow a specific set of criteria to discern if the investment measures up. I use the acronym CAPTAIN to help me make educated, well-thought-out decisions. The more criteria met by the investment, the better the investment is likely to perform. This is especially useful when evaluating real estate opportunities, but is applicable across sectors.

- C - Cash flow
- A - Appreciation
- P - Principal reduction
- T - Tax benefits
- A - Advantages of leverage
- I - Inflation hedge
- N - Non-correlated assets

For each investment opportunity in front of me, I'm looking at each CAPTAIN concept individually, asking, "Will this investment give me [insert letter in acronym]?"

For example, "Will this investment give me Cash flow?"

CAPTAIN
Will this investment give me Cash flow?

Cash flow - Cash flow is what differentiates the truly successful from less successful investors. Few asset classes have the potential for predictable, long-term cash flow like real estate does, but debt funds, private equity funds, and oil and gas can provide excellent cash flow as well.

Important point: **not all cash flow is equal**. Cash flow from a single-family unit is going to be much different than from multifamily, which is different from a single-tenant net lease, which is different from an Airbnb. All of these vehicles create cash flow, but at differing levels. You need to understand your goals and your why, and leverage your pillars to see which is the right investment for you. This is cash flow that you can use to pay for life expenses or buy more assets that create further cash flow. Before you know it, your cash flow outpaces your expenses and you are financially free!

CAPTAIN
Will this investment give me Appreciation?

Appreciation - Real estate generally appreciates over time. However, with investment real estate, you are able to drive the appreciation by increasing revenue and decreasing expenses. Understand that there are two ways to appraise real estate. The typical residential appraisal uses the comparison approach where like/kind properties in the area are used as a benchmark for the value of the property in question. With investment properties, you can take advantage of the income approach appraisal method, where the appraiser looks at the NOI (net operating income) and divides that by the prevailing market Capitalization (Cap) Rate for that asset class to come up with a value.

Let's imagine that a neighboring property is a junkyard. It's really going to hurt the value of your personal residence that's appraised using the comparable approach. However, if you have an apartment complex in the same location, it will be appraised using an income approach to value the property, giving you a much higher valuation.

The more you can increase your NOI by increasing revenue (i.e., raise rents, add garage parking or storage onsite, allow pets for a fee) and decreasing expenses (i.e., utilize solar, bill back utilities to tenants, water walks, implement efficiencies with management) the more your property is worth. If you increase your NOI at your apartment complex by $50,000 by implementing some of these strategies, and the prevailing capitalization (cap) rate was 8%, you just added $625,000 ($50,000/0.08) of value to your asset! This is not just magic money.

You can refinance the apartment complex, pull the equity out, and buy more assets. That's the value of appreciation in real estate!

CAPTAIN
Will this investment give me Principal paydown?

Principal paydown - As you are enjoying the cash flow and the appreciation you are driving in your property, your tenants are paying down the note, so your equity is increasing as well. Most investment properties have a mortgage. As long as the rental payments are more than the mortgage payments and all the expenses, you are positively cash flowing while tenants continue to pay down your mortgage for you. You get the benefits of cash flow while your outstanding loan balance continues to decrease every month. The difference between what you owe on the property and what it's worth is your equity. By having tenants pay your mortgage for you, this amounts to a 2-4% annual return, depending on your interest rate and if you have any interest-only period.

CAPTAIN
Will this investment give me Tax benefits?

Tax benefits - Real estate is unique in how many tax benefits it offers. You may be able to take advantage of tax benefits such as deductions for expenses, mortgage interest, and property taxes while capitalizing on tax-advantaged passive income, depreciation, and 1031 exchanges. Passive rental income is taxed at a lower rate than your ordinary income, and depreciation can be used to offset that income to where it can be tax-deferred or even tax-free. Accelerating depreciation through cost segregation analysis can really amplify the amount of depreciation you receive in the first couple of years of ownership. Either you or your spouse having full-time real estate professional status (REPS) can supercharge these benefits even further as they will carry over to offset your W-2 income as well. This will potentially result in you getting most or all of the federal tax you paid back in the form of a refund at the end of the year. This is an IRS designation and there are criteria to meet, but they can be found in full at cashflowmd.com/how-to-qualify-as-a-real-estate-professional/.

An example of the power of REPS: Let's say you are a full-time real estate professional, and your physician wife made 400k in income. You own an apartment complex (managed by a third party; NOT YOU) and you do a cost segregation study on the asset. This gives you 400k of accelerated depreciation to take in year one. Since you are a full-time real estate professional, you can offset dollar for dollar your wife's income to where her effective taxable income is now $0, so you get ALL the federal income tax paid that year back as a refund. The federal income tax rate is 32% as of this writing, so that would be $128,000 returned to you in the form of a tax refund. Powerful! Income tax is the thief of generational wealth. Being able to pull these tax levers can keep more income in your pocket and change your life.

Another tax benefit is how you can harvest equity from your assets. A refinance is a tax-free event. Loan proceeds are not taxable, so the money you put in your pocket can be used to do whatever you want...I would suggest using it to go purchase other assets that cash flow, but that's just me. You can do this because your real estate holdings are a business, and the bank views them as such. Your home is a different story. Ever try to get a home equity loan when the stock market is down and housing prices are stagnating? It's difficult at best, but when you have investment real estate, it's a completely different way of valuing, and it becomes a great tool to use to harvest equity and go shopping for more assets on sale during these times!

It's also important to remember your real estate holding is an actual business that you can deduct expenses from. I recently deducted my trip to Hawaii because I spent more than half the time in real estate pursuits. Meeting brokers, lenders, seeing potential properties, driving to development sites, and dinners discussing potential partnerships all count as legitimate expenses. I loved seeing the island and had a blast meeting with the broker touring potential investments and enjoying some Acai bowls along the way! I also created several online videos, content, and blogs while I was there. Additionally, since my wife and my kids are employees in my business, I was able to write off a large portion of their expenses as well. (Please note: I confirmed all of these deductions with my CPA…you should too!) These tips are not some shady backdoor accounting. They are not loopholes. This is tax law. This is yet another benefit of owning a real estate business.

Last but definitely not least: 1031 exchange tax benefit. This allows you to cascade up to larger and better assets, all while deferring or maybe even eliminating the capital gain taxes altogether! This is one of the most powerful tools to create generational wealth at our disposal as investors.

CAPTAIN
Will this investment give me Advantages of leverage?

Advantages of leverage - Real estate investors can use leverage (i.e., borrowing money) to acquire property, potentially magnifying their returns greatly. Notice I said leverage and not debt. As discussed earlier, there is a difference. Leverage can be defined as "using a debt to multiply the potential return on your real estate investment."[11] Breaking it down simply, debt is taking on a liability (such as a home mortgage) to pay for an expense (example: your second home). This use of borrowed money with no return will drain your bank account very quickly and leave you in a situation where you have to continue to trade time for money. Leverage is different. While it's still borrowed money, it's all about what you do with it that changes its meaning. Leverage is using a liability (such as a commercial loan) to pay for an asset like a mobile home park) that will provide cash flow over and above paying off the liability. Not only that, you stack the benefits of what I just talked about (driving appreciation, have others paying off your mortgage, and get amazing tax benefits) to really supercharge your returns! For example, If you invest $100k in the stock market, you own $100k of stock. If you invest $100k in real estate, you could own a $1 million dollar property that you can control to a large extent what it's worth when you sell it. Just like the example above, if you increase NOI by $50k, at an eight cap, you've added $625k in value that can be accessed tax-free through a refinance or a sale. When was the last time you heard of someone turning $100k in the stock market into $625k in two to three years? If they did, it was a one-off, unicorn event. An exception, not the rule. With real estate, this can be the rule with every asset you purchase.

The scenario of taking on debt has *you* personally paying off the debt with *your* income. The scenario of using leverage to purchase assets has your *tenants* paying off the leverage you have on your asset with *their* income while providing extra cash flow at the same time. There's a big difference.

It's important to know the risk profile when considering how much leverage to use. Generally, the "safer" the asset, the more leverage you can deploy. For example, if I have an investment-grade single tenant with a fifteen-year absolute triple net (NNN) lease like Dollar General, I feel much more comfortable placing higher amounts of leverage on that asset because I know they are backed by the full faith and worth of a BBB+ rated national company. Even if they close my particular store, that lease will still be paid for fifteen years by the company.

Contrast that example with a fix-and-flip investment. There is nothing wrong with these investments at all, but you just need to understand the economic climate you are in when venturing into this space. If days on the market are increasing, home prices are stagnating and it's a higher interest rate environment, putting high leverage on a fix-and-flip isn't a good idea.

CAPTAIN
Will this investment give me an Inflation hedge?

Inflation hedge - Hard assets, especially real estate investments, serve well as a hedge against inflation as property values and rental income tend to increase in value as inflation rises. Real estate is very stable, is in demand, and has the highest risk-adjusted returns of any asset class. It can give you economic cycle protection you don't get from the stock market. There's a reason AAA+ life insurance companies both lend and invest in this space, and historically the foreclosure rate has been less than 1.5% throughout decades of economic cycles. As interest rates rise and inflation rages, the prices of home ownership become less affordable, so rents get driven up. This is the perfect storm for owners of hard assets like real estate, and can be the perfect hedge against inflation.

CAPTAIN
Is this investment Non-correlated with the stock market?

Non-correlated - One of the reasons I invest outside the stock market is the volatility it experiences. One of the aspects I look for in my investments is to be non-correlated to the stock market. It all gets back to reducing risk. I want to diversify and make sure I am investing in something non-correlated, so that when the stock market takes a pause, my overall portfolio is not at high risk. Once again, real estate investments can have a low correlation to other assets, such as stocks and bonds, which can help to reduce overall portfolio risk. Investing in real estate is a great diversification play to an investor's portfolio, spreading risk across multiple asset classes.

You now understand how you can be the CAPTAIN in terms of discerning the opportunities you'll be greeted with in your efforts to ensure you have a solid investment strategy in place to secure your financial stability outside of medicine.

This next section of the book will explore the details of investing in specific vehicles within the Investable Universe: real estate investments, businesses, mineral rights, and a host of other exciting and interesting investment options available. Using the Five Pillars of Financial Freedom as your guide, you can unlock serious (and lucrative!) opportunities to help you get out of the trading-time-for-money cycle and start having your hard-earned money work *for you*.

With that, let's go forth and explore the investment options inside the Investable Universe!

SECTION OUTLINE

Real Estate 147
- Multifamily 149
- Single-Family 177
- Short-Term Vacation Rentals 189
- Mobile Home Parks/Manufactured Housing Communities 199
- Recreational Vehicle (RV) Parks 215
- Triple Net Leases 229

Mineral Rights 243

Working Interests 257

Timberland 269

Car Washes 283

Self-Storage 297

Opportunity Zones (OZs) 311

Debt Lending and Private Equity Investments 319

Businesses 331

Additional Investment Options 339
- Residential Assisted-living Facilities 339
- Maritime Shipping 341
- Heavy and Light Industry 342
- Land Entitlements 343
- Land Flipping 344
- Art 346
- Carbon Credits, Mine Reclamation, Conservation Easements, and Pipeline Investments 347
- Stocks, Bonds, Mutual Funds, and ETFs 349
- Advanced Option Strategy 353
- Plan B Strategy 354

INVESTING IN REAL ESTATE

There are countless investment options in the Investable Universe, and it can be hard to decide which is best for you. One of the main asset classes I always recommend is real estate. There are a ton of reasons why: from great cash flow, to being able to drive appreciation, to having tax-free equity. It basically fulfills every part of my CAPTAIN discernment tool. Investing wisely in real estate can give you the freedom to live a life of purpose and generosity.

When talking about real estate, you're going to hear the important term "capitalization (cap) rate" referenced repeatedly, so before we dive in let's take a moment to define this term (and a glossary has also been included at the back of the book for easy reference if you need to refer back to find the definition of any key terms as you continue reading). The capitalization or "cap" rate is used to indicate the rate of return that is expected to be generated on a real estate investment property. The measure is computed based on the net income, which the property is expected to generate and is calculated by dividing net operating income by property asset value and is expressed as a percentage. It is used to estimate the investor's potential return on their investment.[12]

One of the reasons I fell in love with real estate is because it is so scalable. I discovered very quickly that an apartment complex with solid property management was a whole lot easier to own than having to manage even one single-family home by myself. If you know the basics and invest with the right team who can be on the ground running the daily operations, real estate can be a huge win.

We'll start with one of my favorites—multifamily—and then move on to single-family and a variety of exciting real estate vehicles thereafter.

MULTIFAMILY INVESTMENTS

A multifamily property is a single building that has been divided into multiple units to accommodate several renters. There are a number of different types of multifamily properties to choose from. Let's discuss the main categories:

Duplex/Fourplex: A building divided into two or four adjoining units. Each unit has its own entrance. Duplexes often have separate yards and garages.

Condo: A building with a large number of individually owned units. The owner of each unit is responsible for maintenance and fees. When the unit is rented, tenants sign a contract that requires them to pay rent on a monthly basis and may include other responsibilities, such as utilities and lawn maintenance.

Townhome: A property where residents share conjoining but separate units. These buildings tend to have two to three stories.

Apartments: These buildings can range in size from four to hundreds of units. They can be highrise, garden-style, or anything in between.

CLASSES OF MULTIFAMILY

As with most investments, there is a spectrum that corresponds to workload and potential financial gain in the realm of multifamily as well. It is important to know exactly what you are getting into before you decide to buy. You will hear discussions about different "classes" of multifamily, so I want to explain the nuances of each so you can make a more informed decision about where you'd like to start investing.

Class A

- These are new builds (or relatively new builds, less than five years old) going after the highest paying renters—typically young professionals.
- These buildings can have covered parking or parking garages, storage options, and facilities such as workout facilities/ gyms, pools, conference centers, business offices, outdoor hospitality spaces, etc.
- Each unit is separately metered, so all utilities are directly billed to the tenant.
- The locations are in nice areas where crime scores are low and school scores are high, and they usually have great walkability.
- The median household income in the area is usually well above the national average.
- These demand the most expensive rents.

Class B

- This investment is considered the "workhorse" of multifamily.
- These buildings were constructed after 1980 or 1981 (after 1979, builders were aware of asbestos, and requirements changed).
- The buildings generally are two- or three-story garden style with a pitched roof and often have private balconies or

outdoor spaces. They usually have open hallways, with each unit having its own entrance.

- There are fewer amenities in Class B than in Class A, and they may or may not have been updated.
- They are located in neighborhoods with good (low) crime rates, good schools, and good incomes.
- These are not top buildings. They are average, middle-of-the-road, well kept. They often require new roofs, repainting, and repaved parking lots to give them more appeal.
- There is a high opportunity for value-add with Class B. You can often add granite countertops, new appliances, and flooring to drive rents. You might be looking at $8k-14k in renovation costs per door, which can be a heavy lift if you are buying a hundred-unit apartment complex, but you'll be able to push those rents to a point where you can potentially get a two- to four-fold return.

Class C

- These buildings were built before 1980 and generally have quite a bit of deferred maintenance.
- You will potentially be dealing with asbestos, outdated electrical systems, and building code issues when implementing value-adds in Class C.
- All utilities are often included; submetering can be expensive and onerous in older buildings, making it difficult to transfer these costs to tenants.
- This is usually considered workforce housing, Section 8, or other low-income housing.
- It's harder to push rents with this clientele.

- The most important thing to consider with these Class C investments is location. Look and follow trends. You want to purchase only if it's in an up-and-coming area.

Class D

- D stands for "Don't buy"!
- These properties are really, really heavy lifts, and you need to know what you are doing. You must have deeply insightful information about the area and operational expertise.
- These buildings will generally stay Class D no matter what you do in terms of value-add.
- There are often demographic issues: the median income does not meet a viable standard, crime may be high, and therefore school scores are likely low.
- The tenant base in Class D is typically difficult, and rents often go unpaid.
- Buildings can have one shared entrance with outdated common hallways.

Upgrading classes

When it comes to Class C and D multifamily buildings, it becomes very difficult to upgrade because you can't change what already is. It's difficult to make structural changes—like adding balconies to modernize—to these types of structures. You also can't change the location, and these assets are often in less than desirable areas. This makes it hard to implement any type of program to increase the value. It becomes nearly impossible to push rents and drive appreciation.

It's very difficult to upgrade classes, but it's very possible to find Class B multifamily opportunities that present an opportunity due to mismanagement, poor marketing, deferred maintenance, or a multitude of other reasons. I typically begin with the location, otherwise known as the Metropolitan Statistical Area (MSA), and then drill down on a submarket that fits my criteria. We'll discuss MSA in detail later in this section. Then, I search for assets in my defined area that are Class B or greater that can be upgraded. **Find the right location first, then find the right asset; that's where the biggest value-add opportunities are.**

Tip: Engaging a knowledgeable broker can significantly aid your investment journey. Consider inviting them for a lunch meeting, where you can delve into focused questions that will advance your property search. Clearly communicate your acquisition criteria during these discussions, and share your investment background or readiness to invest, ensuring they recognize your serious intent. Brokers can keep you abreast of what's going on in that specific market and let you know when some assets might be coming up. They may also have off-market deals that haven't been offered to the public yet. This approach is part of the strategic insights you'll gain in the "Cash Flow Prescription" course, designed to equip you with the tools and knowledge for successful real estate investment. Explore more strategies and deepen your understanding by enrolling in the course using the QR Code at the back of the book.

WHAT I LOVE ABOUT MULTIFAMILY INVESTMENTS

1. Great place to start

Multifamily investments are near and dear to me because it's where I got my start. If done correctly, these investments fulfill every parameter of my CAPTAIN investing strategy. This asset class is known to perform well over time and is a logical starting place for new investors. The benefits of investing in apartments far outweigh any drawbacks (both of which we will dive into).

As I mentioned in the introduction, in our first foray into multifamily, my business partner and I jumped right in and went from owning zero to owning over 300 units in a very short timeframe. We bought three different apartment complexes, and we were off to the races!

Despite our bold move, we were well prepared to make this step. The tools our mentors had provided to us in our real estate residency were paramount to our success. They taught us proper acquisition criteria, how to evaluate an MSA (Metropolitan Statistical Area), introduced us to the various types of financing options, and explained what they look for when evaluating deals, doing due diligence, undertaking operations, and exiting the deal—the gamut. We basically had a nine-month crash course: an intense program where our mentors opened up their entire portfolio, their underwriting, their resources, their network, their attorneys, their tax team—everything.

This was invaluable in our journey. Finding good mentors compressed our timeline dramatically and was the key ingredient to success. Embarking on your investment journey with the right guidance can transform your path. "Cash Flow Prescription" isn't just a course; it's a conduit to financial freedom, offering insights and strategies honed from real-world experiences. If you're poised to transition from learning to action, this course might be your next pivotal step. This course opens up my playbook for you and jump-starts your path to financial freedom.

2. Appreciation and scalability

When you invest in multifamily, you are buying a business—and it's valued as such. You can drive appreciation virtually overnight.

As you are able to drive appreciation with these types of assets, they are valued using an income approach. As you increase rents and decrease expenses, your NOI (net operating income) grows. This increases the value of your asset.

Multifamily is also easy to scale rapidly. Let's say you want to grow your portfolio by twenty units. With single-family, you'd have to deal with the hassles of finding and completing due diligence on twenty different homes. However, it's very easy to find an apartment building with twenty units. When it comes to due diligence on every property you purchase, going through it once with a twenty-unit apartment complex is much more appealing than going through it twenty times with single-family homes.

3. Tax advantages

Tax advantages are numerous with multifamily. Whether investing passively as a limited partner or being actively involved as a sponsor/owner, tax advantages abound. Multifamily is one of the best asset classes to realize tax benefits across the board. Whether it's deducting expenses like mortgage interest, insurance, or property taxes, leveraging cost segregation analysis to accelerate depreciation and offset income, or utilizing 1031 exchanges to defer capital gains or even negate it altogether, multifamily offers many avenues to realize massive tax advantages and passive income that's taxed at a much lower rate than ordinary income. And let's not forget about tax-free equity harvesting events we can realize through refinances, either! Hopefully you're starting to realize the power of investing in this asset class!

4. Management options are plenty

A massive added benefit of investing in multifamily is that it can be relatively hands-off.

An integral part of the business of multifamily is hiring good people to run your properties, and because the multifamily market is vast, it has attracted great operators. As a result, you'll have plenty of solid, reliable people and property management companies to choose from.

You want to find operators that are trustworthy, skilled, super connected, and hungry. I leverage my network initially and then have a list of questions I like to ask potential property managers. Delving into "Cash Flow Prescription" could offer you a refined set of these crucial inquiries, subtly guiding your interactions to ensure meaningful engagements and informed decisions.

As an overview, I look for things like time in market, how many units they have under management, reviews from other owners, their ability to lower operational expenses, value-add strategy, and success with other assets, to name a few. If you have a really fantastic property manager who is on the ground solving problems and dealing with daily operations, it makes life much easier for the ownership group.

With a larger multifamily property, you can take advantage of economies of scale, meaning it can support its own maintenance staff, grounds crew, leasing agent, etc.

5. Reliability

Multifamily is an evergreen asset class. The favorable demographics for multifamily are undeniable. Increasingly, Baby Boomers and Millennials are choosing renting over home ownership. These are the two largest generational populations that will need housing for many years to come.

6. Commercial multifamily options

Larger (typically one hundred plus-unit properties) apartment complexes are generally referred to as *commercial multifamily*. These bigger properties are a "self-contained business" as soon as you buy them, meaning that they create enough economies of scale to be profitable and support their own staff (property manager, leasing staff, maintenance personnel, etc.).

You can also potentially claim full-time real estate professional status by owning one large apartment complex, or being a general partner on the deal with other partners. This status comes with massive tax benefits (refer to the Glossary of Terms & Key Concepts to learn more about this status).

7. Plenty of exit strategies

Multifamily also offers lots of exit possibilities:

- There is a large pool of buyers for multifamily.
- Banks and other lenders love to lend on this asset class because of its historically low risk and foreclosure rate.
- Strategic refinances can help you harvest tax-free equity to get your initial principal back. After you receive your initial capital contribution back, you can enjoy an infinite return and put your retrieved capital to work in another asset!
- Selling a portion of the asset to recover your investment is another option, or bringing in limited partners who will give you capital in return for a piece of the investment is another.

- Utilize brokers or your network to sell the asset to new ownership and scale up to larger assets using a 1031 exchange.
- Larger multifamily deals can be positioned to be attractive to institutional investors and family offices.
- There's nothing wrong with keeping it and cash flowing it, as well. Upon your death, the cost basis resets to market, which allows your family to enjoy the cash flow without having to sell the asset to pay the taxes. Want to learn more about this? Visit cashflowmd.com/1031-exchange-a-powerful-wealth-generation-tool/ for more information about the benefits of 1031 exchanges.

With so many juicy exit opportunities, you can see why multifamily is one of the darlings of the investable universe.

Keeping the exit in mind is paramount. When I look at possible opportunities to invest in, the first thing I consider is the exit. I don't want to buy someone else's mistake; just because I *can* fix it doesn't mean I *should*. While there is definitely money to be made in inefficiencies, there are also fortunes to be lost, so always be very cognizant of your exit strategy.

THINGS TO CONSIDER WITH MULTIFAMILY

1. Competition

The multifamily market has a ton of competition and is a consolidated market. Roughly 55-60% of Class A and B multifamily assets are owned by institutional, private-equity, and syndication investors, so competition is tough. This consolidation has pushed prices higher, often pricing the assets out of the reach of individual buyers or small syndications. There are still deals out there, but they are harder to find, and there is generally more competition for them once you find them.

2. Rising prices

Capitalization (cap) rates are very compressed, making these assets potentially overpriced. Because of the consolidation mentioned above, cap rates have fallen—or *compressed*—because institutional investors are willing to pay more for the perceived safety of multifamily. As prices rise, it squeezes out smaller investors—raising the barrier for entry to often unattainable levels for the average investor.

Despite these two factors above, I firmly believe there are many more positives than negatives to investing in multifamily. When you compare it to other asset classes, the track record of multifamily holds up very well.

WHAT A GOOD DEAL LOOKS LIKE IN MULTIFAMILY

I'm asked about this all the time from people just starting out. It's important, because it's the foundation of your search. Once you know what you're looking for, you're easily able to eliminate other opportunities that don't fit your criteria.

It's nuanced for every investor, but as mentioned earlier, I always start with the MSA (Metropolitan Statistical Area) and work backward to find the deals. MSA is a defined geographic area that consists of a large city and all of its linked communities and resources encapsulating the area. There are almost 400 major MSAs in the U.S., so there are plenty of areas to evaluate. Not all MSAs are equal, however: there are many variables that make up a good MSA. A few I find very important include:

- population
- population growth
- unemployment rate
- median household income
- employer variability
- average rents
- renters as percentage of population
- single-family home vacancy rate
- affordability
- how many new units are coming on the market

I then evaluate specific submarkets within that MSA. I get very granular now, looking at:

- crime
- schools
- walk scores
- local jobs, etc.

to determine the best submarkets within the MSA. Then, *and only then*, do I start looking at deals.

Once you've narrowed down your MSA and submarkets, it's time to go to work looking for deals. What does a good deal look like? Dive deeper into defining and refining your acquisition criteria with the "Cash Flow Prescription" course. Uncover the strategies that will guide you in identifying the deals that best align with your investment goals. Enroll now and start shaping your path to finding the right deals for you.

HOW TO INVEST IN MULTIFAMILY

There are numerous ways to jump into multifamily investing, and the spectrum ranges from active (do it yourself) to passive (done for you), with varying levels of engagement in between. Most people are familiar with the terms "active" and "passive," but there's a third investing option I refer to as "passively active" investing. Passively active investing can be a subtle sweet spot that fits in between. With this approach, you'll work "on" your asset and not necessarily "in" it, using a property management company, for example, where you are managing the managers, not the tenants—or creating strategic partnerships where everyone brings different talents and the work of operating the asset is delegated amongst those partnerships. For more on this topic, you can read about it at cashflowmd.com/passive-vs-active-real-estate-investing/. Suffice it to say, passively active investing can give you the best of both worlds, where you're able to take full advantage of the profits and tax benefits that active investors do, while having property management/your capable team dealing with the headaches.

The majority of your success is going to be based on who you invest with. If you plan to do it on your own, your due diligence and property management team(s) will be the main factors in your success. If you are going to invest with a syndicator (a partner who is responsible for strategy, operations, funding, and disposition of the asset), then your due diligence focuses on vetting the sponsor of the syndication you are working with. You want to make sure their underwriting is accurate and that you understand the business plan. If you don't understand the business plan, you need to walk away. There will be plenty of other deals. Want to learn more about vetting syndications? Visit cashflowmd.com/dd-checklist-resource/ for my free resource guide on completing due diligence for syndications.

MULTIFAMILY CASE STUDY

Do Your Due Diligence!

After we had purchased 300+ units, we felt like we were getting our feet under us pretty well. We had systems in place for evaluating assets as well as adding value, and we had a strong property management team. We had completed our real estate residency, and we were feeling pretty good about ourselves.

Though our plates were full with the assets we were currently improving, another opportunity came our way (remember: when you do one deal, other deals tend to follow—often rapidly!).

On the surface this looked like a good deal, as well. The sellers needed a buyer who could close fast. In retrospect, that should have been an alarm bell. While it's good to be able to move quickly, having it as a condition of the sale is not a good idea. My "Spidey-Senses" were already going off—and I should have listened to them.

As we began implementing our due diligence program, a few additional red flags went up. Two of them were pretty important: crime and schools. When considering an asset that has mainly two- and three-bedrooms, crime and schools are a big deal because the likelihood is that families with young children are going to be your main tenant population. Even though these are important parameters, we had other assets in the area that were doing really well, so we decided we could mitigate these issues and we moved forward. Even though we were trained to make better decisions, we deviated from the norm. We felt the price was very fair, and we didn't want the deal to fall out of escrow, so we pushed it through.

In order to expedite the process, we leaned pretty hard on a third-party management team to help with due diligence. The main mistake was that we didn't interview the tenants or talk to contractors who were used in the past. As part of the due diligence process on older apartments, another very important step is to get camera studies done on the sewer system. We were pressed for time and didn't do this.

Very soon after the deal closed, we encountered a six-figure sewer issue that would have been discovered if we had completed the camera study. Additionally, we were having trouble hitting our occupancy targets because families didn't like the school district, and crime was a concern. We were in trouble. We had to fix the sewer issue, but we couldn't change the location. Lesson learned: you can't change the market you purchase in. No matter how great the deal looks, if the location is a dud, move along. There's a reason that "location, location, location" is universally regarded as one of the key factors for investing in real estate: the importance of it simply can't be overemphasized!

We were able to bring in an equity partner to help with the costs of sewer mitigation. We continued to struggle with occupancy, and finally sold the complex at basically a break-even price to a group who likely thought they could overcome the market as well. That apartment complex continues to change hands frequently, and will likely continue to do so. If we had not brought on an additional equity partner, the situation could have gotten very scary.

The moral of the story is: develop your due diligence method and stick with it. We are all going to make mistakes, but so many can be avoided by sticking to your due diligence principles and process. When investors fail in real estate, it usually comes back—at some point—to a lack of due diligence.

Some of the best deals are the ones you never do because they save you from inheriting someone else's problem.

STUDENT HOUSING

Student housing is a nuanced genre of multifamily. While it looks like and mostly operates as traditional multifamily, there are some key differences.

The lease cycle on these assets can often be nine-month leases, to mirror the school year, and they tend to be amenity-laden and close to universities.

The renter population is obviously younger, and often this is their first taste of freedom outside of their parents and/or dorm life. Consequently, you'll need to charge much higher damage deposits and do walkthroughs more often, as these assets tend to take on more wear and tear. You can imagine a working couple with two kids might take a little better care of their housing than four college students living together potentially for the first time. Don't act like you don't know what I'm talking about… we were all in college once!

In terms of management personnel, you will need to flex staff according to peak times—generally May and August, which are move-out and move-in months. Consequently, you can complete a lot of your capital projects and/or repairs in June and July.

Another consideration is occupancy. If you are at a big university with a large renter population, your occupancies generally do really well. If you are in a tertiary market—mixed between students and working-class people—then you are alienating a large renter pool by designating it as student housing. Once you are branded as student housing, it's difficult to get families with small children to move in. In the right location, however, you can benefit from a captive audience. Students want to be where the action is. They want to live close to the university to be able to walk to and from classes, events, and entertainment options. Finding the correct locations means investing in student housing near the right universities. Large state universities and established private schools that are financially secure, for example, would be good characteristics, and you may want to consider the universities with major draws like being in Power Five athletic conferences, strong academic giants, or the flagship state schools that are always going to receive the funding they need. I caution against small private schools, as they are usually the ones where student housing takes a hit if there is an economic recession, for example. With larger schools, they have many contributors to keep their enrollment steady, and consistent enrollment is key, so make sure you are investing in a demographic that will always value higher education. It's not a bad idea to underwrite the university and look into the student population. Is it growing or leveling off? Has there been a loss of a key field of study in the university? Does it offer strong and/or unique graduate programs like architecture, medicine, pharmacy, or veterinary? Those things aren't going away. These programs anchor a university and attract the student demographic you will be looking for.

One of the other unique aspects of student housing is that the leases are often secured with parental guarantees. This is different because not only do you have the student bound to the lease, but you also have the parents. It drastically lowers eviction costs and non-payment issues, because the parents act as guarantors as well.

MULTIFAMILY DEVELOPMENT

Multifamily development investing (a.k.a. "new construction") is quite different from purchasing an existing multifamily asset.

Your exit timeline will generally be longer on a development deal than with a value-add multifamily deal. It takes many months to even years just to get the proper entitlements, zoning, and utility infrastructure in order to even *begin* a development project. During this period and then during the actual build phase, there is no cash flow, so you (or the sponsor, if you're investing in a deal passively) need to be very well capitalized. You need to understand this investment payout will be very heavily backloaded, meaning you will make the majority—if not all—of your profit upon exiting the investment.

The ideal submarket for development of new multifamily is usually different than for value-add, as well. If you are developing new inventory that will demand premium rents, you need to be in a location and have the demographics to support this. Most development is in established areas or known up-and-coming areas with much higher median incomes than surrounding areas. If you want a median income of $60-90k for a Class B investment, then you'd likely want a median income of $70-100k+ for a development project. It's much more important to have a high white-collar employer mix with plenty of established high-paying jobs in the area that aren't going anywhere.

Taking the above into consideration, development can be super lucrative, and I think it is worthwhile to consider adding to your portfolio.

WHAT I LOVE ABOUT MULTIFAMILY DEVELOPMENT

1. Less competition

As multifamily has become the darling of institutional and private equity investors, competition for value-add projects has gotten out of control as large investors seek to take advantage of short-term market opportunities. In contrast, development projects may face less competition as large investors are more cautious about taking on long-term projects that are years from completion. With value-add, there are fewer uncertain variables as you already have zoning, entitlements, utilities, and some rental history in place. Development offers none of these, so there is less competition and more opportunities to be in the MSA and submarkets you want to be in (albeit it may take longer to realize your profits).

2. Attractive potential for financial returns

Development projects often have a fixed cost structure, which means that the cost of building the project is determined at the outset. Things like labor rates, cost of goods, loan rates, and other major variables can and should be negotiated upfront with a maximum variance agreed upon by all parties. This ensures the project is not substantially affected by changes in inflation or interest rates. In contrast, value-add projects may have variable costs that can fluctuate with inflation, interest rates, or the current labor market, which can make it more difficult to forecast the project's profitability accurately.

Development projects generally come to market at lower cap rates, as they are brand new with minimal to zero deferred maintenance, have all the latest technology, and are in super desirable areas. These assets are very appealing to large family offices, private equity, and other institutional investors as they will require little to no maintenance and give them a good return on their money for years to come. For these reasons, development projects tend to command higher prices than value-add projects, which makes these opportunities very attractive to investors. This is even more true during inflationary times. As inflation increases, asset prices tend to rise, and a development project that is completed during an inflationary period may appreciate in value even more than anticipated at the outset.

3. Less volatility

Development projects typically have a longer-term time horizon than value-add projects, which can make them more resilient to short-term economic fluctuations. At the writing of this book, inflation is still on the minds of investors, and there are worries of a recession. Interest rates are high and people are nervous about placing capital in value-add multifamily projects. Inflation and rising interest rates can cause short-term volatility in the markets, wreaking havoc with short-term multifamily notes (a.k.a. bridge debt), so I think caution in the value-add space is definitely warranted. However, a long-term development project can benefit from a fixed loan rate and eventual economic recovery and growth, making it a great investment during uncertain economic times.

THINGS TO CONSIDER WITH MULTIFAMILY DEVELOPMENT

1. Time commitment

Development is not something that will offer a fast return on investment (ROI). It is usually a capital commitment from at least three years to up to five to seven years, depending on the size of the project. As mentioned earlier, development requires a heavy amount of groundwork to be laid before the first hammer hits the first nail in construction. There are entitlements to obtain, planning and zoning boards to win over, environmental impact studies to be completed, financing to obtain, architectural renderings to be approved, revised, then approved again… you get the picture! This all has to be done well before considering going vertical with the project. You can see how this process could take many years, and often does. However, when done correctly, it can still be one of the best ways to get a solid return on your investment over time.

2. Limited cash flow

If you are looking for cash flow to replace your income, development is *not* the investment for you. If you are looking for a large return on your investment that you can wait four to seven years to realize, then it's an outstanding option. Instead of using Cash-on-Cash return (CoC) as a parameter when evaluating these deals, I look at equity multiple and internal rate of return (IRR). If I can get 2.5 to 3x my passive investment over a period of five years and a 20%+ IRR, I'm very happy with that. *Mixed with other investments that cash flow*, development can make very good sense.

3. Getting in too early

When I consider a development deal, I'm looking for one main parameter before I dive in too deep: is the deal shovel-ready? If not, it's simply too risky. There are plenty of other investment opportunities that don't involve the risk of an "early" development deal. Ideally, I would like to come in as an investor once the loan is closed, all entitlements have been obtained, planning and zoning has signed off, and the project is going vertical (or at least nothing is preventing it from going vertical). The construction plan, with variances accounted for and spelled out in the contract, should be signed off on by both operator and builder.

One of the areas where I've screwed up in the past is getting in too early, investing in ground-up development. I just won't do it anymore. The time horizon is too long before I see my money back, and the risk of the project failing at any preliminary step is too high. You take on a lot of risk. Remember all the things we just discussed about entitlements, zoning, etc.? Any one of those things can delay or completely derail the investment altogether, putting your hard-earned capital at risk. Development is super risky from the outset, but the further you get down the pathway, the more it becomes de-risked and a powerhouse to generate awesome returns. I choose to invest once I know the project is shovel-ready and the risk has been virtually eliminated.

4. Choose your team wisely

This is ALWAYS key, but especially in development: those you invest your money with *need* to know what they are doing. This is NOT a sub-class I recommend newbies start out being active in. There are too many variables involved that will eat inexperienced operators alive. Finding the best-in-class operators is imperative here. It's often said your success in real estate is about 70% dependent upon your property management company. With development, I suggest that number is closer to 90%. I cannot stress enough how important your operator and builder are in this equation. Simply put, if they do not have a strong track record, you need to just stop right there and move along. You don't want to be an investor on the first deal, no matter how enticing the numbers look. Physicians spend countless hours in education, preparation, and training before seeing their first patient on our own. Pilots put in countless hours of flying and simulator training before taking their first commercial passenger in the air. Unfortunately, there's no such training requirement for developers, so it's up to you to make sure the developer can pilot this project to a smooth landing. There are a lot of people out there with amazing-looking proformas and offering memorandums, but the main thing you need to know is their track record.

WHAT A GOOD DEAL LOOKS LIKE IN MULTIFAMILY DEVELOPMENT

I've evaluated hundreds of development deals over my career, and there are certain parameters most development deals I invest in have in common. First, the location is premium. I mentioned earlier the factors that go into evaluating an MSA, and they are super important here. The last thing you want to do is build a nine-figure development deal in the wrong place. I want high median income, excellent employment options, good local tax environment, growing population, low competition, operator familiarity with the area, low single-family home vacancy, high rental income potential, and no threats looming to any of these parameters.

Next, I look for amazing operators with track records over many deals and market cycles. Honestly, anyone could have done well from 2016-2021, but I want to know what you were doing in 2008-2011 during the

Great Recession. What did you learn? How did you improve operations based on what you learned? How have your deals done before, during, and after? An operator with a strong track record makes the investment much more attractive.

Additionally, I want the opportunity to be as risk-free as possible. The closer it is to actual construction, the less risk the deal involves. Remember: the more you remove risk from the equation, the higher your chances are of realizing an excellent return on your investment.

Lastly, while this may not be super intuitive, I like the opportunity to be able to use my Self Directed IRA (SDIRA) as my investment vehicle of choice. Most sophisticated operators offer this avenue for investing. I like using my SDIRA for development deals for a couple of reasons. First, I don't want my money in the volatile market where it will have wild fluctuations and low actual returns. I'd rather invest that money in hard assets that are predictable and offer a good return. Second, I believe in using tax-advantaged investment vehicles (i.e., SDIRAs) with tax-disadvantaged investments. Real estate has amazing tax benefits, but development is probably one of the least favorable. There is little cash flow during the lifetime of the investment, and the nature of getting all the profit after the sale can set you up for a bit of a tax issue. Even though it will be taxed at capital gains and not ordinary income, if the long-term rate is 20% and you make $500,000 on the investment, that's still $100,000 of taxes that will be due. However, if you invest using your SDIRA, those profits roll back into your SDIRA tax-free, allowing you to capitalize on the velocity of money much faster and put those funds you would have paid in taxes back to work in another investment.

HOW TO INVEST IN MULTIFAMILY DEVELOPMENT

I think it's pretty clear I don't suggest going it alone with this subclass of real estate. Finding the right partner with the characteristics above is paramount in development.

Passively investing as a limited partner is probably the easiest way to dip your toe in the water. Use me as a resource! You can go to www.cashflowmd.com and look at our offerings, check out our fund page, or just set up a time to connect with me to discuss options.

If you want to do this on your own, I highly recommend partnering with someone who is super experienced in this area. Let them teach you the operations side of the deal while you offer value in any other area(s) that you can. Maybe you could be a signer on the note (key partner), contribute capital, or even help to raise capital. An experienced partner can also help you navigate the painful headaches of preconstruction and compress your timeline to proficiency in this space.

Regardless of how you decide to move forward in this space, actively or passively, it can be a very rewarding and financially sound investment when thoughtfully done.

MULTIFAMILY DEVELOPMENT CASE STUDY

The Importance of Experience

I was involved in a development deal in Hawaii many years ago. It was early stage, and I was enthralled with the potential returns. The area was amazing, the renderings were beautiful, and—I didn't know the proper questions to ask. What could go wrong…right?

The developer had a strong track record in the past but, unfortunately, had not done any active development EVER in Hawaii. I later found out he had not completed a successful project in over a decade, as well.

The project was a planned community with golf, swimming, shopping, a large clubhouse, villas, bungalows, and hiking. In all the development deals the operator had completed in the past, the scope of this was WAY larger than anything he had completed in the past. Did I ask this question? Nope.

This was offered as a "ground floor" opportunity with tons of incentives included for early investors. By ground floor, I mean this was basically an idea on a piece of paper at this point. No entitlements had been secured, no approvals from planning and zoning had been obtained, no environmental impact studies had been conducted (SUPER important in Hawaii), and there were no strong lending contacts in Hawaii.

Had I known what I know now, this opportunity wouldn't have even got past my assistant's email filter. But I didn't, and it did.

It wound down before it even got the chance to wind up. The project was unanimously rejected by planning and zoning, and local protestors made sure there was not a second hearing.

Thankfully, I had not invested too much in this deal, but it was still an expensive lesson. At the time, it turned me off to development in general because I didn't know what I didn't know, and I just assumed all development was super risky based on that experience.

Thankfully, over the years my Mindset evolved, I was able to Learn much more about this asset class, I developed a strong Network (including amazing mentors), found better Deal Flow, and eventually took appropriate Action using the strong foundation my Five Pillars of Financial Freedom has afforded me.

SINGLE-FAMILY INVESTMENTS

A single-family home is designed for one family and has its own kitchen and unshared utilities. In most cases, it is an independent structure that sits on its own piece of land. However, the U.S. Census Bureau includes certain attached dwellings, such as townhomes, in its definition of "single-family home."

For a dwelling that is attached to other homes to be considered a "single-family home," it must be separated from an adjacent unit by a ground-to-roof wall and able to function on its own as a single unit.

Types of single-family investments:

Fix and Flip: Buying a property, renovating it, then selling at a higher price.

Buy and Hold: Investing in a property and holding it long-term with the goal of appreciation and cash flow.

Single-Tenant: An agreement between a sole renter of the property and the owner.

Short-Term Rental: Normally stays of seven days or less, not to exceed thirty days.

Long-Term Rental: Stays of more than thirty days. One- to two-year leases are very common.

WHAT I LOVE ABOUT SINGLE-FAMILY INVESTMENTS

1. Versatility

The beautiful thing about single-family is that it is very versatile. You can do many things with these properties: flip them, hold them, rehab/refinance them, or turn them into Airbnbs. If you have one single-family house, that's a nice start, but hard to justify calling it a business. Once you get two, three, or more, you have a strong argument for this being a "portfolio." Once you have a portfolio, other investors become interested, and the assets start to stand on their income rather than their surrounding comparables. Remember the first "A" in the CAPTAIN acronym (Appreciation)? When you have a portfolio with rental history, the SFH (single-family homes) become valued using an income approach rather than a comparable approach. You can market these assets to investor networks, mom-and-pop buyers, or end-user buyers. Your exit strategies are very robust.

Your renter population is very versatile, as well. You can obviously rent to families, but you can also market to travel professionals and charge a premium due to shorter lease agreements. You can market to university students and command a higher rate, as well, by renting it per *room.* If you have a four-bedroom, two-bathroom dwelling, for example, that rents for $1,200 per month, you may be able to rent it to students at $400 *per room per month*. That's an additional $400 monthly. If there is a medical school or law school nearby, this approach is ideal. These tenants would be less likely to have parties and tear up your property because they are too busy studying; they tend to be more responsible than your average college student and generally will take better care of the property.

Lastly, if you are in a destination city or desirable area, you can easily turn your single-family home into an Airbnb. This is especially true if you are within walking distance to attractions. There are a ton of benefits to Airbnbs that we'll get into later.

Single-family homes can be one of the most chameleon-like investments in your portfolio.

2. High demand

There is very high demand for affordable single-family housing in the United States. We're also (conservatively) three million housing starts behind current demand at the writing of this book. As a result, there is a massive supply and demand mismatch—creating a housing shortage in the United States. The consequence is consistently increasing rents over time. Compound rising rents with low affordability for first-time homebuyers, and that is a recipe for very nice profits for SFH owners for many years to come.

Just like in multifamily, there is a class system for single-family investments. You can use the same parameters for A, B, C, and D, but your rents are generally higher per door regardless because of the demand for SFH. People pay more for things like privacy, better school districts, not sharing a wall, having a yard, or having a garage. People like their own space: a yard to have a cookout, and walls that aren't attached to their neighbor.

3. Liquidation options

If you own single-family properties and find yourself in need of cash, SFHs give you the flexibility of selling an individual property rather than the whole portfolio. In comparison, if you only have multifamily properties, you are limited in liquidity events to a refinance or an outright sale. You can't just sell a single apartment unit if you need to.

As mentioned earlier, you may get more for the SFH you sell as well because they are valued using an income approach. This valuation approach will help you harvest equity from the properties much more consistently than using the customary single-family home comparison ("comp") appraisals you would have to use if this was not an income-generating property.

4. Not consolidated

There is less consolidation in SFHs when compared to other subclasses of real estate like multifamily and self-storage. What do I mean by "consolidation"? This is basically where well-funded buyers (think private equity, life insurance companies, family offices, REITs) purchase massive amounts of an asset and subsequently gain an inordinate amount of market share. For example, institutional-type investors now own over 60% of multifamily assets in the U.S. This drives prices up for smaller buyers and raises the barrier to entry.

Contrast this with single-family homes. Of the more than 80 million single-family homes in the U.S., fewer than 5% are owned by institutional investors. This statistic is changing daily as larger investors are taking notice of this asset class, but at this time the barrier to entry is much lower than multifamily, and there are many opportunities for "smaller" investors to be active in this space.

THINGS TO CONSIDER WITH SINGLE-FAMILY INVESTMENTS

1. Maintenance

With more square footage under one roof and landscaping or a yard to take care of, repairs and maintenance costs are naturally going to be higher with single-family. Considering the individual costs for each home's HVAC, water, plumbing, sewer and electricity, and property taxes, these costs will also likely be higher per capita compared to multifamily. Your management fees will go up as well when owning just a few SFHs because there is no true economy of scale, so the management group must charge a higher percentage of rents for it to make sense for them to manage your property. This changes as you have more SFHs, however. For example, if you own ten or more SFHs, you can likely negotiate the management fee down to what a multifamily property manager would charge. Maintenance fees are going to run higher per door overall.

2. Turn times

The time from when a current renter vacates the property until a new renter occupies it is referred to as the turn time. This cost can vary greatly and needs to be weighed when evaluating both the property and the property management group. From the property standpoint, I want to know how long homes stay on the rental market in that area before being rented; and when discussing with potential property management, I want to know what their specific turn times are and how that compares with the norm in that market. Turn times can eat profits, so minimizing turns is best. You can do this by incentivizing tenants to stay longer by keeping rental increases below market, making sure property management responds quickly to requests, setting up incentives and building community by having gatherings for tenants annually, or even offering a scholarship program for the tenants of your properties. The bottom line: when renters leave, it can be expensive. I generally tell people to budget the turn cost being $1,500 per year of the tenant living there. If you rent a property for three years, for example, budget $4,500 for the turn cost and the rent lost while that turn is happening. If you have only three units and you've got one down, you've lost a third of your income. The best defense is a good offense, so keep on the offensive in making sure your tenants are happy and stay with you.

3. Location, Location, Location!

We discussed a lot of the location parameters to look for in the multifamily section, so refer back to that section or read it if you skipped it initially. I will point out that with SFHs, crime and school rates are much more important because families with kids make up a large portion of the renter population for two- and three-bedroom homes. What's most important to this group of renters? They want their kids to attend good schools and live in safe neighborhoods.

Other things like good walkability scores (shopping/entertainment within walking distance), trendy neighborhoods, and public transportation are important as well, but it's very difficult to overcome poor schools and high violent crime. I noted violent crime for a reason. This includes armed robbery, murder, and assault. If you have an area that has great schools, is a trendy area, and is close to nice outlet shops, you might still see that it has a high "crime" rate and come to the conclusion it isn't a good investment. I encourage you to dig a little deeper because the high crime rate may be coming from being so close to malls and outlet shops where cars often get broken into or there is shoplifting. The website neighborhoodscout.com will break the crime score out for you and maybe keep you from walking away from a good investment!

4. "Different" due diligence

Let's say you've found a three-bedroom, one-bathroom walkout ranch SFH, and it seems perfect. Don't forget that it likely has eaves, dormers, an attic, and a crawl space. That's a lot more due diligence. And then you need to get a property inspection.

Whereas multifamily has a lot of codes and city involvement from the very beginning, single-family is different. The house may have been built in 1941 when there weren't many codes. This is why it's important to hire someone who really knows what they are doing to check out the structural integrity and help you navigate the specific and "different" nuances in the due diligence process for each specific SFH property. If you are buying a large SFH portfolio, this can be pretty cost-intensive, so budget accordingly!

WHAT A GOOD DEAL LOOKS LIKE IN SINGLE-FAMILY INVESTMENTS

A good deal is somewhat subjective. Basically, if I can purchase an asset for seventy cents on the dollar compared to its market value, I feel like that is a very good deal. How do you find these types of deals, especially when it seems like everyone is trying to buy investment property?

I begin by looking at preforeclosure opportunities. Using websites like propstream.com to identify distressed properties or getting a list of preforeclosures from the courthouse is a great start. You can then use a trusted skip tracing service to locate owners of these properties and begin a conversation to see if there is mutual interest.

Let brokers in your area know your acquisition criteria, and incentivize them to bring you a deal you can close on. If a broker brings me a deal, I often give them a 5-10% bonus over and above their normal commission if I end up purchasing the asset. This greatly incentivizes them to bring me deals first and to price them aggressively to get my business. Once you close one deal and the broker sees the extra 5-10% commission in their pocket, they become a very loyal lead source. You can do the same thing with wholesalers as well, as we'll discuss below.

You can't just purchase any home, however. To be a good deal, it must check all the boxes of your set acquisition criteria. The clearer you are with your criteria, the less time you, your broker, or the potential seller waste.

To me, most deals can be "good deals," provided you buy in the right location and are decisive. It's the old adage that "you don't wait to buy real estate; you buy real estate and wait." It's about asking:

- Does it cash flow?
- What do my return metrics say?
- How does that compare against my investment criteria?

Returns are a big part of discerning if it's a good deal or not. If I'm investing passively, I may strive for a 20% return. If I am doing something actively, I may want a return of 30% or higher because it requires more work from me. It isn't necessarily about the price, but if it fits your criteria. Price sometimes can scare away those who don't know the potential. There have been times when I may have paid too much for an asset, in some people's opinion, but it was great for me because it met all my investment criteria and return parameters.

HOW TO INVEST IN SINGLE-FAMILY INVESTMENTS

Elaborating on what we just talked about, one of the best ways to get your foot in the door with active single-family investments is to contact a wholesaler in the area. Wholesalers are generally considered to be middlemen between homeowners who need to sell quickly or own distressed property and investors who want to pay "wholesale" prices for real estate in order to maximize profit. Wholesalers have their fingers on the pulse of their local markets and can get you actionable data quickly. I don't mind paying a wholesaler a few thousand dollars on a deal because if my return metrics are a hit, everybody wins. Just like with using brokers above, I often incentivize wholesalers over and above the fee they are asking for if I close on the deal. It's a great win-win.

There are many different ways to get in touch with a wholesaler. If I'm starting out in a new area, I'll start with the property managers. They tend to know many good wholesalers and are generally incentivized to put you in contact with them (if you buy the property, they can manage it). Local real estate organizations usually advertise wholesalers on their websites, as well. And once you buy an asset, you are on their radar. I don't know how many texts I get every day from wholesalers, but it's a lot! There is a ton of power in doing that first deal, even if it isn't the best deal, as you are now a part of the network. Once your name is on the scoreboard, people find you.

Other ways to invest in this space include passively investing in a single-family home syndication or buying turnkey rehabbed homes in a "passively active" manner, as we'll discuss below.

SINGLE-FAMILY INVESTMENT CASE STUDY

Passively Active Investing

A colleague of mine has established an amazing vertically integrated company that allows active investors a very passive experience. By working with him I'm able to purchase distressed SFHs before they are rehabbed at an agreed-upon price much less than that of ARV (After Repair Value). They complete the full rehab, and then we put the asset into a rental program. How can he do this? Volume and experience. They purchase and have 75-100 of these in progress each month, and they have been doing this for over fifteen years, so they are able to offer better prices to their investors because of the volume they are doing. Their investors are super happy with the finished product as well because they are good at what they do! Most "flippers" have to make much more per home to make it worth their effort because they are flipping fewer homes. Flippers are also usually selling to end users. My friend's company sells exclusively to investors, and most of the houses are pre-sold by the time they start rehabbing them.

Once the rehab is finished, you have a newly renovated, turnkey, beautiful home ready for tenants. This is where their property management group takes over for a very reasonable fee. They have tried-and-true methods of finding excellent tenants and employ strategies to retain tenants and decrease vacancy and turn costs.

One of the reasons I love this process is it allows me to be "passively active." What does that mean? This is a nuanced sweet spot. I own all these properties outright in some sort of entity (usually an LLC). However, I don't get the headaches of tenants, toilets, and trash. This is where the property management company comes in. I delegate the actual "work" of the property to the management company. My job is to direct the management company and look for other value-add opportunities within the portfolio. It allows me the full tax benefits of being an active investor in the eyes of the IRS while not having to deal with the troubles that come along with being an active real estate investor. Win for me, win for the property management group, and win for the tenants!

SHORT-TERM VACATION RENTALS

People absolutely love to stay in places that have a personal touch. Hotels can be vanilla—very plain—and if you stay in them a lot, it's sometimes difficult to even remember what city you're in and where you are when you wake up each day with the lack of differentiation and personality. Don't get me wrong, there are plenty of nice hotels out there, but you are also sharing a wall with someone—who may be a noisy neighbor. The rooms never seem to have the right amount of space to put away your clothes, and you often park, walk through a lobby, and ride an elevator to get to your floor.

Short-term rentals, such as Airbnbs, give customers a completely new and unique experience. They feel personal. And—they make money.

WHAT I LOVE ABOUT SHORT-TERM VACATION RENTALS

1. Versatility

Short-term vacation rentals are versatile and offer value to a lot of different people. The ability to charge a daily fee means the client can rent for a few days, a week, or even up to a few weeks. As the owner, you get the benefit of being able to control the calendar and decide when you'd like to use it yourself versus renting it out to others. It also allows you to be generous. I let my church group use one of my Airbnbs for free whenever I don't have existing bookings, for example, or someone else could choose to provide value to friends and family by offering a reduced rate for last-minute getaways during open slots on the booking calendar.

2. It's lucrative

With short-term vacation rentals, you can charge more than you could for a month-by-month rental. Renting by the day is much more lucrative than having a long-term rental tenant. One of the biggest benefits of renting short-term is that there is generally three to four times the cash flow as compared to a long-term rental. And, right now, the market for short-term vacation rentals is hot, with many travelers preferring Airbnbs over hotels. If you have value-adds and a destination location—a log cabin at the side of a mountain, or a cottage with private beach access—the potential for rent goes up. Looking for these value-adds is crucial in my decision-making process because my bottom line with short-term vacation rentals is always, *What is my potential average daily rate and occupancy?*

3. Tax benefits

If you are in San Diego, for instance, and purchase a $750,000 Airbnb, you can do a cost segregation ("cost seg") analysis on it and get close to $200,000 of accelerated depreciation upfront. That offsets your active income as a physician, or whatever active income is on your W2. Short-term vacation rentals are very unique in this regard.

The reason this strategy works is short-term vacation rentals are considered to be a business. Active "losses" offset active income. This is huge for people who don't qualify for REPS (Real Estate Professional Status). Since owning a short-term vacation rental is considered active investing, you can buy one and reap all the benefits of owning a business. With this, there are still some obligations to be met:

- You have to materially participate in the business for one hundred hours per year. This is only a little over two weeks and a very easy hurdle to jump.
- The average length of your short-term vacation rental guest needs to be seven days or less.
- Guests who wish to stay longer than seven days must remain for less than thirty days, or else you need to provide substantial services like mid-week linen service or booking your guests for a local experience in the community.

In my opinion, the best way to get involved and fulfill the material participation requirement is to operate the business for the 100-hour minimum and then turn the rental over to a property management company and to exact your plan for the future. The last quarter of the year is generally a slow time in real estate, so I always look for deals in October/November/December. If you want to keep your holiday season open, feel free to exact this plan earlier in the year, but my system works for me and I consistently find good deals this time of year. I operate it for the 100 hours required and then turn it over to a property management company and reap the benefits of tax advantages, cash flow, and building the NOI for an exit or refinance. Do this exact same thing every year, and you can build your short-term vacation rental (STVR) portfolio, realize amazing tax advantages, and reap the benefits of cash-flowing assets! It's a super ninja move.

THINGS TO CONSIDER WITH SHORT-TERM VACATION RENTALS

1. Regulations and laws

One of the risks of owning a short-term vacation rental is that the laws can change. Planning and zoning can pull the rug from underneath you and say, "Nope. We're not going to allow this anymore." This is happening more and more in larger cities.

If that happens, all is not lost as there is still potential to turn it into a long-term rental. My suggestion is that when you buy, underwrite it as both a short-term and long-term rental. This just improves the property's versatility. I underwrite my purchases as if they are *going* to change the rules on me, and it definitely saves me a few headaches in the long run.

Let's take Boise, Idaho, as an example. Boise has gone through quite a "boom-bust" cycle in the past few years. Imagine you paid $2 million for a short-term vacation rental, and then all of a sudden the market shifts, and no one is flocking to Boise. Then your loan comes due, and you need to refinance. What are you going to do? You paid $2 million! Do you think someone is going to rent it long-term for $8,500 per month? Probably not. Are banks going to refinance this loan with comparable sales dropping and no appreciable NOI to show because the Airbnb business has slowed? Probably not.

This is the reason I caution those buying a short-term vacation rental to set a reasonable threshold—half or three quarters of a million dollars—and stay below it. You want to protect yourself against risk. If something happens and they change the laws or economic winds change, you want to be able to maintain cash flow by converting it to a medium- or long-term rental. The more diverse your asset can be, the more hats it wears, the more your downside risk is protected.

2. Market consolidation

At the time of writing this book, we are at the front end of market consolidation. There are still opportunities for smaller investors, but large operators are figuring out systems and processes to make these assets super attractive for larger investors like private equity and other institutional investors. There are already large funds starting to gobble up short-term vacation rentals as large operators have made them more turnkey and very attractive acquisition targets. I see the consolidation not happening in a decade, but more like two to three years. There are a lot of big funds out there with deep pockets that the average investor simply can't compete with. They can utilize professional management, designers, economies of scale (they can take less margin because they have 100 million under management), technological/automation advantages, infrastructure, capital, and full-time dedicated professionals who ONLY do this. They are cherry-picking all the best assets and driving up prices, making it more difficult for smaller operators to enter and sustain their business.

It used to take forever to consolidate a market, but the virtual world we live in has accelerated this process greatly. Deals are done over Zoom and walkthroughs can be done remotely. Contracts are put in place site unseen. With everything online, business is happening at lightning speed.

3. Management

Another consideration when looking at short-term vacation rentals is the operators. Unless you personally want to keep your finger on the pulse of what the renter wants, you need a very skilled property manager or property management company.

The consequence of missing the mark is a bad rating, which can get you removed from STVR platforms like Airbnb. One of my properties had a 4.7 rating, which fell below the 4.8 average. The platform looked at us as an "underperformer" and we were at risk of being canceled. Crazy, right?

Many short-term rentals hire professional designers and have professional management. These experts can analyze a thousand data points, which people like you and I can't even imagine. I've seen people put a golf simulator in their rental because *they* think it's cool, but they didn't take into consideration that no one wants to stay home and play golf when they are hiking or at the beach in a prime outdoor location. Sometimes, we completely miss the mark thinking about what we would like and not understanding what our customers want. Professionals see these things we may not consider.

If you are deciding whether to manage your short-term vacation rentals yourself or hire a professional management company, refer back to the *"How much is your time worth?"* exercise at the beginning of this book.

If you haven't completed it yet, now is the time.

WHAT A GOOD DEAL LOOKS LIKE IN SHORT-TERM VACATION RENTALS

A good deal in this category really is location specific (not unlike most real estate investments: location, location, location!). What is the property's proximity to attractions? Is there access to those attractions? What amenities could I potentially add? What is the competition offering? If you're on a beach, most renters don't care about amenities other than a pool, perhaps. If you're in the mountains, you need a hot tub. You should also consider the size of the property. If it is a larger rental space, it will likely attract families, so having games and entertainment options is important. Each property holds its own possibilities; what works in coastal Texas may not work in the foothills of the Blue Ridge Mountains, but you want to be thinking of ways to increase the rent to its maximum potential no matter where the property is located.

Another thing to consider when looking at short-term vacation rentals is the average occupancy, ADR (Average Daily Rate), and projecting occupancy going forward (Pacing). These numbers are super important; they tell you the current situation and a glimpse into what the future holds.

Last but not least, look for low seasonality. I like to have all four seasons booked in my short-term vacation rentals. In New England, for example, people visit in the spring and summer for hiking, but they also go in the fall and winter for hiking and winter sports. Let's say you are in a place that doesn't have a lot of snow; it just gets cold and dreary (like central Ohio). You may have to run your rental only for nine months a year and shut it down for a season, which is definitely not ideal. Model for these variables, and you'll find yourself very happy with your investment!

HOW TO INVEST IN SHORT-TERM VACATION RENTALS

There are several ways to enter this space. You have to decide whether you want to be active, passive, or passively active.

Active: You can create your own STVR empire. This would involve building out your own systems, processes, and management team. This is a heavy lift and no joke. It's an active business and must be treated as such. It can be time-consuming and super labor intensive but has many financial benefits. This is by far the most profitable way, but most labor intensive. If I can make over 30% CoC, then I usually deem it worth my time to take on an active role. If the returns are less than that, I usually look for a way to invest passively or passively active.

Passive: Remember the funds I talked about just a few minutes ago? Well…they are great places to invest for passive investors as well. They have taken care of all the upfront work that we don't have time to do, or simply don't want to do. There are funds, fund of funds, and syndications that are giving investors excellent returns and requiring zero work. The CashFlowMD has several partners in this space, and you can go to https://cashflowmd.com/ to see what offerings we currently have available.

Passively Active: This method is described above using the super ninja move of doing some initial work upfront to be able to realize the benefits on the back end. If you are willing to do the work upfront to find these deals, set up, operate initially, and then transfer responsibilities to a competent management company, you can achieve the tax advantages, cash flow, and appreciation benefits most only dream of.

This book is an excellent resource for what and why, but if you want to go further into *how* I did this, my "Cash Flow Prescription" course may be for you. This course will help you unlock the full potential of passive income in the world of STVRs. The course offers exclusive insights into leveraging STVRs for tax advantages, cash flow, and appreciation. Don't just dream about financial freedom; make it your reality. Enroll in "Cash Flow Prescription" today and embark on a journey to build your STVR empire with the knowledge and insights that fueled my own success.

It will fully equip you to jump in and start your journey to building your own STVR empire!

SHORT-TERM VACATION RENTAL CASE STUDY

Remove Emotion from Investing

One of my core investment rules is, "Don't get emotional about assets." I broke that rule once.

I had a short-term vacation rental in Gulf Shores, Alabama, that ended up being my worst performing asset. This place had one of the best views in Gulf Shores and was drop-dead gorgeous. I tried to convince myself the numbers worked and it would be a great short-term vacation rental when really I was simply letting my emotions guide my investment decision—bad move.

I did my normal due diligence and knew the numbers didn't work. I stretched the proforma and based my purchase price on what I thought it could generate in revenue rather than what it was actually generating. My broker even told me she didn't think we could get as much as I was projecting. But...I was in love. I was like, "We'll just put some bunks in there and increase occupancy." Even with the bump in occupancy, the margins were still super tight. Did that stop me? Nope!

I struggled with cash flowing this asset for three years before finally selling it. Thankfully, it was a good market when I sold and I still made money overall, but it was a super heavy lift and definitely not the highest and best use of my time.

Not only did I learn the hard way the importance of removing emotion from investments, I also learned another investment principle from that experience, too: vacation where you want, invest where you make money. It's so important to make financial decisions based on where the money is, not where you want it to be.

MOBILE HOME PARKS/ MANUFACTURED HOUSING COMMUNITIES

Mobile home parks, otherwise known as manufactured housing communities, are different from any other real estate class. (The difference between the two names is centered around the date they were built. Ones built prior to June 15, 1976, are considered mobile homes, and ones built after June 15, 1976, are manufactured homes, which were subject to new construction standards after the HUD code came into effect on that date.)

In manufactured housing communities, the owner rents out pieces of land to tenants (called "pads") so a home can be placed on it. Communities generally have a mix of tenants who either own or rent their manufactured homes, and a mix of how utilities are handled. Some communities offer all utilities included with renting a home, while others pass along all utility expenses to the renter. If the tenant owns their own home and is just renting a pad, the tenant is usually responsible for paying all utilities, either through direct billing or by getting billed back from the community owner. Interesting fact: manufactured homes aren't actually classified as real estate properties, so tenants are unlikely to get a mortgage from a traditional financial institution when purchasing their home.

Manufactured housing is about six times cheaper to build than single-family homes. You can buy a manufactured home and place it in a park much more economically and quickly than buying a lot, having utilities run to the lot/home, building the home, and then paying the resultant property taxes annually. Manufactured homes are the least expensive form of detached housing we have. And nowadays, these properties are really good quality housing. With manufactured homes now being built with the same standards and zoning regulations as regular single-family homes, it is a much better answer for affordable housing. And when an investment is cheaper and faster, that is going to give you higher Cash-on-Cash returns as an investor.

From low-maintenance property management to a very high profit potential to the overall affordability for tenants, I don't know of many reasons *not* to consider this asset class for investment.

WHAT I LOVE ABOUT MOBILE HOME PARKS/ MANUFACTURED HOUSING COMMUNITIES

1. Low level of involvement

Initially, it may take purchasing a park where the park owns a lot of the homes and converting it to tenant-owned homes. There are definitely nuances to this, but understand the goal is to get it to a position where it can be very hands-off. Once stabilized, the investor simply owns the land but none of the actual homes. As a result, it is up to the tenant to care for their own home, utilities, and other expenses, saving the investor the capital expenditures and deferring maintenance costs.

2. Low financial risk

I don't want to underestimate risk because it's inherent with any investment. However, these assets, when operated well, are generally low risk. This population tends to stay put quite a bit more as they have fewer means to be mobile, and given the opportunity to live in a safe, clean, and affordable community, they choose to stay put. Also, these assets are comparatively cheaper to purchase than any other subclass of real estate. Combine this with purchasing a larger park (over 100 pads) that can absorb some vacancy while you are making improvements, and the financial risk of the investment is generally quite low.

3. Lots of opportunity

Mobile home parks are literally everywhere, and the majority are still owned by mom-and-pop types who aren't necessarily super-sophisticated real estate investors. They may have missed the incredible cap rate compression we saw from 2020-2022—one of the best selling opportunities they were ever going to have—which means they are now having to consider operating for several more years before the economy is in that position again. So…now may be a great time to negotiate a purchase using seller financing! Mom-and-pops are generally more reasonable in their asking prices, and they have the flexibility to be much more creative with their financing because they likely don't own a ton of parks and usually don't have a ton of debt to pay off once they sell. A sophisticated buyer could educate them on the benefits of seller financing. If you do an installment sale, for example, where the owner sells a property but gets a lump sum upfront and the rest is paid over a set time, mom-and-pops avoid the huge tax hit they would have if they sold the park outright. It's easier to do tax planning for a $200,000-per-year income versus a $3 million one-time lump sum payment, and this strategy truly can be a win-win for both parties.

Seller financing is "a real estate agreement in which the seller handles the mortgage process instead of a financial institution. Instead of applying for a conventional bank mortgage, the buyer signs a mortgage with the seller."[13]

4. Other smart investors are already in the game

I always like to look at where other smart investors are putting their money.

Warren Buffett owns Clayton Homes, which is the largest manufactured housing supplier in the United States (possibly even the world). He also owns 21st Mortgage, which is one of the largest manufactured housing lenders in the world.

The late billionaire Sam Zell, one of the country's largest individual apartment owners, was also a prolific manufactured housing community owner.

I personally can't help but feel I'm in good company when I'm investing alongside these guys.

5. Evergreen investment

I love investments that are evergreen. We've talked about multifamily being evergreen, and I think mobile home parks are probably as evergreen as they come.

There will always be a heavy demand for workforce housing. Statistics from 2022 show 28% of American households with an annual income of less than $25,000, which means tenants can afford approximately $650 a month *tops* for rent—yet the average two-bedroom apartment is more than double that. Some municipalities around the country are finally trying to address this issue. Many cities are eliminating single-family housing zoning altogether because they understand we are in an affordable housing crisis. This makes it a prime time to invest in manufactured housing communities; the significant demand for affordable housing and the trend of going away from single-family houses is only just beginning.

THINGS TO CONSIDER WITH MOBILE HOME PARKS/MANUFACTURED HOUSING COMMUNITIES

1. Reputation

Even though I love them as an investment vehicle, it's not all roses with mobile home parks. Being fully transparent: they typically have horrible reputations. Bringing them up as an investment at a dinner party may get you some side-eye looks.

Cities don't love these communities either, because they drain resources and don't bring in much income to the municipalities and towns they occupy.

First of all, the community owners may pay property tax on the park they own, but these assets are valued much lower than shopping centers and apartment complexes, for example, so they bring in comparatively much lower tax income to the cities where they are located. If the tenants do own their home, they may only pay a couple hundred dollars per year in taxes because mobile homes are considered chattel (tangible *personal* property), not real property. They are taxed like a car or an RV, not a home. And most of these parks are packed with kids. In 2022, federal, state, and local governments granted $15,120 per pupil to fund K-12 public education,[14] which means that with the limited taxes coming in and the big expenses going out, this is not a winning proposition for a city in terms of their ROI.

Secondly, these parks have a bad reputation for drugs and crime, which is another reason cities just don't want them. As an investor, you need to come in with a plan and show the city that the community can be an asset.

The good news is, there are systems you can implement to ensure the park runs well. You need to find a key person to run it, and establish reporting mechanisms to make sure management is held accountable. The cosmetic appeal of a park encourages people to take pride in their homes, and it changes their mindset. This is important for them—and for the park. You can put park regulations in place that tenants need to abide by; if they don't, you can come in and spruce the place up and then charge the tenants for it, so you can control the park's curb appeal across all units. For about $1,200 you can make cosmetic improvements, such as installing skirting, painting the deck and the roof, and covering the hitch. If the tenant can't afford the $1,200, you can charge them ten dollars a month until the cost is recovered. The pride they feel with these simple improvements and the drastic difference it makes to the overall appearance of the unit and, therefore, the community is immeasurable.

2. Aging infrastructure

Most of these parks were built between the 1960s and 1980s, so they often have failing infrastructure. You need to know what you are doing when it comes to underwriting and looking at the infrastructure because they are old and likely haven't had much improvement.

The age of the homes is also something to watch out for. If the mobile homes in the park were constructed before 1976, you legally cannot move them. They need to be trashed, and it becomes an added expense (it costs anywhere from $5,000 to $7,000 to take a trailer to the dump).

Additionally, in my experience, the older parks often have cesspools and lagoons. They are unsightly, they smell, and they are a hazard to kids. It's hard to complete proper due diligence on a cesspool, as not many companies service them anymore. If you want to do that, if you are an expert, and that's your niche, go for it. But most of the time, I personally stay away from it. I'd rather see a sewer or well-maintained septic tanks.

3. Limited management options

You also need to think about the management piece. There aren't a lot of great management companies when it comes to manufactured housing communities. If you buy a mobile home park, you need to hire someone who knows what they are doing. With multifamily, you can interview three companies and take your pick, but it's not the same with mobile homes. There are just not enough options available. I don't think that should stop you from investing in this asset class, though—you simply need to understand there may be a little more of a lift upfront (but the return most often makes it worthwhile).

4. Limited financing options

Borrowing can be a challenge, especially for smaller parks. There are more national groups now (like Security Mortgage and 21st Mortgage), but those are mainly for the mobile homes themselves, not necessarily for buying the actual park.

Right now, a lot of people are buying manufactured home communities for value-add, so they are utilizing mainly bridge debt (funding to purchase and stabilize). Being able to obtain bridge debt often depends on the asset, the operator's history, the cash flow in place, and the overall economy, to list a few factors. When the economy stagnates and interest rates rise, the same happens to bridge debt—it stagnates and commands a very high interest rate. Additionally, if strong cash flows aren't already in place (which they usually are NOT if you are purchasing a value-add mobile home community), the financing may be even more difficult to obtain. Since this is not an asset class as familiar to lenders as multifamily, for example, interest rates are generally higher and terms are not as attractive.

With my years of experience in the space, I've learned there are private equity, community lenders/brokers, and regional banks that will usually lend for our purchases. However, my goal for exit is to make sure the park qualifies for agency/nonrecourse debt. (Note: A nonrecourse loan permits the lender to seize only the collateral specified in the loan agreement, even if its value does not cover the entire debt.[15]) This is truly asset-based lending, where the lender will lend on the merits of the park itself, and the buyer does not have to be a guarantor. Most parks have to be at least 65%+ tenant-owned homes to qualify for this type of debt, so with parks I purchase, I need to make sure I can make this a reality. If I don't feel I can get the park to a position where it's attractive to all buyers, including those seeking nonrecourse lending, then I simply move on to the next deal.

With any deal, you have to keep the exit in mind. So, you want to position your parks to be attractive to as many buyers as possible. You are smart, creative, and strategic, and you can probably do well with the park, but unless you want to retire there and give it to your kids, you have to be able to sell it at some point. You need to plan ahead at the time of purchase and know it could be financed after you complete all of your value-adds. If you don't have a plan for where it can be financed on exit, don't buy it. You may be simply inheriting someone else's problem.

5. Master meters

A master-metered park is where all the electricity comes into a building that you own and then goes out from that building to service everybody else in the park. As the owner, you are responsible for everything in the park past that master meter. You can imagine if a tree falls or a fire burns the master-meter building down, the results would be catastrophic.

A master meter means you are essentially becoming an electric company for your park. It's near impossible (or very expensive) to implement any sort of a bill-back system, so you are ultimately paying for people's electricity. This is a dealbreaker for me personally—if the park I'm looking at is a master metered one, I'm immediately out, no matter how good the rest of the deal looks.

6. Weather

States with high incidences of severe weather should warrant caution as well. When looking in coastal areas, remember it is very difficult and expensive to get wind-driven rain coverage and hurricane coverage. Flood coverage is available, but it is super expensive if your prospective park is in a flood plain. Suppose a natural disaster like a tornado comes through and knocks out all of your manufactured houses. In that case, you will likely be successful in recovering damages from the insurance company, but you will also probably be dropped from their policy soon thereafter. It is hard enough to get one insurance company to take on a whole community to begin with, but if you have a large claim, you will have to delve into the "high-risk" pool. That could make the margins for the park untenable and put you in a really bad position. It's the price of doing business in bad-weather-prone areas, and it's too steep a price for me to want to pay, personally.

WHAT A GOOD DEAL LOOKS LIKE IN MOBILE HOME PARKS/MANUFACTURED HOUSING COMMUNITIES

Manufactured housing communities are selling at higher cap rates than their counterparts in real estate, especially with the way the economy sits currently. When you are a buyer, you want to purchase at a high cap rate. When you are a seller, you want to sell at a low cap rate. With bridge debt options being fewer in this subclass, seller financing becomes a very prominent avenue I look for when acquiring parks. Using seller financing can help force leverage a little higher on the park, which means more cash flow on these investments.

I prefer to buy parks where at least 50% of tenants rent their homes from the park as opposed to owning them. This gives me the opportunity to unlock value by being the one to turn the tenants into homeowners. It's easy to approach a tenant and say, "We want to give you the pathway to home ownership, and we'd like to sell you your home for $10,000." Chances are, the tenant doesn't actually have $10,000. So in that case, I would ask, "Well, how much *do* you have?" Even if they only have $500, you can put them on a payment plan that enables them to own their home. So, when investing in a manufactured housing community, my advice is to make wise concessions and renovations to the park-owned homes and turn them into tenant-owned ones. This has two benefits: people feel more pride for something they own themselves, and it will decrease your cost to run the park. The owners are happy, and the tenants are happy. It's a win-win.

You do need to be aware of the laws so that you don't become a lender, however. There are ways to establish a rent-to-own or a master lease that creates a feasible path to ownership. What that does for you is take all the repair and maintenance off your balance sheet and put it on to the tenant's. *They* become responsible for their homes. Due to the aging homes generally found in most parks, repairs and maintenance can be your biggest expenses. Once you've renovated homes, if they are still park-owned, the repairs and maintenance costs are much lower. If you can sell the home to the tenant, it's an even bigger win.

Most tenants will want to get on board with this plan. In my experience, these are good people—hard workers who want to own and to stay in their community—and home ownership to many is still a fundamental tenet of the American Dream. If they don't like this option, you can certainly ask them to leave. The people who leave are most often the drug dealers, the transients, and the people you don't want there anyway. We're not trying to give affordable housing to just anyone; we're trying to give affordable housing and homeownership opportunities to people who deserve it, want it, and will be good citizens in the community.

Generally, the difference between renting the home and owning the home may only be one or two hundred dollars per month. This is not a huge deal for most people, and the ROI is huge for everyone. They get to own their home, and you don't have to pay for their repairs and maintenance. Even though tenants are now responsible, they generally use less water, less electricity, and less heat because they are now paying for it instead of somebody else paying. So the park becomes more eco-friendly as well.

The size of the park and the surrounding community is another consideration. My personal sweet spot is 100 pads or more. It makes sense for the economies of scale, and it can support a park manager who is either paid or lives on the premises for free. A community this size will also support its own maintenance person, absorb inevitable vacancies, and be attractive to institutional and larger investors when I position it to sell.

I like to invest where the population of the area is 100,000 or more and where the park is within thirty miles of a large metropolitan area. That's how far most people are willing to drive for work. Having a sense of employment in the area is important. You can Google the top ten employers in the area and see what type of workers are needed in that area. We are looking for both a variety and an abundance of blue-collar employers.

I also like to see a housing vacancy of less than 10% in the area, with houses selling for at least $160,000 and above. That tells me it's a high barrier to entry to purchase a home in that area because supply is low, home prices are high, and people will be looking for more affordable places to rent.

Most importantly, I want my investment to be within five to ten miles of a Walmart. Nobody does better demographic due diligence than Walmart. If there is a Walmart in the area, that's a strong assurance that I'm looking in the right area.

HOW TO INVEST IN MOBILE HOME PARKS/ MANUFACTURED HOUSING COMMUNITIES

You can jump into investing in this category in several different ways. The heaviest lift would be to buy your own park. Still active but less work would be to rehab and flip mobile homes in other people's parks. Park owners generally like people to do this because they get pad rent and a renovated home in their park with a good tenant. Many times, I've had park owners just give me the mobile home to renovate because they aren't making any pad rent on a dilapidated vacant home. Lastly, you can invest with syndicators. (Real estate syndication refers to a pool of funds gathered by multiple investors; "syndicate members join so they can invest in properties they may not have been able to afford or that they would prefer not to manage on their own."[16]) You could also use a fund. Several funds are buying mobile home parks—including my own.

If you want to invest in this exciting asset class through my fund that puts YOU in the driver's seat, visit investor.avestorinc.com/cashflowmd for more information on how you can invest in mobile home parks and various other opportunities in the investable universe as well!

It's an exciting time to invest in these affordable housing options. With the relatively low barrier to entry, the large demand for affordable housing, and tons of different ways to be involved, the options are plentiful!

MOBILE HOME PARKS/ MANUFACTURED HOUSING COMMUNITIES CASE STUDY

Due Diligence is a MUST

Bad deals are so often a result of improper—or a lack of—due diligence. It's easy to get shiny penny syndrome and just jump in. But proper due diligence is a MUST.

Not researching local zoning laws and restrictions as a part of your due diligence can (and will) really bite you. This step is simply not optional. It only takes a quick call to planning and zoning, or you can take the time to bring some donuts to city hall—whatever you need to do to get the information you need.

A colleague of mine bought a park on the outskirts of a major city, thinking the land was not within city limits—but it was. (Okay, I know everyone talks about what happened to their "friend," but I promise this wasn't me. That doesn't mean we can't learn from it, though!)

Because it was within city limits, the property he bought fell under the city's local zoning laws and restrictions. As I mentioned before, if the city doesn't have a housing crisis, municipalities often don't like mobile home parks. The ROI isn't there for them because of the lack of property taxes paid, and they only want "nice" houses within their city limits (the perception of a "trailer park," as these communities are often called, is anything but nice in the minds of many people—especially lawmakers looking to protect the reputation of the city's image).

Unbeknownst to my colleague, the zoning laws and restrictions in this particular area did not allow replacement mobile homes or manufactured houses to be moved. They only allowed renovation of existing homes. (Essentially, if you move a mobile home out, you cannot replace it.) It might sound crazy, but it's actually pretty common.

My colleague found this out when he had removed four mobile homes and went to replace them with ones he'd already bought in anticipation of being able to do this. Thank goodness he had other mobile home assets in the area where he could put them instead. His only other alternative would have been to fight with the city on the basis of fair housing laws. He may have won, but it would have been tied up in the courts for months or years, draining resources and income. All of this could have been avoided by simply doing his homework around zoning laws and regulations.

He eventually got out from underneath the park after about a year of renovating enough homes to get occupancy to a level attractive to a new buyer. He spent more money than he should have doing so, and missed all of his return parameters for the investors. The investors ended up getting their principal back, but my colleague didn't personally make any money on the investment.

What did he learn? Do your due diligence!

RECREATIONAL VEHICLE (RV) PARKS

Some investors make the mistake of thinking recreational vehicle (RV) parks are just like mobile home parks. While there are definite similarities, RV parks are more nuanced as an investment class. With mobile home parks, tenants often own their homes but on leased land. Similarly, at an RV park, customers usually rent space for their recreational vehicle instead of owning the property. RV parks are often in desirable destination areas and vary in acreage. Also, RV parks generally offer many more amenities (pool, sports, playground, restaurant, clubhouse, etc.) than manufactured home communities, but that's not always the case.

By definition, a recreational vehicle is a broad category of motor vehicles and trailers that include living quarters designed for accommodation and can be readily towed or driven from one location to another as needed. Per the root of the first word in the name, they were originally designed for *recreation* (an activity done for enjoyment, typically when one is not working). Mobile homes, on the other hand, are designed to be predominantly stationary as a fixed structure in a mobile home park or manufactured home *community* (even the term "community" implies you'll be living there with enough permanence to have an ongoing, longer-term relationship with others living in the same place). Even though manufactured homes *can* be moved, it's very costly and time-intensive to do so.

Over the years—and especially since COVID-19 changed the travel industry—RVs have become increasingly appealing to North Americans.

They've made road trips and traveling around the country exciting and affordable for millions of families. In the past, when you thought of an RV, most people associated renting one for a family summer road trip or owning one in retirement (the "recreation" definition). In recent years, especially with the prominence of remote working, we've not only seen RV ownership continue to rise in all stages of life, but also an increase in Americans embracing this as a *lifestyle*—living in their RVs for several months (or even years) at a time.

A recreational vehicle *park* (sometimes also called a caravan park, RV resort, or RV campground) is a facility for temporary stays in allocated spaces known as "sites."

There are multiple types of RV parks:

Transient parks - The majority of the clientele in transient parks are seasonal workers who might be repairing roads, building a bridge, working as traveling nurses, etc. They want to stay for one, three, or six months, or whatever the duration of their job is. This type of RV park is run similarly to a mobile home park as it has more long-term clientele.

Pass-through parks - These parks appeal to people traveling across the country, such as maybe driving from Kentucky to Wyoming. Travelers are looking for an overnight spot. These are increasingly becoming online transactions and with automated entry and exit. People book online, and then when arriving at the park, they simply present their credit/ID card, drive through the security gate, and go to their assigned spot. Their credit card gives them access to water, electricity, and sewer. It's low-amenity, but it efficiently gets them from Point A to Point B.

Destination parks - These are usually found in or around national parks, state parks—anywhere people want to go on vacation. Some are quite primitive: campgrounds with only tent sites, maybe electricity and water, and a dumping ground. It's basic camping. Then there are other parks that offer more: utilities at your sites, a sewer dump station, a bathhouse, and potentially a few amenities. There might even be a store. Then there are resorts. The differentiator between a "park" and a "resort" is definitely amenities. Resorts offer playgrounds, fishing ponds, swimming pools, golf cart rentals, hiking, arcades, and activities for the kids. They may also offer other ways to stay, including cabins or RVs you can rent.

With RVs steadily rising in popularity, and people needing a spot to vacation with these RVs, this investment opportunity has the potential to diversify your portfolio and maximize your returns in a big way.

WHAT I LOVE ABOUT RV PARKS

1. Growing industry

RV parks fall into the outdoor hospitality asset class—and it's booming.

There has been a huge increase in RV ownership over the last twenty years. 2021 recorded a whopping 362% increase, as compared to 2009, and then 2022 saw an additional 16% year over year increase in the United States.[17] That was the highest number of new RVs sold in a year since they've been recording this data. There are more than 90 million camper households in North America alone, and another 10 million households expect to buy an RV within the next five years.

The demand is really outpacing the supply at this time and doesn't seem to be slowing anytime soon. The majority of campers are Gen Zers, Millennials, and Gen Xers, which means there is a long runway for this subclass. We aren't talking about Baby Boomers living out their golden years here—we're looking at young families who desire to get outdoors (many of whom are relatively new to camping).

2. Fragmented industry

To give you a sense of the numbers, roughly 13,000 privately owned RV parks and around 1,600 state parks cater to RVs in the USA.[18] As mentioned above, this doesn't come close to meeting the current demand, and—as an added bonus—the industry remains fragmented at the time of this writing.

Most of these parks are still owned by mom-and-pops who own five parks or less. That type of fragmentation creates an opportunity for smaller buyers to enter the market. Interest rates and purchase cap rates are both rising, which can be good news for buyers. A lot of these owner-operators are nearing retirement years and don't want to be operating these parks for three or four more years until the interest and cap rates normalize. This means they are much more willing to get creative with financing options including things like seller carrybacks, repair credits at closing, or financing the entire purchase through an installment sale.

3. Ability to drive appreciation

Very few asset classes have the potential to drive appreciation like RV parks. They generally have good cash flow to begin with, but there are a ton of additional opportunities. For example, you could optimize your merchandise sales by diversifying inventory to increase sales of clothing, candy, fishing equipment, camping supplies, or snacks. Implementing golf carts is a huge value-add. (Tip: Buy new carts with great warranties so when they need repairs, they are covered.)

You can also use dynamic pricing and site lock fees. *Dynamic pricing* is where as occupancy increases, so does the rental price of the space. On peak weekends such as the 4th of July, this means you are increasing cash flow (often significantly). Dynamic pricing also drives people to book early—in November, for example, for July 4th—which makes your cash flow more predictable. *Site lock fees* allow renters to secure a preferred location (i.e., lakeside). For an additional fee, you can lock in your exact site so you can book with friends or family to ensure your sites are beside one another or just to ensure you're exactly where you want to be.

If you choose to add more amenities, you can charge a premium. Expanding the park by adding more playground areas, upgrading the pool, putting in a restaurant, installing patios, converting sites to concrete—these things all add value, and people are willing to pay more. Dog parks and paid attractions such as ziplines, mountain coasters, and lake inflatables can also bring people to your park and increase income.

The bottom line is: The more ways to drive appreciation, the more I'm interested in the park. If there are limited options to drive appreciation or expand, it can feel more like a mobile home park instead of an RV park. Be smart and tactical about your investment.

4. Marketing

The good news is, with a good website, booking software, and social media initiatives, your marketing efforts are pretty much covered with RV parks. A well-planned and consistent Facebook marketing campaign will drive tons of business to your park. One of my parks is currently running a Facebook ad that basically says, "Hey, share this ad and tell us why you love our park in the comments." Each time people share our post, they are entered into a drawing to win a free weekend stay. This drives up the search engine optimization for Facebook because people are organically sharing our post and their pictures, and tons of people end up visiting our website because they love giveaways. We get the benefit of social proof, testimonials, and a buzz surrounding the park, which leads to—you guessed it—bookings!

I also advise aligning your park with a nationally known RV membership group (Good Sam, KOA, etc.) as well because many avid RV owners generally join these clubs for membership perks. Members receive 10% off (for example) a stay at participating parks. The exposure you get to their membership base is definitely worth giving a 10% discount to members.

THINGS TO CONSIDER WITH RV PARKS

1. Cost of employees

With destination and pass-through parks, one of your biggest expenses is going to be the cost of your employees. RV parks require a more sophisticated customer service-oriented employee than mobile home parks. They need good communication skills because they are dealing mostly with vacationers. Vacationers can sometimes be not-so-nice—you know, people who try to get a free night's stay because their Wi-Fi isn't working. Also, there are generally more transactions with an RV park (camp store, propane, golf cart rentals, etc.), so you need to have a sophisticated employee who can handle both communication and customer service and can be trusted with finances. These employees cost a little more and are more difficult to find.

There are ways to offset this increased employee cost. We often give our park managers free rent, for example, to live onsite at the park. We generally build a site very close to the camp store for the park managers. One of my parks has an amazing park manager, so I even offer one of my Airbnbs for the cold winter months for her and her family—it's a beautiful location to celebrate the Holidays with their family and a much warmer way to spend December through February. Winter is a low-rental season at this park anyway, so it makes sense to offer this perk—it's a great incentive!

2. Park type

While banks love transient parks because they have "reliable income," I tend to disagree. The income is not that reliable when renters live in vehicles that have wheels and can leave anytime they want. I think there is a false sense of security there. I personally prefer destination parks with a history of demand.

And while it seems like a four-season park would be better for consistent cash flow, when you have a park that is open year-round it can be really hard to do major capital improvement projects needed to drive appreciation. Inevitably you will disturb the ambiance and experience of your guests, and as a result, you might get bad reviews and/or a bunch of squeaky wheels vying for free amenities and services as compensation for their "hardship." I don't want to discourage you from four-season parks, but I don't want to steer you away from seasonal parks either. Both can have their advantages and challenges.

3. Quality of bookkeeping

Banks want to see clean balance sheets, income statements, and T12s (a detailed financial statement showcasing the income and expenses for the previous twelve months broken down in categories[19]), but sometimes mom-and-pops don't keep very good books. Often they're pretty rustic and "old school"—they might only have a written ledger instead of electronic records, for example.

In the situation where they don't have traditional financials, I ask for bank statements. A seller should have those, and I can at least validate revenue and verify expenses they run through the bank account. If a seller cannot confirm revenue in any way, it's an absolute no-go for me.

If they do produce financials, you'll want to verify everything as well. Reviewing bank statements, seeing tax returns, and contacting utility companies and vendors to verify expenses are very important steps. Most utility companies and vendors are happy to release that information to you with the seller's permission. Do this even if the financials they give to you look pristine as a way of verifying or "double checking" where you can, since it is highly unlikely you will be given audited financial statements.

Low-quality books make it difficult for you to really understand the numbers, so you'll need to do extra due diligence wherever possible to vet the deal and see if you can figure out how close or far off the numbers may actually be.

4. Environmental issues

In some areas of the country, people are converting former farming, industrial, or mining sites into RV parks. Where there has been industry, farming, or mining in the past, chemicals leach into the ground. Or, if the park is sitting over a former gas station or mechanic shop, you could be walking into a potential hornet's nest of environmental issues. You need to do your due diligence, or you could easily inherit a problem that could be a big issue when you try to sell. Always obtain a Phase I Environmental Assessment. If you don't get a clean Phase I report, you may not be able to sell your asset, as banks want this information when they are financing—especially in protected areas. One of my key rules for investing is to have several exit options. Having a troubled environmental impact study will greatly decrease your buyer pool.

5. Infrastructure

Are there adequate dump stations situated strategically throughout the park? Are the utilities set up in a beneficial way? Does each site have full hookups? If the answer is no to any of these questions, you could be looking at thousands of dollars to implement the critical upgrades necessary for the answers to be yes. It's not a deal breaker and can be an opportunity for great value add, but you'll need to budget for the improvements and adjust the purchase price accordingly.

Also—city sewer is much preferred to septic. Septic tanks require maintenance and need to be pumped regularly, which can give an unpleasant smell to your vacationers trying to enjoy their burgers on the grill! There is also a strong likelihood of damage from overuse. No matter how good the tanks, entering repeatedly for pumping will inevitably cause damage that is costly to repair.

I would stay away from RV parks with master meters because—as we talked about with mobile home parks—I don't want to become a utility company. Things will invariably go wrong. If you have a master-metered park that gets struck by lightning, for example, you could lose electricity for an indefinite amount of time, and everyone is calling *you*, not the utility company.

WHAT A GOOD DEAL LOOKS LIKE IN RV PARKS

As mentioned above, I personally prefer parks in established destination areas. I look for inefficiencies in operations, layout, use of land, amenities, or any other gaps I see in the customer experience. I believe there is excellent value to be found in inefficiencies.

Location is super important because it's the one constant about the park you cannot change. So, I look for a desirable area to vacation or an area that is in the path of growth and recreation. You can find a lot of these areas through a short-term rental search on your website of choice. I often use Airdna.co because it has a ton of data. It's a paid subscription, so just looking at popular Airbnb locations will be a good start to see where people are choosing to vacation.

When purchasing an RV park, I use my "rule of three" to find good deals. First, the park needs to be less than three hours away from at least three major metropolitan areas of greater than three hundred thousand people. This ensures I have a large vacationer population within a reasonable driving distance to market my park to.

Increasingly important is making sure guests have access to reliable internet, especially as more and more people are hitting the road long-term and working from their RVs. If people are staying for a week or two, they expect great internet service. Make sure you can run fiber optic or do something to boost the signal strength so people can stream and work. Some of these mountain parks simply can't get great service, and if they can't, that's going to be a liability, given the day and age we live in.

Lastly, I look for any other "meat on the bone" that makes the deal more attractive. Similar to the inefficiencies I mentioned earlier, this is more low-hanging fruit that I can implement immediately to increase cash flow and drive NOI. Is the park charging way below market rates? Are they charging monthly utilities for longer-term tenants? Could I implement dynamic pricing? Can the website be improved to drive more traffic? Are there underutilized sites I could put a camper on and rent as an STVR? The more meat on the bone there is, the more hungry I am for the deal.

HOW TO INVEST IN RV PARKS

As with several of the other real estate subclasses we've discussed, there are many ways to invest in this exciting asset class. A quote from the great NHL player Wayne Gretzky reminds me why I love this subclass of real estate so much. When asked how he continued to be so great even in his later years of playing, Gretzky famously said, "I skate to where the puck is going, not where it has been." I believe RV parks are where the puck is going.

There are many ways to get in the game. You can go out and buy an RV park yourself and can achieve some individual achievements on your own. But, just like in hockey, to win championships, you need an amazing team. Whether it's on your own or putting together your own investment group, your team is everything. I've built a championship team over the years of being active in this space. There are syndicators and other funds to choose from for sure, but you need to exercise caution as many of these folks are just starting out and don't have a great track record. When you invest in the CashFlowMD Capital Fund, you'll have the peace of mind of knowing my money is going right alongside yours, and I've done the heavy lifting of the due diligence upfront before we offer anything to our investors.

RV PARK CASE STUDY

The Power of Amenities to Add Value and Drive Appreciation

We bought an RV park with forty-five sites in a destination area where avid outdoor enthusiasts love. We immediately understood the demand and expanded to seventy-five sites the first season. We also improved fifteen of the existing sites to be pull-through concrete sites with patios because feedback from big-rig customers was that backing in wasn't desirable for their large, forty-five-foot diesel pushers.

We then revamped the website to make it more professional and user-friendly, implemented a Facebook marketing campaign, leveraged the existing email database for more targeted marketing, and bought user-friendly booking software.

I often like to add cabin homes or tiny trailers that are decorated to be retro-cool. People love to stay there! We did this here, adding seven short-term rentals ranging from vintage RVs to rustic cabins. We wanted to make sure we had something there for everyone.

We added an arcade, stocked the pond for fishing, improved the aesthetics, built a restaurant onsite, and brought in high-speed internet. We began offering weekend activities such as crafts for kids, and we built a playground to encourage more families. Then we made arrangements with local vendors so our customers could get great deals in the area.

We also decided to sell some of the land that was in a flood plain to a local entrepreneur in the area. We put deed restrictions on it so they couldn't build something undesirable, unsightly, or noisy. The deal articulated that anything built had to be aesthetically pleasing, like an artisan's courtyard. The buyer ended up opening a donut and coffee shop, and a gem mining business the kids all love! These improvements added great value to our park.

All in all, our improvements increased NOI by 35% in the first year, adding about $1.5 million in value in only twelve short months.

TRIPLE NET LEASES

A *net lease* refers to a contractual agreement where a lessee pays a portion or all of the taxes, insurance fees, and maintenance costs for a property in addition to rent. Net leases are commonly used in commercial real estate.[20]

There are different types of net leases: single, double, and triple. Let's explore all three.

Single net lease - A commercial lease agreement that requires the tenant to pay property taxes in addition to rent. The landlord is responsible for all other operating expenses associated with the property.21

Double net lease - In this agreement, the tenant takes responsibility for the property taxes as well as the insurance. The landlord retains responsibility for structural maintenance costs like roof, parking lot, and mechanicals.22

Triple net lease (NNN) - This refers to an agreement where the tenant pays all the expenses of the property: real estate taxes, hazard insurance, liability insurance (naming the landlord as an additional insured, which is very important), maintenance, HVAC, plumbing, and electric. This is above and beyond their rent and utilities. As this definition has been "massaged" by brokers over the years, there is a new, more descriptive term, absolute triple net, which means the landlord has absolutely zero responsibilities and zero liabilities. No roof responsibilities, no parking lot responsibilities; truly NO responsibilities.

WHAT I LOVE ABOUT TRIPLE NET LEASES

1. Excellent tenant pool

Triple net agreements are very advantageous to the landlord, especially with larger, investment-grade tenants. An "investment grade tenant" means the tenant or entity in the lease has a favorable credit rating—one that lenders find really attractive. Think Dollar General, Walgreens, Fresenius, and other BBB+ rated national organizations. This is attractive because if your location has any issues, there is no danger of default—the debt will be paid by the company acting as the guarantor.

This is a really important factor when venturing into triple net leases. Lenders for this will often give high-leverage, nonrecourse lending and other favorable terms because the tenants are backed by their respective national corporations.

2. Diversity

I like triple nets as a diversification play. It's a great asset that is going to produce consistent checks no matter what's happening in the short term. Unlike multifamily or other tenant-based investments, triple nets offer huge security, no repair costs, and no management hassles. Because the tenant is responsible for all of the maintenance and repairs, they generally take care of the place better than most tenants.

3. Hands-off investment

Triple net leases are essentially what investors like to call "mailbox money." Investors use this term when they've secured a lease that requires little to no responsibility on their part—they simply receive a check in the mail every month. No phone calls. No dealing with tenants. No fixing toilets or a leak in the roof. For a busy physician, this type of investment is wonderful because it leaves time for them to focus on their main job: medicine. You hear the term "mailbox" money thrown around quite a bit, but this is what is truly meant by the term.

4. Low liability

I also can't stress enough the incredible benefit of having low to no liability. The tenant is not only required to have the building and their business insured, but to cover you as well as an additional insured. Since the tenant pays for this insurance, it cuts down on a major expense associated with real estate investing.

5. Financing Options

We touched on this above, but another reason I love triple net leases is because they qualify nicely for nonrecourse debt. This means the bank's only recourse is the asset itself. You are not required to be a personal guarantor in this investment, which frees up your balance sheet to go find more investments.

THINGS TO CONSIDER WITH TRIPLE NET LEASES

1. Fixed rents

With triple nets, you can't drive rents like you do in other subclasses of real estate, so you are often stuck with fixed rents and rent escalations. Rents are fixed, and returns are fixed for a set amount of time. If you are in an inflationary cycle in the economy, these rent bumps often do not keep up with market rents. It's fairly common for a company such as Dollar General to not have *any* rent bumps for the first fifteen years, but they generally have a higher operating cap rate, meaning they pay higher initial rents than other potential tenants would. Other tenants will offer 2% annual rent bumps, while others may have rent escalations every five years. Generally, however, they will always lag behind market rents. This is a trade-off for the stability and security you get with these tenants.

You may be allowed to put less equity on these assets, however, as banks are willing to give higher LTVs for investment-grade tenants. So, this may allow you to get two Dollar General stores as opposed to just one asset that would have a noninvestment grade company as a tenant.

2. Tenant quality

One of the risks with this type of investment is that the tenant could go out of business and leave you with a vacancy. If the economy was one of the reasons the tenant went out of business, good luck finding a replacement tenant. No tenant = no income. No income means this is a liability, not an asset. Let's avoid this scenario!

I'm not a fan of single-tenant net leases with noninvestment-grade tenants for this exact reason. Even a multiple-tenant strip mall wouldn't sit well with me unless it was anchored by an investment-grade tenant. I know these tenants are harder to find, but, using stock market terminology, I look at NNN investments as my "bond" investment. The safe investment that will continue to pay no matter what the economy looks like. If I allowed less stable tenants to rent for more money, it would go against the reason I invested in NNN in the first place. I want a "set it and forget it" asset that only good quality tenants can give me.

3. Smaller rental pool

You will probably find yourself with a much longer wait time between tenants if and when one leaves, because the pool of replacement candidates is much smaller.

In multifamily, you can get another tenant in a relatively short amount of time.

When a Dollar General, Kroger, or a large anchor store decides to leave, however, it could result in a lack of income for a considerably longer period of time while you're trying to fill it, potentially costing you thousands of dollars. This is why it's important to make sure you have ten, fifteen, or even twenty years on the tenant lease when you purchase an NNN asset.

4. Interest rates

When interest rates rise, so do the rates for triple net, which creates a buying opportunity. When interest rates fall, so do the cap rates, and that is a great selling opportunity. NNN assets are very interest-rate dependent, but other factors can come into play that make these assets more or less desirable.

I bought a Dollar General at a 7.5% cap, which is around the historical average over the last decade. I was okay with that rate, because the interest rate on the loan on the property offered me great arbitrage and good cash flow. However, as the economy shifted and investors were seeking security, this asset became much more desirable. Interest rates had not changed much, but sentiment did. This enabled me to sell that asset eighteen months later for a nice profit. I'll go into more detail below in the case study. I used that profit and 1031'd into another NNN, increasing my "mailbox money" and getting a new asset.

Fluctuating interest rates definitely affect the value for triple nets, but make sure you keep abreast of consumer sentiment and appetite as well so you don't miss out on nice profit-generating opportunities.

5. Nonpermanent locations

Test locations don't always work out. A lot of national companies will build smaller "test" stores to see if it's a market they want to be in. If the concept is proven, they then build a larger store, oftentimes in a different location that's more visible, larger, and desirable. If you are the owner of the "test" building, then you could be left scrambling for a new tenant to fill the space vacated by your tenant! Not a great position of negotiation to be in.

Avoid this by making sure you're buying a new NNN structure with a long lease by an investment-grade tenant. If they do move on you, they're still on the hook for the rent, and you have time to find a suitable replacement for them.

WHAT A GOOD DEAL LOOKS LIKE WITH TRIPLE NET LEASES

I can't stress enough the importance of an investment-grade tenant. On top of that, I want the business to be recession-proof and thrive in all economies, like a Dollar General or a Walgreens. There are some great automotive companies out there as well as dental chains that are decent, too. Essential services such as dialysis centers can also be great investments.

An absolute triple net is a must for me. As I stated before, I look at these as my "bond" investments. I expect them to be completely hands-off mailbox money. The only way I know to ensure that is to verify it's an ABSOLUTE triple net deal.

I also want a long-term lease of fifteen years. I generally do cost-segregation analysis on these assets for accelerated depreciation benefits. After about five to seven years, the depreciation is usually bled off, so I want to sell them and 1031 into something with a higher basis to take advantage of the accelerated depreciation in the new asset. If I only have a five- or ten-year lease, the asset may be harder to sell because it's up for lease renewal relatively soon. If the lease is fifteen years, the new buyer still has another eight to ten years left on the lease before the tenant can potentially move out.

Location is very important. A lot of Dollar Generals move to a bigger location right across the street from the old one, as I mentioned above. For this reason, I don't buy "test" stores. I look for their "relocation" stores. These are stores where they have tested the market, decided it's where they want to be, then built a larger (relocation) and more permanent store they will use long-term. When they have proven they can thrive in a neighborhood, they look for more permanent locations. These stores are really strong investments, as they generally extend past their initial fifteen-year lease term because they are in a proven market.

HOW TO INVEST IN TRIPLE NET LEASES

A broker is going to be a key piece to this puzzle, and that person needs to be regional. Most brokers are boots on the ground and may have a territory that spans the entire state. You need to have someone who has a direct pulse on the area you're looking at.

You want a broker who is super-communicative and has great deal flow. They should have tons of off-market deals. They don't have to be the biggest player in the game, but you want someone who has adequate transactional volume so they have lots of sellers in their circle. If you have someone who is starting out and who is hungry, they don't generally have the relationship capital to get you what you are looking for with these types of deals.

Not only are there triple net brokers, but there are ones who are specific to each type of investment, too. For example, there are Dollar General brokers who have worked in the business to the point where they may be selling dozens of these per year. They know the nuances to these deals and can really compress time for you.

NNN brokers usually get paid 1% or 2% commission, so they deal in sheer volume. While your broker may be busy talking to people and trying to cook up a hundred deals, it's probably not the highest and best use of your time to see all of these. You're looking for quality over quantity. This means your broker needs to listen to your acquisition criteria and only send you assets that check all the boxes. If they spam your inbox and disregard your criteria, they're probably not the broker you want to be dealing with.

If you are working with a savvy broker, they will likely have a good relationship with tenants and parent companies. As I mentioned, there are brokers who do nothing but Dollar Generals, for example. My broker can even go as far as to look at the financials and forecast which stores are going to extend their leases because he's been at it for so long and is such a deep expert on Dollar General's practices. If he lets me know there is a Dollar General for sale that's in year twelve of a fifteen-year lease, but they are most likely going to extend, I can likely get it at a very nice price (high purchase cap rate). I purchase it and will immediately negotiate a lease extension (known as blend and extend). I can then do two things: keep it and cash flow it for an extended period while getting the benefits of accelerated depreciation, or turn around and sell it at a much lower cap rate since the lease has been extended. It's a nice play that can give you cash flow and multiple exit options.

You'll also need to consider your lending options. I encourage you to go to your regional bank and ask them for nonrecourse debt (which means the loan is secured by using the property as collateral).[23] Sometimes banks will want you to be on the hook personally until the property appreciates to a 60% loan-to-value ratio (the ratio of the loan amount to the market value of the property) before the asset will stand alone and become a nonrecourse product. You will need to ask your lender how the asset can become nonrecourse debt because every regional bank has different terms. They don't love to do it, but they *can*. You just need to ask the question. Once you develop a big enough portfolio with them, you can demand it or move your business elsewhere. Having a portfolio of $5 million to $10 million allows you to start flexing your negotiation muscles with lenders. If they don't want to offer nonrecourse lending options, triple nets are very easy to get long-term permanent debt at a very low interest rate from agency lenders as well.

Another thing I recommend is hiring somebody to do a risk assessment on your asset early. You can catch some deferred maintenance upfront and get the tenant to fix it. If a tenant moves out in year seven of a fifteen-year lease, it's going to be much more difficult to get them to abide by the terms of the lease while they aren't occupying the property. Many of these businesses are a part of large organizations, so there is a lot of bureaucracy and red tape. Do an assessment as soon as a tenant signs the lease, and keep your eye on the repairs and maintenance throughout the duration of the lease—this is definitely something you'll want to stay on top of.

I also always hire an attorney who is well-versed in real estate and who has done some large, sophisticated deals. You want an attorney with several clients who work in the NNN space. It's a subclass full of institutional investors along with their attorneys, so your attorney needs to speak fluent "corporate bureaucracy." I often find my attorneys through the broker's recommendations. My initial interview would be based on questions about triple net leases: How many have they done? Are they licensed in different states? What business sectors are they involved in? I also ask for their references. It's the same principle as finding any good advisor. The more deals you do, the better legal team you'll build.

Once you find the right broker, asset, and team, you are ready to take down your first absolute NNN investment!

TRIPLE NET LEASE CASE STUDY

Triple nets are somewhat inelastic, meaning their value usually goes up and down with interest rates in a linear fashion.

One of the things I love about triple nets is they are a great place to park 1031 money. If they are guaranteed by an investment-grade tenant, they are easy to finance and have stable, predictable cash flow while you are trying to figure out your next move.

I had a 1031 exchange and decided to invest in an absolute triple net with Dollar General. I didn't have a super long runway for the 1031, but my broker found a brand-new relocation store (which means Dollar General had already established the market with a test store a block away) with a fifteen-year lease. My purchase cap rate was 7.5%.

I could have put permanent or nonrecourse debt on it, but I wanted more flexibility because I was planning to sell in two or three years (once I figured out what I wanted to do with that capital), and I didn't want to worry about the fees that come with nonrecourse debt when you exit early.

I was able to complete the sale and did a cost segregation study, which netted me quite a bit of depreciation upfront to use to offset gains that I had from other assets that year. Since I was a full-time real estate professional, it also offset my wife's W-2 income, so we retrieved all her federal income tax back in the form of a tax refund. Simultaneously, the market began to shift, interest rates dropped, and the world found itself in the middle of a global pandemic. While triple net assets are generally inelastic, the flight to security and businesses deemed "essential" by the U.S. Government drove cap rates on Dollar Generals down even further than they should have been. Remember, low cap rates are GOOD for sellers, BAD for buyers.

I knew this series of events set up well in my favor, so I had a decision to make. I decided to harvest the profit and put the Dollar General on the market. I had purchased it for a 7.5% cap and was able to sell it eighteen months later at a 5.9% cap. The really cool thing was I had a ton of net operating losses (NOLs) held over from previous years, so I was able to offset my gains from the sale of this asset (including depreciation recapture) with these NOLs and ended up owing absolutely zero in taxes when the dust cleared!

NNN assets offer flexibility, are sought after as safe investments, and are great places to park 1031 exchanges for several years while you figure out your next move!

INVESTING IN

NON REAL ESTATE INVESTMENTS

In real estate, we've all heard the phrase, "Location. Location. Location." When it comes to the Investable Universe, your mantra should be, "Diversification. Diversification. Diversification."

By adding diversity to your portfolio, you are mitigating risk by spreading your investments across various asset classes. While real estate holds many profitable options, this next section will dive into non-real estate investment opportunities which should protect and sustain your cash flow.

Non-real estate investments offer flexibility, liquidity, and the potential for significant returns, getting you one step closer to financial freedom.

MINERAL RIGHTS

In inflationary times when market volatility is increasing, hard assets tend to become more appealing than ever. When the price of everything increases, so do the returns on hard assets. One category of asset investing that allows you to feel the benefits of rising prices is mineral rights.

Mineral rights investments refer to the acquisition of the rights to extract and/or sell minerals found within a particular tract of land. These minerals can include anything from coal and oil to gold and copper. Unlike surface rights, which allow the owner to cultivate the land for agricultural or residential purposes, mineral rights entitle the owner to own and mine any natural resources *below* the land.

The problem is that not many people understand these assets well enough to invest in them confidently. And rightly so. Mineral rights investments can be highly lucrative, but they can also be highly complex and require significant expertise to navigate successfully.

"Mineral leases differ from other real property leases in three important aspects. First, the lessee has the right to use the land and to take substances of value from it. The same cannot be said in a typical landlord-tenant arrangement, which only entitles the tenant to possession of the property. Second, rights conveyed in a mineral lease are not always limited by time. Third, a lessee's rights to use and access the property where the subsurface minerals are located must be shared with the surface owner.

While leases are governed by the straightforward rules of property conveyances, mineral leases are hybrids between contractual agreements and conveyances of rights. A mineral lease is a property conveyance because the mineral owner grants a transfer of possession, easements or other property rights through the document. On the other hand, a mineral lease is a contract because it contains legal promises regarding compensation, use and other aspects of the developer's use of the land.

Courts treat mineral leases differently depending on whether the state law tends to treat such leases under principles of property law or contract law. Some states, such as oil-rich Texas, see mineral leases as creating interests as fee-simple property estates on behalf of the developer-lessee. Other states, such as Oklahoma, Kansas, and California, instead classify the lessee's interest as a "profit á prendre," which is an agreement that creates rights to others' lands to take value from them. Courts in still other states treat oil and gas leases as both a conveyance of mineral rights and as a contract between the property owner and development company."[24]

- From "Mineral Rights Leases: Form and Function" on lawshelf.com

The unique thing about this asset class is that finding somebody you can trust to do business with can be hard. It really is buyer beware. You need to work with someone who has been in the business a long time, understands the nuances, and has a track record of proven success.

WHAT I LOVE ABOUT MINERAL RIGHTS

1. Great earning potential

One of the main advantages of mineral rights is their potential for high returns. If the mineral deposits on a particular parcel of land are significant, the owner of the mineral rights can stand to make a substantial profit by leasing those rights to a mining company or selling them outright. And, as oil and gas prices go up, so do your royalty checks.

This investment generally responds linearly to price, supply, and demand. So, it is another non-correlated asset class as it mirrors the economics of commodities more than the stock market.

The way it works is that companies that lease the mineral rights extract oil, natural gas, and other minerals from the land you own and pay you—the mineral rights owner—royalties on the amount they extract. The royalties can generally range from 18.5% to 25%, and the value of the mineral rights is based on the amount of royalty income you receive as well as the residual value of what's still left after extraction.

The oil extraction companies look at what the anticipated production of that net mineral acre is going to be, then offer a lease price to the owner of the mineral rights based on their projections. If the operator and mineral owner come to an agreement, the oil company will start with the extraction process. As they extract oil and gas, the royalties come to the mineral right owner as monthly cash flow.

2. Legacy creation

When you invest in mineral rights, you will receive a mineral ownership record, which is basically a property deed that grants you the rights to the land and outlines ownership of all the materials below the surface. When you lease the land to an exploration production company, they make an upfront payment followed by royalties. The average lease cycle is twenty to fifty years. These leases are so long because oil and gas exploration companies invest a lot in geophysical research and constantly develop new technology to enhance extraction. They want to hold on to these leases as long as possible to maximize extraction using technological advances. You hold onto the rights forever, unless you sell them. So, during the time you own the rights, you may go through a few different lease cycles, but you will receive an upfront payment when each new lease is signed.

Some of these oil fields have been active for over a century. With continued production potential averaging thirty or more years, these royalties can roll on seemingly forever, and the wealth generated through royalty payments can be passed down to your heirs. This further helps to secure the financial future of generations to come, and creates a legacy deeded asset that you can pass down to your kids and their descendants.

3. Accountability

One of the fantastic benefits you have as a mineral rights owner is that companies must mine the land or they will lose the right to mine the minerals. If activity goes dormant for a certain amount of months or years (depending on how the lease is spelled out), you have the option to resell the rights to someone else.

4. Residual land value

There's also residual value in the mineral rights during and after an extraction cycle. As discussed above, extraction technology is advancing virtually every day. Ten or fifteen years ago, no one knew what horizontal drilling was, but now it's the gold standard for resource extraction, and companies are still developing sophisticated ways to extract more efficiently. They used to drill straight down in a vertical line, and if they hit a big patch of oil, woo hoo! We now have the knowledge that *several* layers in the earth produce resources, and all of these levels are so much deeper than they've ever previously explored. They are just now realizing how to efficiently and effectively drill down to procure the resource. As one company that leases the mineral rights may focus on one layer or resource, the next leaseholder may have technology that is able to access an entirely different layer altogether. This helps the mineral rights retain value and even increase over time as inflation increases the prices of hard assets.

5. Minimal liability

Another reason I love this type of asset is that it is basically liability-free. Oil and gas extraction can be dangerous, and people get hurt. Those concerns fall 100% on the company that leases the mineral rights, not you. When you buy mineral rights, there's no need to insure against liabilities or property damage. You don't have to purchase them using a limited liability company, or LLC, because there is no "personal responsibility for its debts or liabilities."[25] So, when the inevitable happens and there is a workplace accident, you can sleep sound knowing there is zero personal liability to the mineral right owner.

6. Deductions

While I wouldn't consider mineral rights a strong tax-advantaged investment, there is a tax perk investing in this asset class worth discussing. With mineral rights, you get a depletion allowance, which refers to deductions from gross income allowed investors in exhaustible mineral deposits for the depletion of deposits.[26] Your depletion allowance is about 15% annually, and it basically acts like a deduction. So, if you make $100,000 on mineral rights, it's as if you only made $85,000. This is a non-tax guy's explanation, so please run this by your tax team to understand how it would affect you individually.

The theory behind the allowance is that an incentive is necessary to stimulate investment in this "high-risk" industry.[27] The government incentivizes the private sector to do what it doesn't want to do itself.

Just like real estate, mining oil and gas has tons of tax advantages. In the oil and gas space, working interests (discussed next) have even more tax incentives than mineral rights.

You can also use your SDIRA to invest in mineral rights as long as the operator you are investing with agrees to this type of investment vehicle. This allows your money to grow tax-free and even be harvested tax-free if you implement the right strategy.

Lastly, mineral rights are considered real property, so they are 1031 eligible. You can mitigate taxes on a sale by doing a 1031 exchange into mineral rights or implement the strategy when selling mineral rights, just as you would with real estate.

THINGS TO CONSIDER WITH MINERAL RIGHTS

1. Lack of liquidity

One of the biggest cons with mineral rights is that the money invested is not liquid. There is just no robust marketplace for mineral rights exchange. Some are being developed, but as of this writing, there is no Dow Jones or Nasdaq to exchange or sell your mineral rights. While there *is* an upside being that it can be a great generational investment, the downside risk is that it is one you might not be able to sell quickly if needed.

2. Subjective pricing

Determining the value of mineral rights can be highly subjective and can depend on a range of factors, such as the quality and quantity of the minerals present, the cost of extraction, and the demand for those minerals on the market.

As part of your due diligence process, you will want to get expert advice on the value and potential of the mineral rights, including seeing geological surveys and market analyses. There are many unsavory characters in this space, so make sure you choose wisely who to take advice from. Our partners have been in this space for decades and have a track record of honesty, character, and performance. Go to https://cashflowmd.com/our-affiliates/ to set up a call with them today!

3. Regulations

Regulations surrounding mineral rights can be really complex and can vary depending on the country or region. For example, mineral rights in the United States are usually separate from surface rights, meaning that a landowner may not necessarily own the rights to the minerals beneath their property. It's a complicated process separating mineral rights from surface rights, and it takes a specialized team to do this. Make sure your team is well-versed in this process and has a successful record.

4. Environmental and social impacts

There are potential environmental and social impacts associated with mining activities. You need to understand if the operators have a history of being good stewards of the land. Our leaseholders leave the land better than when they found it.

Unscrupulous mining practices can have consequences such as deforestation, water pollution, and displacement of local communities. If you are invested with this type of company and they get involved in a lawsuit, while you won't have liability, you *may* find your operator shut down and cash flow halted. There is such better technology available now than in years past, so there is really no excuse to use outdated extraction methods. Make sure you attach yourself to a group of good stewards of the land.

5. Operator risk and middlemen

There are a lot of bad operators out there—and a lot of "middlemen," so to speak (manufacturers, distributors, and reps).

If a company is multifaceted and is involved in carbon sequestration, pipelines, or conservation easements as well as oil and gas, chances are they are spread too thin, and they aren't really best in class in any of those things.

Many times, you'll have brokers or commissioned representatives try to sell you anything they can make money on without truly knowing the operators or the fundamentals of the deal. These brokers will line up opportunities in working interests, mineral rights, pipeline opportunities, carrier companies, or anything they can make a commission on. While some may be worth investigating and even investing, always remember that they are a third-party seller, so their motivation is to sell, not to perform.

Good operators in this space are very hard to find. By operator, I mean a company that can acquire good mineral rights, working interests, and other oil and gas investments desired by large exploration companies. We'll cover more about good operators in a minute, but understand the most powerful oil companies—ExxonMobil, Chevron, Shell, BP, Ovintiv, and TotalEnergies[28]—want to deal with operators they know will consistently offer productive net mineral acreage for lease. It costs a ton of money to take a well from exploration to production, so they want to work in proven tracts that they know contain oil deposits.

Good operators acquire these tracts, and the exploration companies know this. Make sure the operator you choose has an excellent working history with these companies as part of your due diligence.

WHAT A GOOD DEAL LOOKS LIKE WITH MINERAL RIGHTS

As I've already stated, it is important to choose a laser-focused company that knows what they are doing. A good deal starts with choosing the right group to invest with. What does that look like?

You need a company with decades of experience, and operators who have a stellar record with clean professional background checks. You want to know they are using the most current technology to locate the best tracts to purchase, what their balance sheet looks like, and that they have geologists and experts on staff verifying the presence of rich mineral tracts. Any company you work with must have strong environmental and social policies in place that comply with local and national regulations as well. Once you've narrowed it down to a few potential groups to invest with, reach out to current investors to get testimonials of their experience. If the company can't give you a list of names to reach out to, that's a big red flag.

If you do your homework and invest with good operators who find land known for rich oil production, you reduce the risk of having a "dry well"—one that costs a TON of money with ZERO results to show for it.

Once I feel comfortable with a company and I'm interested in an opportunity they are offering, how do I know what they are offering me is real? It's super difficult to establish ownership for mineral rights, as we discussed earlier. It takes a whole lot more than a simple title search. I need to be able to see the geographic location of the mineral tracts, history of production, and API numbers of working wells and wells they have capped waiting for prices to rise. I only move forward in the process if they can produce API numbers and legal descriptions for every producing well on all tracts being offered. API numbers are like serial numbers for the wells, proving their existence. Kind of like a VIN on a car, they are the unique identifier numbers for every producing well in oil and gas. These digits give you lots of information. The first digits in the API number refer to the specific geographical location of a well, while the last digits record the well's operations. When read from left to right, the numbers start with the two-digit state code, followed by a three-digit county code, followed by the five-digit unique well identifier number. Using this information, I can verify the wells are where they say they are. If the company refuses to provide API numbers, it's a full stop and I move on.

Assuming the company and the investment pass due diligence, here's what I look for in a return model: I want the investment to at least pro forma out to 10% CoC return, meaning if I invested $100,000, I would expect $10,000 annually in cash flow. Mineral rights are not super liquid, as we discussed earlier. I look at these as legacy investments, meaning I'm a "never seller." After eight to ten years of owning this asset, you have received your principal back, are in the "infinite return" realm, and have created a generational asset. However, in the spirit of "never saying never," I want to make sure there are at least some liquidity options. A good deal will at least offer the potential for the operator to buy back your rights at some point, or offer some sort of peer-to-peer platform where you could sell your mineral rights if unforeseen life events happened. With that being said, if I were to sell my mineral rights and receive a 20% annualized return on the investment, I would consider that a good investment. Make sure you discuss your expectations with the company you are investing with and, whatever your return parameters are, ensure they have a pathway to get you there.

HOW TO INVEST IN MINERAL RIGHTS

This is not a space you want to go it alone, and it's definitely an asset class where experience and track record are vital ingredients in choosing who to invest with. Sure, you can hire a "landman" or a broker to sell you just about anything individually, but in order to have the best chance at success, you want to invest with a company that has a long record of success in the oil and gas space for decades, not just days.

This asset class has a very high barrier to entry. You could go to school/ training to be a landman, go out and hire geologists and surveyors as well as attorneys to do mineral right title searches, approach the owners (who haven't been shrouded in such anonymity whereas you could actually find them), offer them what you hope to be the correct price, and then have the fun of changing over the royalty rights, which start with hundreds of pages of paperwork and bookkeeping. Then, you have to reconcile this every month to make sure they are not shorting you, OR you could invest with a known group who has been in the space for over thirty-five years.

Using the criteria we have already discussed, I completed due diligence on several companies offering oil and gas investment options. I narrowed it down to one group that I do the majority of my oil and gas investing with, and you can find it at cashflowmd.com/our-affiliates/.

MINERAL RIGHTS CASE STUDY

Take Action, Diversify, and Play the Long Game

Investing in mineral rights is just like investing in real estate—you don't wait to buy; you buy, then wait. "Buy" is a verb, which necessitates action on your part! You can't build a robust mineral portfolio unless you combine your knowledge with action. Let's look at how this mentality has worked for me in this space.

I've averaged high teens cash-on-cash returns on my mineral rights investments. I've not sold one single net mineral acre since I started investing, either. The key to these returns is understanding dollar-cost averaging. This investment strategy involves investing the same amount of money in a target security at regular intervals over a certain period of time, regardless of price. By using dollar-cost averaging, investors lower their average cost per share and reduce the impact of volatility in their portfolios.29 As long as I dollar-cost average over several tranches of mineral offerings, or I buy one large tranche that covers several areas, I'm continually increasing my holdings and remaining well diversified.

The more you invest over a variety of offerings, the more likely you are to find oil activation, and the more likely you are going to get a good return. Some of my investments have produced over 60% annualized return, and others only 6-8%. By continuing to accumulate and diversify, I still find myself winning the game in the long run with excellent returns.

The economy is going to ebb and flow, but the good news is that oil and gas economics are not necessarily tied to the stock market. It's one of the things I love about this industry, and it's a huge advantage over the volatile stock market. Times of recession can surely affect short-term returns, but we are playing the long game here, remember? So, take action. Diversify. And play the long game.

WORKING INTERESTS

While there are different types of working interests, the term really refers to a true ownership stake or a share in an oil and gas lease, or on the property itself. In this type of investment, you are an active investor with a proportionate share of costs, rewards, risks, and everything associated with the exploration, development, and production of the land.

As you read through this section, I want to be very straightforward with you: **I don't recommend working interests for new investors.**

When an oil and gas property is developed, there are a lot of moving parts. You've got oil companies, investors, landowners, mineral rights owners, and many partners. Each one of them has a specific and different interest in the project.

As a working interest owner, you are responsible for contributing a portion of the capital required, and you are going to bear a portion of the risk involved. Maybe there is a dry well, or the project is way over on cost, or there are massive fluctuations in the commodity prices. These factors make people pucker, and can create a (sometimes significant) capital call. But, on the flip side, you get a portion of the revenues generated, and that's where everyone gets excited.

The exact percentage of a working interest varies depending on the terms and agreements between the mineral rights owners and the operators. There are people who invest talent/expertise, people who invest work, and people who invest capital. The return is going to be commensurate with what is contributed, respectively, to the project.

The bottom line, and one of my foundational rules, is, "Don't invest in things you don't understand." With working interests, the reward is high, but the risk can be as well due to the steep learning curve. So, unlike the other sections in this book, this chapter is a bit of an advanced class.

You can't do this on your own. Good working interest investment opportunities will feature excellent management by professional oil and gas companies. They will have invested a ton of their capital, time, and talent into this industry. Incredible expertise and valuable resources are fundamental components of developing these lucrative assets. These opportunities differ from mineral rights in that you have to vet the extraction company along with the company organizing the offering. Similar to mineral rights, you want to work with companies that employ geologists, engineers, landmen, and certified industry professionals who all work to assess the potential of an oil and gas asset and collaboratively determine the best method of extraction while sporting an exemplary returns history.

WHAT I LOVE ABOUT WORKING INTERESTS

1. Huge ROI potential

As long as you are well educated and prepared, there are a ton of advantages to this type of investment. First of all, there is a chance for astronomical returns—hundreds of percent of return on your money, especially if the economy is good. If the operators are skilled, know what they are doing, and keep the costs low, you can really generate substantial cash flow.

2. Diversification

Working interests are a great way to diversify your portfolio.

When you have a diverse portfolio—real estate, stocks, bonds, mutual funds, gold, cryptocurrency, oil, and gas—you are reducing the overall risk, and you are more likely to have upward steady returns over the long term.

3. It's fairly hands-off

There is *some* active involvement required in this type of investment, as you need to do your due diligence and figure out who to invest with. However, once you connect with the right people, working interests can generate passive income.

The oil and gas companies are not going to call you and say, *"Hey, what do you think we should do about x,y,z based on these metrics and flow rates we're finding?"* They're the experts, and they are just going to take action. So, the investment can offer a very steady income stream without the need to be actively involved in any form of day-to-day management.

4. Depreciation benefits

One of the biggest reasons people invest in this asset class is the depreciation benefit.

You can be 100% passive from a time and talent standpoint, but 100% active in the government's eyes, which allows you to write off your entire investment without the depreciation recapture.

Note: Depreciation recapture is the gain realized by the sale of depreciable capital property that must be reported as ordinary income for tax purposes.[30]

This is the sweet spot of passively active income.

With the U.S. government backing domestic energy production, oil investments have significant advantages. Drilling costs are 100% deductible in the year incurred. These costs generated through working interest are considered *active* income and can be offset against other forms of income (W-2 wages, interest, and capital gains).

I'm not a CPA, but in layman's terms, the main government requirements to be considered actively investing is that you must be materially participating (time) and have money at risk (liability). With every working interest investment, you are an "active" partner, meaning you are on the hook for cost overruns, dry wells, and other unforeseen costs, as well as liable for any debts incurred by the exploration company related to the well. If you choose wisely based on your due diligence, you will align yourself with a group that budgets for cost overruns and has a "zero dry well" history. This de-risks the investment greatly and allows you the tax benefits of active investing while remaining passive from a time component. The perfect "passively active" investment!

5. It's a legacy investment

Similar to mineral rights, working interest investments have a long lifespan. Some fields are productive for many, many decades. A good operator will know when to ratchet production down and when to turn it on based on global economic conditions.

Additionally, you have first right of refusal on any other wells they want to drill on the lease you own together. If they have done their homework and are in a bountiful area to drill, you have the opportunity to continue investing not only for *your* lifetime, but into your children's lifetimes, as well.

6. Demand

Another advantage is the huge demand for these assets globally. Crude oil, natural gas, and other minerals are essential for everyday use. Your car, your phone, food service, manufacturing, you name it—oil and gas are a part of it all. Worldwide, we have a very strong dependency on these assets, and in my lifetime, my kids' lifetime, and my grandkids' lifetime, oil and gas will remain major players, creating ongoing generational demand.

THINGS TO CONSIDER WITH WORKING INTERESTS

1. Capital calls

A capital call, also known as a *drawdown or a capital commitment,* is a legal right of an investment firm to demand a portion of the money promised to it by an investor. You really need to think about what percentage of your investable funds you want to invest in working interests, and also set aside 10% of what you invest for potential expenses so you are not caught off guard with a capital call. Even the best operators run into unforeseen circumstances out of their control (i.e., a global pandemic). If you bite off too large of a working interest investment, you could get a capital call for your pro-rata share and find yourself in a financial pinch.

2. Who you partner with

Your partners are one of your biggest—and most important—risks. Many working interest owners participate in projects through partnerships or joint ventures. These collaborations involve risks associated with the actions, decisions, and financial stability of other partners.

You need to know who your partners are. If one member of the partnership can't pay their share of expenses, and it goes down the line to the next person who can't pay, you could be on the hook for a huge amount of money, even though you only own 1%. Every partner is joint and severally liable for the entire project. This means, for example, if all the other partners can't pay their portion of expenses and file for bankruptcy, the financial burden of the entire project could fall into your lap.

3. The unknowns

There are additional risks with working interests that I'll simply classify as "the unknowns."

First, there's the dry hole or exploration risk. There is always a level of uncertainty when it comes to oil and gas. Even if the companies have done tons of above-the-ground work, they never know *for sure* what lies below the surface. The way I mitigate this risk is by not investing with *fringe drillers*. These are drillers who drill several wells around the outskirts of known mineral-rich basins, hoping at least one of them will strike oil. Hope is not a strategy. I want to know if a company is drilling in well-established basins, where they have previously discovered oil, if they are using the latest extraction methods, and where they plan to dig next. I don't want to work with an *explorer extraordinaire.*

Next, even if a successful discovery is made, you are still liable for production risks. There are dangers involved. There are technical difficulties. Even the pandemic hit us with unexpected costs—shipping went through the roof, and all of a sudden a $5 million rig became a $10 million rig. A myriad of unexpected costs can arise in exploration, drilling, production, trucking, etc., and can eat into your profit. When you are part of an investment team, the expenses incurred go into your share of the return.

Last but certainly not least, there are also market fluctuations to contend with. These are based on global supply and demand, or on geopolitical events (like Russia and Ukraine going to war). We are living in unpredictable times, which puts us at risk for many things that are unknown, unforeseen, and unexpected.

4. Regulations

You also have to deal with environmental regulations that change depending on who is in political office. The oil and gas industry is subject to extensive bureaucracy, which can directly impact your operation and increase your costs.

5. Capital-intensive

Working interests are a very capital-intensive investment category, and you need to understand that upfront. Banks often don't lend in this space, and private equity's appetite is finicky as well, so you need to depend largely on investor capital for exploration. As lucrative as it may be, the upfront capital is always at risk. Your revenue is directly correlated to your production. If the investment is not producing because the well is dry or due to any number of factors, you won't be getting paid, and you may lose the entire investment to fees and other costs. Remember Warren Buffet's first two rules of investing here!

WHAT A GOOD DEAL LOOKS LIKE WITH WORKING INTERESTS

After reading all of the risks, you may be thinking, *"Why on earth would I venture into this, Danny?"* The answer is because when you can understand what makes it high risk, you can mitigate those risk factors and reap great rewards. It all starts with doing your proper due diligence.

First and foremost, a good deal needs to meet your own personal investment criteria. *How many years will it take to get my principal back? How much do I want as a return? How much depreciation will I benefit from?* If it is checking all of your boxes, it's worth investigating further.

Secondly, you want to look for basins that are proven reserves and for partners who are knowledgeable and proven as well. This will give you the best chance for success. As with any investment, a number of factors can affect your cash flow: regulatory changes, economic collapse, changes in administration, natural disasters, etc. If you've partnered with a large operator who already has an industry presence, they tend to weather the storms and stand the test of time better. They generally have uncompleted wells (DUCs: Drilled Uncompleted Wells), which can be turned on easily during economically beneficial times and turned off when returns aren't as good. They generally drill several DUCs during good economic times when cash flow is plentiful. They keep these in their arsenal during down economic times and reap the benefits during good economic times by putting them into service. This process helps absorb seismic shocks to the economy, which inevitably occur while maintaining profitability.

A good deal will offer an excellent return over and above the depreciation benefit I receive. I caution against deals that seem too good to be true, however. Oil and gas can make you really wealthy, but if someone is making a *promise* of returns, I would be VERY skeptical. There is no such thing as a guaranteed return. Yes, there is history—a record of what has been done in the past. But if someone is guaranteeing an outlandish return, they better be able to back that up with data, not promises.

As mentioned before, a good investment is rarely found with fringe drillers. Good deals are usually found in the "meat" of oil and gas basins with proven operators. Using the meat analogy, you want the tenderloin, not the sinew or the fat layers. Some companies drill *around* the right basins, and they hit a good spot every now and then. They are hoping that out of five drills, one is going to pay off. As I said before, that's not a strategy, it's simply hoping. Anyone who is fringe drilling basically doesn't have the chops to drill with the big folks. They haven't proven themselves yet, and I would avoid them.

The groups I invest with have clean, professional background checks. I urge you to spend the time or money to conduct these on every operator you are seriously considering. These will show you if there is any history of fraud, violations, or litigation against the potential partner. If you've been in business long enough, you're likely to get sued for something. I get it. If something comes up on the background check and the potential partner can explain the situation to my satisfaction, it's not necessarily a deal killer. But, if whatever the issue is cannot be readily explained, that's an enormous red flag.

HOW TO INVEST IN WORKING INTERESTS

If you are just starting out, I suggest you get into mineral rights first, in order to understand more about the oil and gas industry before jumping into a working interest.

Once you've done that and learned through experience, the only way I suggest investing in this category is to partner. As I mentioned earlier, you can't do this on your own.

We've already discussed the importance of partnering with the right people. For working interests specifically, I want to partner with someone who has capital riding right alongside mine, so they have their own skin in the game.

As with all investments, you want to partner with someone with a rich working history. I want to work with someone who has forgotten more than I will ever know. These aren't the people wearing coats and ties, doing awesome webinars—they are the people on the ground. They have landmen and geologists. They have hit dry holes and understand the ramifications of that. They know the perfect operators to partner with. If they haven't cut their teeth in those realms, I would wish them the best and move on. They might do just fine and even go on to make a killing, but not with me.

Because this type of investment carries heavy risks, you also want to make sure your partner values communication. It has to be paramount because changes happen quickly with working interests. Among other hurdles, there are cost overruns and regulations that can really stymie production. You need to be in the loop because you are ultimately on the hook for all of it. I don't want to be hit with a six-figure bill that's due next week. I want to understand what's going on, where we are in the stage of the process, and why we are over budget long before a bill arrives.

This is a complex and difficult space to wrap your mind around. The partners on my affiliates page have met the criteria I've discussed and invest their money right next to mine. Feel free to reach out to them from my website or set up a time to discuss this further with me.

WORKING INTERESTS CASE STUDY

Ask a LOT of Questions

When I was living in Alaska in 2012, four physician colleagues approached me about a possible drilling investment. At the time, I didn't know much about oil and gas, but I knew a little about investing. I was smart enough to ask a few basic questions such as, "Where are they drilling? Is there a big oil basin there?"

They explained that it was an exploratory play near a large basin, but there was very good data and a good team involved—good everything. They felt like it was a home run.

I continued to ask questions. "Who brought this opportunity to you?" (It was an Alaskan broker who apparently had unique access to the deal.) "What kind of well is it?" (Vertical.) "Is there any other way to drill? (Nope.) How long have they been in business? (First venture but years of experience.) How much money has the broker put in himself? (He would have invested heavily but was short on cash.) What's your liability on this?" (My colleagues explained they didn't have any liability. They had formed an LLC.)

I decided to walk away. The more I asked, the more questions I had. I didn't know much about the space, and it seemed the broker wasn't being upfront with his information, as the answers were vague and full of deflections from the original question.

Turns out, my colleagues invested in a dry well. They got zero dollars from this "investment" and ended up on the hook for the $2 million in decommissioning costs, which was double their initial investment. Their LLC did protect them personally from liability, but it did not protect them from the financial obligation as each of them had signed as guarantors. Remember the "joint and severally" liable nature of these investments? Three of the four of my colleagues declared bankruptcy. The fourth was left with a massive bill that he was forced to pay in lieu of filing bankruptcy as well.

This is a cautionary tale of knowing what you are getting into, knowing your potential liability, and knowing who you are working with. You need to go in with eyes wide open…and ask TONS of questions.

TIMBERLAND (A.K.A. "TIMBER")

"Timberland" refers to land that is primarily used for growing and harvesting trees for timber production. It typically consists of large tracts of forested areas, often owned by private individuals, companies, or government entities. These timber resources can be harvested and used for construction, paper production, and fuel.

This type of investment can offer potential financial gains through both the sale of timber and the appreciation of land value over time. It is a long-term investment, with growth and yield potential. Investing in timberland is a strategy for individuals and institutional investors looking for long-term returns and diversification.

WHAT I LOVE ABOUT TIMBERLAND

1. Diversification

Adding timberland to your investment portfolio can help diversify risk and reduce overall volatility. This investment is influenced by factors unique to the timber market, such as housing construction and demand for wood products, but is not directly affected by what's happening in the stock market. For instance, in down economies, people more often renovate than build. In good economies, new construction often outpaces renovation. Good news: Timber is needed for both! It's resilient in good and bad economies.

It's a great tangible asset, which adds a lot of value and is resistant to inflation. As the prices of goods and services rise, the value of timber tends to increase as well, making timberland a potential hedge against inflation.

2. Sustainability

It's also a great renewable resource.

Let's say you buy a 4,000-acre timber stand, and you break it up into 20 tracts and one tract is harvested annually. By the time you cycle through all 20 tracts, it's been 20 years since you harvested the initial tract, and it's ready to be harvested again! It's the ultimate sustainable resource!

If the managing company is thoughtful with its strategy, timber investments can offer a steady stream of income for a very long period of time—forever, even!

3. Tax advantages

Depending on the jurisdiction, timberland investments may offer specific tax advantages because the government desires to protect the land as timberland. To do so, they'll make your property taxes very low—in some cases, almost free.

Along with reduced property tax, there are special valuation methods for qualifying timberland. You can get an agricultural designation, for example, which encourages the preservation of forested lands. The government doesn't want companies going in and stripping the forests, so the IRS allows for special provisions related to timberland. If you meet the criteria, your profits are essentially treated as long-term capital gains, which are lower than ordinary income tax rates.

You can also deduct the cost of timber depletion over the period of growth, which is usually around 15%. You can basically play the game one of two ways: recovering some of the cost of acquiring and growing the timber in the form of a tax deduction, or offsetting the taxable income generated from sales.

Timber is real property, so it is 1031 eligible. A 1031 exchange can mitigate taxes for many years or even permanently when structured correctly. Timberland is considered a hard asset, so—just like you can do a 1031 into apartments, for example—you can do so with any sort of land investment.

There are also estate tax benefits to consider. You can get favorable treatment because this investment is considered a working asset, which means it provides a valuable resource to the economy. Various estate planning strategies, such as conservation easements and agricultural districts, can be set up to help mitigate estate tax liabilities for timberland owners.

It's a good idea to talk to your CPA and asset protection team for more information. They will know the specific tax regulations and guidelines in the jurisdiction your timberland is in.

4. Environmental stewardship

Owning timberland can provide many opportunities for conservation and environmental stewardship. While that is likely not the number one reason people are investing, it's nice to know your investment is helping to create sustainable resources and taking into account conservation principles.

If you use proper forest management practices, you can have a positive impact on the habitat and help it flourish. There is potential to preserve, restore, protect watersheds, enhance biodiversity, and sequester carbon dioxide.

5. Recreational opportunities

The topography of timberland generally lends itself well to fishing, hiking, and even swimming if you have a lake or a pond on the land. If you own an apartment complex, you don't necessarily want to go and sit and bask in its courtyard, for sure, but if you own timberland, you may actually *desire* to "get away" and enjoy the great outdoors and the wildlife on your property.

You can also explore the opportunity to lease the land and monetize hunting and recreation rights on it to further cash flow this investment, as well. If you have 10,000 acres, for example, this can add up to a really nice supplemental income. A desirable area may bring anywhere from $20-80/acre/year in supplemental income.

6. Legacy investment

Timberland is an intergenerational wealth play that can be passed down over generations as a long-term family asset. This is not a get-rich-quick scheme or an investment you are going to flip—it's one where you'll be playing the long game.

Different studies have shown that timberland investments have well-outpaced inflation. Historically, there have been attractive long-term returns. They've also exhibited lower volatility compared to other traditional asset classes like stocks, bonds, mutual funds, and ETFs.

While it's true that the main value proposition of this investment is the timber itself, there are many extraneous ways to monetize the land if you take advantage of the added opportunities.

THINGS TO CONSIDER WITH TIMBERLAND

1. Associated costs

You need to carefully evaluate the financial requirements before jumping into this investment vehicle. Many costs are associated with owning and managing timberland: property taxes, harvesting expenses, replanting costs, and management fees, to name a few. These things all need to be considered when looking at net returns. While there is cash flow, the return parameter I look to most in this asset class is annualized return over a cycle, which is usually 20 years—as that is the minimum time between harvesting an area.

Timberland investments carry significant upfront costs just from the land acquisition, because banks don't generally lend more than 40% to 50% loan-to-value. With banks putting up less and less of the leverage, it is cash-intensive, and you need to make sure you are well capitalized. This makes timber a good asset to utilize 1031 exchanges, especially if you have a lot of equity in the asset you're selling. The more equity you have inside the 1031, the less money in the form of a loan you'll need from a bank.

You also need to budget for reforestation costs, especially if you purchase in the southern regions of the United States. For example, pine trees need to be completely replanted after harvesting, which drastically cuts into your net profits. Hardwoods in the Northeast are more expensive timber stands to purchase, but they regenerate themselves much more readily than their Southern neighbors, giving you a healthier bottom line come harvesting time.

Property taxes are also something to think about, even though they are relatively low because timberland is considered agricultural land. In some states, however, the taxes are higher if the government knows you are operating a timber business on the land. Make sure you check into local municipalities' laws surrounding taxes before purchasing.

Other costs involved with proper forestry stewardship are spraying for bugs and decreasing the underbrush to prevent fire. You also need to put in logging roads, and there are transportation costs. If your facility is a hundred miles away, that's going to add up.

2. Lack of liquidity

The liquidity of timberland investments can be relatively low, and investors should be prepared to commit their capital for a considerable period of time. If you don't want to invest long-term, or if you want to use a lot of leverage, timberland probably isn't the right play for you. Trees take years to mature, and harvesting and selling timber occurs over extended intervals.

Moreover, refinancing your investment can be a bit tricky. Very few banks are willing to refinance based on the land value alone. It all comes down to the value of the trees grown on the land.

3. Local conditions

The lucrative potential for this investment is highly influenced by what the regional and local market dynamics look like. This includes the demand for timber products and the availability of materials.

You also need to know the regulatory framework in the area. It can be super onerous or super logger-friendly. One end of that spectrum has the potential for fines and shutdowns. There may be zoning restrictions permitting where you can and can't log. Some regions require business permits.

It's crucial that you look at the regulations of where you are buying. I always say that real estate is hyper-local. Even though timber is worldwide, the land is still hyper-local, so you really need to know the community.

4. Environmental risks

Make sure you insure your land and business against any environmental risks you can. This is definitely not an area to skimp on. During due diligence, clearly characterize mitigation plans in place for fires and other natural disasters. Understand how close utilities (especially fire hydrants) are to your land and what the local policy is surrounding fighting fires, avalanche prevention, pest control, and several other areas that could adversely affect your timber stand.

> *Note: Mitigation planning is the process used by state and local leaders to understand risks from natural hazards and develop long-term strategies that will reduce the impacts of future events on people, property, and the environment.*[31]

I've mentioned previously that we lived in Alaska for six years. They don't fight fires in Alaska, for example, unless homes are at risk. If a fire moves through your land, you'd better be insured. In Maine, however, it's totally different. They understand timber is a scarce and needed resource, so they do fight fires.

You also want to be aware of a pest infestation nearby—and if there is one, what is being done to eliminate it. Some infestations can kill hundreds of thousands of trees. In many states, no action is being taken. If you are up in the Northeast, stakeholders will be proactive, but in Kansas, Kentucky, or West Virginia, you are more than likely on your own.

I highly suggest consulting a local forester and using their expertise. You can also contact the U.S. Forest Service or local cooperative extensions, which are usually part of the state agricultural colleges. Either of those options should provide the information you need to understand the environmental risks associated with this type of investment.

5. Market volatility

Timberland is a commodity, so it's subject to market fluctuations. Global pandemics, trade policies, tariffs on imports and exports—these things can all affect lumber prices, which will impact your revenue.

It is important to think long-term. Even if your profitability is affected temporarily, you can still expect double-digit returns over the long term. Short-term issues can be mitigated with a calculated harvesting plan. If timber isn't doing well, you harvest less to keep the costs lower and wait for a better time. It will come.

6. Timber stand improvement (TSI)

Companies want to increase their timber yields and wood-growing potential through a number of initiatives outlined in a timber stand improvement plan, or TSI. Timber stand improvement is achieved through a combination of pre-commercial tree thinning, girdling, and pruning for multiple resource benefits…depending on stand location and site-specific management objectives.[32] The TSI can have a positive impact on your investment, not only because of the increased timber yield, but also enhanced timber value. By selectively thinning the forest and removing defective or lower-quality trees, those remaining have more space and resources to grow, resulting in higher-quality timber. It also means a shorter "rotation" period (rotation being the period from planting to harvesting), which means that investors can harvest and sell timber more frequently—leading to a more regular income stream and potentially faster ROI. TSI also mitigates risk by minimizing potential financial losses. By maintaining healthy forest stands, investors can reduce the likelihood of pest infestations, diseases, and wildfire damage. TSIs can improve the overall resilience of the forest to natural disturbances and environmental impacts.

WHAT A GOOD DEAL LOOKS LIKE WITH TIMBERLAND

One of my biggest considerations when looking at an investment opportunity in timber is the stumpage value. This term refers to the amount of money a timber harvesting company is willing to pay the landowner for the right to harvest and remove timber from the property. Your stumpage value will give the highest indicator of profit potential.

A lot of different variables influence the stumpage value. Different tree species have different market values, based on the quality of wood and the demand for it.

You really need to know the quality of the wood, no matter the species. *Are the trees big? Does the wood have many defects? Does the hardwood have beautiful knots that people desire in tables and furniture?* These characteristics are going to affect the value.

Market demand affects the stumpage value. If there is a housing boom in the area and a ton of construction activity, that has a positive impact. If there is a big furniture manufacturer down the road, that's a great thing. It's supply and demand dynamics.

You also need to investigate the site index (a term used in forestry to describe the potential for forest trees to grow at a particular location or "site." The index is used to measure the productivity of the site and the management options for that site and reports the height of the dominant and co-dominant trees[33]). The site index describes the average height of the dominant tree of that species in a specific area—specified by a number of years. A site index of ninety means the soil occupying that site will grow a specific species of tree ninety feet tall in fifty years. Fifty years is the normative time used to derive site indexes, although timber companies harvest timber in much shorter rotation periods.

It's really important to understand that the site index can be premium in one part of the country and just average in another. An index of a hundred might be considered excellent in one region, while a site index of eighty is considered excellent in another. It's all relative to what kind of return you are expecting.

You might find a property with an average site index of seventy that has an average return of $45 per acre. There might also be a property with a site index of eighty-five with an average return of $110 per acre, or a site index of a hundred with a $250 average return per acre. Notice as the site index increases, so do your returns.

If you are considering a property with a site index of eighty-five, then another opportunity arises in the same area with an index of a hundred for the same price, you obviously will find the property with the higher site index more attractive.

The site index can be a great predictor of success. Similar to using the MSA and looking at the submarket in real estate as concentric rings to narrow down the bullseye on what type of property you want to buy, the site index is a very strong tool to help you make an informed decision with timberland. It's not 100% predictive, but will tell you what *should* grow based on the comparable composition of the land.

State Forestry Commission publications are a great resource that compares site indexes. If reviewing the site index makes you feel like a deer in headlights, you can always find a broker who specializes in forestry and timber. Remember, a broker is only as good as their knowledge base in the asset class. If you ask about stumpage value and site indexes and they look at you like a deer in headlights also, it's best to find another broker.

Timber is a good investment option, but if I can add an additional exit possibility, it becomes an excellent investment option! When searching for timber stands, I find it to be a great deal when using the land for timber may not be its highest and best use. If I can find awesome stumpage value in the path of development, I've just given myself another exit possibility. I may be able to sell to a developer, subdivide myself, or continue to create wealth for my family via harvesting timber. Bottom line, having multiple exit options only increases my interest in an already good investment.

I also look for investments in close proximity to a sawmill. When forest products are purchased from a landowner (timberland investor), certain costs of production must be considered. Many factors affect production costs, and the distance to the mills is perhaps the most important. The further the owner's property is from the mill, the more it will cost to get his product from the stump to the mill. The extra distance means extra expense to the logger, which means less money to be paid to the timber owner. Because a finite amount can be paid for the raw material and the logging company still be profitable, any additional expense incurred by the logger will have to come from the amount that can be paid to the timber owner. Timberland investors can contact their state Forestry Extension Service office to get locations of area mills. You can also talk with foresters in your area to get information about the timber market where you want to buy timberland. They not only know where all the mills are, they will know which ones are the best for the type of product you will be selling.

HOW TO INVEST IN TIMBERLAND

As with many investments, your success in timberland depends upon the quality of the people and the expertise you surround yourself with.

Most people choose to hire professional management, which is definitely my recommendation. There are a lot of things to know as an owner, but you can't know it all, especially if you want to be as hands-off as possible. A good management company will run the day-to-day operations as well as be able to anticipate future needs.

You'll want to find a management group that will give you the most successful return, and this requires forestry expertise. Whoever you hire should know the techniques, the operations, the market trends, and the environmental regulations. They will be knowledgeable about and able to help you understand the known and potential associated costs, and what to budget for reforestation (if any). They will have a pulse on the regional and local market dynamics and regulatory framework in the area. Make sure they believe and practice good land stewardship, and ensure proper regulations and best practices are followed. You don't want to end up in a lawsuit with the EPA because of your property manager's ineptitude or negligence.

The U.S. Forest Service is an excellent resource for finding trusted advisors to help you along this journey. This expert knowledge is essential for optimizing your returns and mitigating the risks. You'd be wise to reach out to them early and often.

TIMBERLAND CASE STUDY

Always Read the Fine Print

As we've outlined throughout this section, the traditional variables I normally evaluate in timber are the stumpage, the reputation of the logging company, the timber report/TSI, the site index, the availability management/logging companies in the area, and the distance to sawmills, to name a few of the major ones.

But there's another category of red flag that only became clear to me through a deal we did: the importance of reading the title "exceptions" and things not covered by title insurance (and understanding exactly why they're not covered).

When you're dealing with timber areas that aren't well populated, you can sometimes find yourself in the midst of long-standing disputes based on arguments over boundaries (which you definitely don't want to find yourself in the middle of).

Years ago, a partner and I bought timberland in Idaho not knowing the full back story of the land. While we did the title search including the title exceptions, we didn't do a good job of reading those exceptions. Lo and behold, one of the exceptions to the title report was that a road we had deeded to the parcel we were purchasing was not included in the title insurance. That should have raised some red flags! We had an easement, but the title company said they wouldn't cover it under the insurance. Then we found out why: the easement was not legally deeded.

We ended up having to sell that parcel of land to the logging company that was located in the middle of their operation. In the end, we worked out a mutually agreeable arrangement, but it could have been financially catastrophic for us.

Moral of the story? Do a record search to see if there is any litigation surrounding a property. Make sure you understand the title, the exceptions, and things not covered by title insurance. If there is no viable plat survey (which is a map that defines the property boundaries and shows any easements or other legal characteristics of the property), insist on having this done before purchasing.

I also strongly recommend getting a Phase One Environmental Assessment before purchasing. As I've said before, you don't want to be buying someone else's problem. If the land doesn't pass Phase One, it's probably best just to walk away from the associated risk. I'm sure there is a possibility it could be mitigated, but I've never seen a failed Phase One turn out well for an investor.

Bottom line (again): always do your due diligence. And when doing so, always read the fine print!

CAR WASHES

I love this space, and it's becoming hotter and hotter—especially since private equity has jumped in. As people's daily lives become busier, amenities such as car washes, which offer rapid convenience, are a sure-fire win.

There are three basic types of car washes, as defined by carwashadvisory.com[34]:

> ***1. Self-Service*** - This is the DIY (do-it-yourself) option where you pull in to use the sprayers and equipment to wash your car yourself.
>
> ***2. In-Bay Automatic*** - These are structures where the vehicle stays stationary during the wash process and the machine or washer moves around the vehicle. This method is also referred to as "non-conveyor."
>
> ***3. Express Tunnels*** - In these structures, the vehicle is moved using an external mechanism (typically a conveyor or belt), and the wash equipment is largely stationary.

For the purposes of this section, we'll direct our focus on express tunnels, as that is where most investment dollars are flocking and is currently the most scalable option. Since the pandemic, express tunnels have remained the preferred method because users don't need to get out of the car. The technology is also improving, so customer satisfaction is on the rise—which is always important for customer retention.

Here are a few statistics to showcase the current industry boom:

- The car wash industry is projected to reach $68.9 billion by 2031. (For reference, the 2021 market was valued at $29.3 billion and in 2022, $38.4 billion.)[35]
- In the last ten years, more than 70% of Americans have switched from handwashing to using car washing facilities, valuing the time saved by the automatic process.[36]
- The USA contributes roughly 43% to global car wash revenue.[37]

These numbers are compelling and make it clear that clean vehicles are important to a large portion of our society. And with a large number of people employed in the industry across the globe, car washes are a strong contributor to the overall economy.

Owning a car wash can be a solid option for investors as it takes a relatively small financial investment to make improvements that substantially increase cash flow.

WHAT I LOVE ABOUT CAR WASHES

1. Fragmented industry

The car wash industry is still very fragmented. Some national brands—like Mr. Sparkle—are gaining market share, but no one really dominates more than 5% of the industry's total revenue. This means the car wash industry is ripe for disruption by implementing technology and creating recurring revenue streams through memberships.

In 2021, 66% of Americans washed their cars approximately thirteen times per year,[38] but only a small percentage of those bought memberships or subscriptions. That's where the huge growth opportunities lie in this market. By selling subscriptions, you can give customers a unique value-add through rewards or points, the ability to use any car wash location in the network, or offering referral bonuses to customers who refer business. As the industry becomes more consolidated and known to private equity, those holding numerous turnkey car washes with recurring revenue streams will likely be rewarded with high exit multiples.

2. Tax benefits

I don't know of any other physical business that gives you more depreciation dollar for dollar. You can realize up to 70% of the total value of the car wash in depreciation loss in year one. This is possible because the entire construction is amenable to acceleration of depreciation through cost segregation. Comparatively, most multifamily assets give you 20% of the total value in year one. This can obviously give you massive tax savings and be a key component in your investment portfolio.

3. Strong cash flow

Car washes have a very favorable revenue-to-expense ratio. These assets drive a ton of cash flow and produce economies of scale by supporting their own manager and employees.

Because the expenses are relatively low comparatively, these assets drive tons of cash flow, and they can support an onsite manager and employees while still averaging an eye-popping 30% cash flow and over 50% EBITDA (earnings before interest, taxes, depreciation, and amortization). These are amazing returns. Add in a recurring revenue model from monthly subscriptions, and this is a great recipe for an amazing asset.

If you have a large portfolio of car washes that have been automated, the turnkey appeal attracts private equity groups that want a plug-and-play investment solution. The larger the portfolio, the larger the exit.

4. An evergreen asset

This investment is recession-proof and performs really well even in down economies.

Part of this is due to car washes becoming part of the very fabric of American life. People have a psychological attachment to their vehicle(s) as an extension of who they are, and a clean car makes them feel good. And having someone else clean your car for you isn't just about convenience—on some level it's a small and affordable luxury that makes people feel powerful and in control, even during times when everything around us feels anything but.

The numbers show us that people don't wash their cars at home anymore, for a variety of reasons. As society becomes a population of home renters instead of homeowners, many tenants don't have access to hoses and car wash equipment in their apartment buildings. And the Environmental Protection Agency (EPA) reports that most commercial car washes use 60% less water *for the entire process* than a homeowner uses just to *rinse* the car,[39] making washing your car at home a losing proposition—for the environment, and for you given the ever-increasing and already uber-expensive residential water bill.

THINGS TO CONSIDER WITH CAR WASHES

1. Time commitment

If you are building from the ground up, this investment requires location expertise and industry knowledge. This can be very time-intensive, which scares off a lot of potential operators because they could start another type of business much easier. Real estate investors, for example, can buy a self-storage or a multifamily home without the hassle of planning and zoning or supply chain derailments. Sometimes it takes eighteen to twenty-four months, or even three *years*, to get a car wash up and running: to find the land, to get it properly zoned, and to jump through all of the other hoops you need to jump through. Not a lot of folks are up for that level of time commitment and deferred return on investment.

2. Capital intensive

Car washes are not for the faint of financial heart. They are very capital intensive, so this scares off a lot of would-be operators as they could start another business much sooner and cheaper than a car wash. All in with land, entitlements, and construction, you could rack up $7-9 million in total costs. This is a very high barrier to entry for a lot of investors.

If you do have the capital, time, and expertise, you may run into lending issues. Banks are becoming more comfortable with this asset class, but most are only willing to offer 50% leverage.

3. Environmental ramifications

The EPA is continually enacting strict water usage guidelines, so it is important to align your investment dollars with operators who are using water reclamation systems. It's crucial that you install better technology for water usage to reduce consumption without compromising quality. You don't want cars to come out dirty, but you also don't want to use 400 gallons of water per wash. These systems can be very expensive to retrofit, so you need to include this cost in the business plan upfront.

4. Operating partners

Personally, I don't want to run the car wash(es) myself, so I need great partners.

There are plenty of operators out there, but you want the *right* operator. You want to be asking questions to make sure your operator is experienced. "What is your plan? What is your experience in this space? Will you have directed social media marketing? Are you getting radio advertising or billboards? What's your sales strategy?"

A great operator will know exactly how to operate and sell. The industry standard for water reclamation is 40%, but some operators are already reclaiming almost 90%! That's cutting-edge. It's not only environmentally sound, but makes for very good marketing as well.

The operator should also be marketing your technology. Car washes can knock off mirrors and cause some damage, so if you have non-invasive equipment, that should be advertised.

Ideally, you want a dedicated salesperson at every location to increase car wash subscriptions. Subscriptions are by far the best-case scenario for operator and customer. They are super convenient and offer the operator consistent income while offering the customer unlimited (if that's the plan they choose) car washes and the ease of just scanning a QR code instead of pulling out and running their credit card every time at a higher price. Convenience and value are everything, and your operator should be selling them.

The wrong employee can absolutely ruin an entire car wash site. The more employees you have, the more likely that one is not a great fit. With express tunnel car washes, you really only need one or two key employees and a great manager to make the business thrive.

5. Preventative maintenance

A good operator will be all about preventative maintenance—taking care of the equipment *before* it breaks.

Tunnels are chain-driven or belt-driven, and each has a rhythm and a system that requires maintenance. Belt-driven tunnels are better because you don't have damaged axles that can result when the equipment grabs the tires and pushes the car forward on a chain-driven tunnel. The car simply gets on the belt and rides. Belt-driven tunnels can also send a higher number of cars through the car wash per hour. Whichever system you choose to utilize, you need to know the industry standards of what is spent on repairs and preventive maintenance, and the maintenance strategy should be evident in the operator's business plan.

I wouldn't recommend that you, as a physician, try to run an express tunnel car wash. The smart play is to partner with someone who knows what they're doing. You don't need to be learning the mechanics of belt-driven versus chain-driven and how to fix it. But your partner certainly does.

6. Zoning restrictions

We've talked about this regarding several different asset classes, and the same is true here: you have to understand local zoning regulations and specific requirements or permits imposed to regulate car wash operations. You must ensure compliance with environmental regulations, water restrictions, and any other local ordinances.

While the car wash industry is booming, it's still in its infancy. There are still plenty of locations to build. But remember the old real estate axiom: location, location, location, and think long and hard about it before choosing your spot. Do you really want to build in California, Arizona, New Mexico—places in the desert with water restrictions already in place? Unless you are super-innovative with your technology, that might not be the best place to build a car wash, as you could find yourself fighting over water more than you are washing cars.

Always ensure you check (and double check) the restrictions and regulations before you get your heart set on a location. A capital-intensive investment such as this could make for a disastrous situation if you get it wrong.

WHAT A GOOD DEAL LOOKS LIKE WITH CAR WASHES

When deciding where to invest, I look at several different parameters. I start with the median income of a community. This gives me an idea of what the disposable income of a household might be. Knowing the purchasing power of the population—what they are able to afford—is super important when evaluating any possible location for investing. Higher median income levels generally indicate a greater ability to afford car washes. For me, that magic number is typically greater than $60,000.

Population density

Volume is crucial in the car wash business. If there are no cars, you have no car wash business. So considering car count is very important. The higher, the better—but at least 15,000 per day would be my starting point. The more eyeballs you have on your location, the more people are likely to stop. There are different ways to find car-count data. In a larger city, the highway department will have those numbers. Paid online services (such as the Car Wash Almanac) are also easily found through a Google search. City planning and zoning are also excellent resources. They do car counts all the time when deciding where to build apartment complexes and widen roads.

Areas with higher population density and significant traffic flow create a larger customer base. I only consider areas with a sufficient number of potential customers in a reasonable radius of the location.

Specific location

"Location, location, location." Are you tired of hearing me repeat that phrase yet? That saying isn't only applicable in terms of regional geography with car washes—it's especially important in terms of local proximity, too.

You want to be close to a major destination center like an anchor grocery store, shopping center, or any other business that people frequent often. People are much more inclined to stop where they shop rather than pull off the road on the way to somewhere else. The majority of Americans are in a rush, and if they are driving down the road and see a car wash with an express tunnel outside a grocery store where they're planning to stop anyway, they will likely take the time to get it done. But if that car wash is half a mile down the road, they will probably think, "*I need a car wash,*" as they keep on driving by…and then get their car washed where they stopped to get groceries.

Site size

You also want to make sure that the site is the right size. Generally, you will need anywhere from an acre to an acre and a half. You need space for a proper-sized tunnel and vacuums. A customer puts a premium on having enough room to clean their car out, utilize free vacuums, and wipe down their car after it goes through the wash. Having enough space to include these accessories is an absolute must to exceed customer expectations.

Competition

Industry experts advise that you want to be more than half a mile from another express car wash. I'm very conservative, so I look for locations at least a mile from the nearest tunnel car wash. If there is a self-serve or in-bay automatic wash closer than one mile, that won't stop me from moving forward, as express tunnels are much preferred. The other forms of car washes will likely just be good advertising for mine!

Education levels

There is a correlation between the education level of a population and the use of car washes. Correlation doesn't equal causation, but if you add up a lot of correlatives, you can hone your funnel to find the best location.

Perhaps the correlation stems from the possibility that households with higher education likely have better-paying jobs, leading to greater disposable income. It might be that a higher income job requires more time, meaning less time to wash their own cars themselves. Whatever the reason, education is a metric I like to use.

HOW TO INVEST IN CAR WASHES

There are three ways to get into this business.

1. Start your own

This option is super capital-intensive, and you definitely need operational experience. It isn't for the novice investor. It's a $7 million to $10 million investment to build a 130-foot express tunnel car wash, so you simply MUST know what you are doing. It's not like buying an apartment, where the property manager is responsible for 70%-80% of your success. With car washes, the key person is *you.* So unless you grew up in a family that owned car washes or you have significant experience in this space, it may be very risky for you to start your own.

2. Buy into a franchise

Not all franchises are created equal. Some have very high royalties—others don't. Some have first right of refusal on the sale—others don't. Some require you to sign long leases, so you could be on the hook even if the business goes bust. Some franchises don't care if you buy the land. (I personally would never let my business be subject to the whims of a landlord. Always buy the land!)

If you are buying a franchise, you need to understand the legalities surrounding your purchase. Can you source where you are going to buy your cleaning supplies and equipment, or are you required to buy them from the franchise? Franchisors, especially in the car wash space, make their money in large part by having you repeatedly buy their products. If you are bound to them, you want to ask what the annual inflationary cap is. If there is no cap, you are basically signing something that says, "I will pay you whatever you want for all of my supplies, forever." Don't do that. You will need to negotiate some autonomy or price caps. If you can't meet in the middle at some place where you feel comfortable, then you need to walk away. If this is the route of entry you are choosing, ensure you do your due diligence on both the company *and* the opportunity.

3. Join a team syndication

A syndication is a temporary alliance formed by professionals to handle a large transaction that would be impossible to execute individually. By forming a syndicate, members can pool their resources together and share in both the risks and the potential for attractive returns.[40]

The benefit of this option is that all of the bases should already be covered, and the chosen operator has the expertise needed to be successful. But due diligence is once again critical here—both on the operator side and on the deal itself.

Due diligence in this scenario with a syndication involves investigating the Private Placement Memorandum (PPM), which is a legal document provided to prospective investors interested in purchasing shares of an LLC. The purpose of the PPM is to describe the terms and conditions of the investment offering and is meant as a disclosure for investors so they are aware of the specifics of the deal.[41]

You will want to see the operating agreement and understand how things like depreciation will be handled. Is it going to be passed along to the investors and, if so, how? It should be pro rata, which means everything is equally divided based on your investment percentage.

What is the sponsor's or operator's experience with car washes? Is this their first or fiftieth offering? What is their track record of success (or lack thereof)? Want to know other questions to ask a potential syndicator or sponsor? You can go to cashflowmd.com/dd-checklist-resource/ and download a resource that covers questions I make sure to ask every sponsor I'm thinking of investing with.

CAR WASH CASE STUDY

The Right Type Matters

I have several peers who love the car wash space and have invested wisely in them over the years. Some invest with me, while others have found varying levels of success on their own. One of my colleagues bought a self-serve car wash—a few handwashing bays and one in-bay machine—several years ago.

The equipment—which wasn't new or innovative—had quite a bit of deferred maintenance and broke frequently. He spent an inordinate amount of time dealing with outdated quarter machines, antiquated vacuums, and freeze-ups because the bays were exposed to the elements. He had to deal with the daily headaches that made it not an investment but just another job...and a bad one at that. He was in misery. The location, the demographics, the car count—everything made total sense, but he bought the wrong type of car wash.

It's expensive to retrofit/rebuild car washes, to upgrade to an app, and to digitize processes and payments. He wasn't making enough money to hire someone or make these capital improvements, so he was stuck. He attempted a subscription model, but couldn't gain traction as customers were looking for better wash technology at attractive prices without having to get out of the car.

Thankfully, the location was awesome, so he was able to sell it to a well-capitalized group that tore down the self-serve and built an express tunnel car wash. They hired a manager who became responsible for the advertising, sales, subscriptions, and maintenance. The new car wash boomed!

The land wasn't the problem. The type of car wash was.

When the deal was done, he didn't end up losing money, but he did lose years off his life working in the wrong type of car wash.

SELF-STORAGE

With the cost of housing on the rise and smaller homes, condominiums, and townhouses becoming some of the only affordable options, storage space is at a premium.

In recent years, self-storage has grown to become an excellent industry to be in, as these units are in great demand. The term "self-storage" refers to the short-term or long-term rental of a space where tenants can store their belongings. These spaces can be a variety of sizes depending on client needs. Central to the storage agreement is the tenant's responsibility for moving their own items in and out of the facility, so don't think you have to start your own moving company along with the storage business! It may be a good combination though…I digress.

Interestingly, self-storage is largely a North American phenomenon. We've got land, means, opportunity, resources, and money in this country. In essence, we have a lot of "stuff." And when life happens, we need a place to put it.

There are four big drivers related to the demand for self-storage:

1. Death
2. Dislocation
3. Downsizing
4. Divorce

The four Ds above are more or less inevitable. Most of us will experience some of these events in our lives. Definitely one of them!

And the National Association of Real Estate Investment Trusts (NAREIT) suggested a new, fifth "D" emerged during the pandemic: "Decluttering." During and after COVID-19, tens of millions of Americans were displaced, some moving voluntarily while others lost their homes due to eviction or foreclosure—unable to pay their rent and mortgages—and needed self-storage to house their belongings. Even for those who remained in their homes, many were "spending more time at home and [were] creating more space for a home office, gym, or classroom"[42]—also utilizing self-storage as a place to store their supplanted possessions.

Self-storage isn't experiencing high demand just from end users—it's also a rapidly growing investment space, too, with billions of dollars flowing into the space. In 2021, Public Storage, widely recognized as the largest self-storage owner/operator in the world and among the largest publicly traded REITs by market capitalization at $52 billion, had revenue of $3.4 billion, a 17% increase over the previous year's revenue of $2.9 billion.[43]

Self-storage has become "the darling" of the investment world, and we now find ourselves in the middle of a market consolidation opportunity. In 2021, the *Self-Storage Almanac* (a great resource, by the way—it has tons of data) revealed that publicly traded companies own less than 25% of the storage market. The trend is rapidly consolidating, however.

In my own career as an investor, self-storage has provided some of my best passive return metrics, returning almost 20%—outperforming other sectors like office and retail.

WHAT I LOVE ABOUT SELF-STORAGE

1. Steady income

Self-storage facilities are generally predictable sources of income. When set up correctly, tenants will be on an auto-pay rent system, giving you automated monthly cash flow.

This investment also seems to be less affected by economic headwinds than other real estate asset classes. Even during the latest recession when valuations were down, self-storage continued to cash flow. During COVID-19, self-storage outperformed all other asset classes except data centers.

Because of the four (now five) Ds, storage needs are ongoing, which means occupancy rates are fairly consistent and cash flow is steady.

2. Flexibility

Many self-storage facilities adjust rents according to their competition and market demand. This flexibility also extends to the type of lease. There's generally no stigma attached to a month-to-month lease versus a six-month lease versus a yearly lease. The longer leases may warrant a slight discount in rate in some markets, but in high-demand metropolitan areas, it's unlikely you will need to give any discount and can continue to raise rents regularly.

3. Low-maintenance management

This is a "plug-and-play" management system compared to other real estate investments. Self-storage facilities generally require less active management, as you can systemize and securitize the facility to operate without any onsite employees.

According to the *Almanac*, a huge percentage of potential users don't want to talk to or even see a person while at their storage unit. They want to find what they need on an app. They want to—and can—get in and out of the facility themselves, on their own time, when they want to.

Day-to-day tasks that involve routine maintenance, marketing efforts, and tenant management can be done via a management company. Most often, this is a passively active investment.

4. Low advertising and turnover costs

Self-storage has a low turnover rate when compared to residential and commercial rentals. Most tenants use the facilities for extended periods, reducing the cost and effort associated with finding new tenants. If your facility is 90% occupied, you don't necessarily need to advertise and pay leasing agents commissions or take prospective tenants on a tour of the facility as you would with multifamily, for example.

Additionally, there is no delay in renting a space once a tenant has left. It's literally a broom and dustpan, and then you are ready to re-rent again.

5. Wide client base

Self-storage serves a wide variety of customers. We all know someone who has been touched by one of the four Ds. This includes individuals, families, businesses, students, military personnel—everyone is a potential tenant. A wide client base helps mitigate the investment risk by reducing dependence on a single demographic. In fact, according to NAREIT, 10% of the American population currently uses self-storage.[44]

6. Ability to drive appreciation

As you improve the self-storage facility, you are setting yourself up for a really nice exit down the road. Whether it's by adding units, an electronic funds transfer service such as Automatic Clearing House (ACH), wider ingress and egress roads, or subscriptions and apps, you are actively driving appreciation that will pay off big time in the long run.

7. Low operating expenses

When people buy apartment complexes, they often find themselves operating within pretty thin margins. If you add a high-inflationary, high-interest rate, high-unemployment environment, operators suddenly find themselves overleveraged. That's how people lose their apartment buildings.

Self-storage facilities are not that way because they have very low operating costs. They don't require utilities for tenants other than electricity and perhaps a common restroom. Electricity in America is pretty stable, so that's not an issue (and you could definitely explore solar power as an alternative—which you'd get a massive tax credit for). You won't be getting a call to fix the plumbing, or that someone's heat went out, or that the waterline has broken. It's a dream come true in terms of simplicity.

8. Consolidation opportunities

This industry is still fragmented, with only about a quarter of facilities owned by big institutions. A good percentage of self-storage is still owned by mom-and-pop operators (those with fewer than five facilities). This fragmentation gives investors like us an excellent opportunity to purchase at reasonable prices.

With a fair purchase price, you then have room to implement value-add strategies.

9. Tax benefits

Investing in self-storage provides some really strong tax advantages. Using depreciation deductions from cost segregation analysis, tax-free refinances to harvest equity, and helping to qualify as a full-time real estate professional are all tax perks you can realize if you own self-storage.

And—when you're ready to sell…it's also eligible for tax deferral strategies like a 1031 exchange.

THINGS TO CONSIDER WITH SELF-STORAGE

1. Tenant quality

Understand the tenant base before you buy. If a significant portion of the tenants are consistently late on payments or there is a high turnover rate, you may be buying someone else's problem. I suggest you review the lease agreements on existing tenants—some may contain unfavorable terms or clauses that could impact your ability to raise rents as well.

2. Associated costs

A lot of people get into self-storage and just don't know what they don't know. You need to ensure you understand all the associated costs with purchasing and operating this type of investment. There will be insurance, maintenance, utility costs, and property taxes, to name a few. If you are developing or rebranding, you must also incorporate a pretty healthy marketing budget.

I highly suggest getting audited financials from the seller. If that is not possible, ask for bank records to verify revenue and expenses.

And be sure to do a structural inspection before you buy. Pay an expert to conduct this so you have an accurate picture of deferred maintenance or neglect, which may lead to expensive repairs down the line. If the inspection reveals that repairs are indeed needed, you can negotiate that cost into the deal.

The bottom line: you need to understand what you are getting into before you sign on the dotted line.

3. Environmental issues

It's important to be cautious and to understand the environmental liabilities associated with a property.

If the land has had a history of environmental contamination, for example, you could inherit the cleanup costs.

Be sure to do a Phase One environmental study before you buy. It is inexpensive, massively informative, and an important part of the due diligence process.

4. Zoning restrictions and pending legal action

Make sure the facility complies with all local, state, and federal regulations, as well as zoning and building codes. There may be accessibility requirements, for instance. Failure to comply can lead to fines and other issues.

You need to be aware of any legal disputes involving the property as well. Purchase the property, but not the entity. Instead of buying the

LLC, I suggest creating your own entity to protect you from inheriting any of the seller's pending lawsuits.

5. Inherited expenses

Ensure you know utility expenses and vendor contracts that may carry over with the sale. You need to know the utility costs of the electricity, water, gas, and sewer. Water and sewer won't likely be huge expenses, but if the units are climate-controlled, you'll want to look closely at the HVAC integrity and understand how much those bills are. If they have just newly added climate control, get an estimate from the utility company of expected usage, and budget accordingly.

If there are outdated systems, the upgrade could eat into your profits. Review vendor contracts with security, landscaping, and maintenance. I strongly recommend you understand the terms and conditions. Sometimes the contracts survive a sale, and you may be stuck with a vendor you don't want or need.

6. Rodents

If your facility does not have climate control with airtight seals, you will likely have to battle a rodent problem. Whether it's a pest control company or you, someone needs to have eyes on the facility as often as possible, conducting routine inspections of the entire facility, including the storage units themselves.

7. Ways to add value

You can add the most value to your self-storage by keeping the facility clean, safe, and well-lit. You can also consider small automated value-adds such as vending machines with candy, chips, water, and soda—many tenants are there for long periods of time loading and unloading, so these can be a welcome addition to the facility. You can even have a small onsite shop that sells boxes, tape, packing paper, easy-to-assemble shelving, etc. if you have an employee on site.

Depending on your geographic location, you could also consider boat and RV storage as a value-add. In Florida, for example, boat and RV storage go hand in hand and are a massive way to create value, whereas in a colder climate or landlocked region, you may want to offer snowmobile/ATV storage as well.

Another consideration with adding value is the space you have to work with. RV storage, for example, needs much greater square footage than normal storage units. They take up a lot more space, so you'll have fewer tenants. You need to make sure the returns you'll realize outpace those of a normal storage facility.

WHAT A GOOD DEAL LOOKS LIKE IN SELF-STORAGE

Undeniably, one of the most crucial factors that is going to determine your long-term success is location. This will make or break your investment. The location of your facility directly impacts your occupancy rate and, thus, your ability to drive revenue.

I look for areas that are in high demand with fast-selling homes. This is a good indicator of how the population is trending. Investigate the average household income and who the main employers are in the area. Knowing your community will help you make decisions, such as whether or not to install air conditioning, or whether you require onsite personnel, for example.

I love an area with a wide variety of potential customers where the mix is residential, student, military, and commercial because all four of these customer bases will utilize storage in different ways at different times. You might also consider a location with a large population of retirees looking to downsize their homes. If you have a good population mix, you will likely retain a strong occupancy rate.

You also want to know the supply/demand dynamics of the area. Does the market already have an overabundance of storage facilities? You want to consider the square footage per capita, which refers to the number of square feet per person of storage space in the area. The lower the number, the higher the demand.

When I'm buying self-storage, I am going to choose a location that's easily accessible from main roads. I want it to have high visibility—close to the freeway or other major thoroughfares. A facility that's easily identifiable with good signage is a huge plus. How many times have you been driving down the interstate and you see the big self-storage sign? There's a reason for that. Out of sight, out of mind—in sight, top of mind!

Another factor I consider is the crime rate. A lot of people visit their self-storage unit after hours, so you want them to feel safe. I install good lighting and implement quality security systems and gated entryways.

Last, I want a good mix of unit sizes. The trend over the past few years has been that larger units are in more demand than smaller units. When people live in apartments, they don't have enough storage space. So, more and more facilities are being built in suburbia, and people are storing their stuff in larger amounts than before.

HOW TO INVEST IN SELF-STORAGE

Self-storage has many ways to invest. This is an asset where being the sole owner can make sense. You would, of course, be responsible for property management, operations, and financials, but direct ownership allows you to maintain full control over the investment. It does, however, also require you to have an active involvement. (You can always hire a property manager or management company to help with your operating systems.)

Alternatively, you can form a partnership with a good operator or take on limited partners (LPs) to raise equity to purchase self-storage. You would still have some level of responsibility, but you would benefit from the expertise—and potentially the time contribution—of your partner(s). Your level of involvement would vary depending on the type of partnership you form: it can be a true joint venture, or you could be a capital partner and bring in a key operations partner. If you had LPs, you'd have an additional layer of responsibility of ensuring a return for your investors.

A third option is to join a syndication, where you contribute equity to a deal and acquire self-storage facilities through a sponsor. Ideally, your syndicators would be experienced in self-storage, property management, and operations so they can (and will) handle the day-to-day on your behalf. This allows you to make a passive investment and rely on the expertise of the professionals.

SELF-STORAGE CASE STUDY

The Importance of Location and Due Diligence (I know, I know. AGAIN.)

I get it. You're sick of hearing the number one rule of real estate: location, location, location. And you're equally sick of hearing me talk about the importance of due diligence.

But if you buy a bad location, you simply can't change it, and it's game over before you've even begun. And if you didn't do proper due diligence, you're going to wind up inheriting someone else's problems after the deal is done. Either way, you're hosed.

I was at a reunion catching up with some friends I had not seen in several years. One of them asked me what I'd been up to, and we started talking about real estate and investing. Another person in our circle of conversation interjected by telling me how dangerous real estate investing was and how it almost ruined his life. Intrigued, I asked him to share why he had such a strong opinion on the subject. He proceeded to tell me about a storage facility he bought a few years ago in a very frothy self-storage market.

He found an active deal in rural Alabama that had quite a few interested buyers, so he felt he had to be very aggressive with his offer. This was a forty-unit facility that was 90% occupied, and he wanted to add another sixty units. He went through most of his due diligence, but decided not to do a Phase I environmental study because he had a sizable, non-refundable escrow deposit (we'd say the escrow money had gone "hard," meaning it was non-refundable) and was in danger of losing the deal as his closing deadline was compressed because the seller wanted a quick close. (In my opinion, the more rural the purchase, the higher the need for a Phase One—you never know what they bury in the ground when there are no zoning restrictions: fuel tanks, pesticides, oil change residue, etc.).

After the purchase, when he went to complete his value add, the bank wouldn't lend any additional funds for development without a Phase I study. The study uncovered quite a bit of environmental contamination: petroleum hydrocarbons from underground fuel tanks. Before the land had become a storage facility, it was a farm. And there were indeed tanks buried underground—that leaked!

His lack of due diligence was going to cost him a ton of money in remediation costs. and to compound the issue, he was already over-leveraged on the purchase.

He didn't have any partners, and capital markets were tightening up. Even when he did find willing lenders, the rates were so high that it wouldn't cash flow even if he did borrow the money. To make matters worse, many of his tenants moved out when they caught wind of the environmental concerns, and he did not communicate effectively to get ahead of the issue. His occupancy dropped dramatically.

He couldn't refinance to absorb the extra cost because he owned the facility for less than a year, and his NOI had dropped significantly since purchasing it.

As you can imagine, this case study does not have a happy ending. He ended up losing his facility to bank foreclosure. His credit was ruined, and it almost bankrupted him.

A couple of important lessons we can take from this experience:

- Don't rush your closing timeline or put up hard money before due diligence is completed—no matter how great the deal looks. There will always be other deals.
- Always complete your due diligence. If not, it usually costs you in the end.

OPPORTUNITY ZONES (OZS)

According to the IRS, *opportunity zones* are an economic development tool that allows people to invest in distressed areas in the United States. Their purpose is to spur economic growth and job creation in low-income communities while providing tax benefits to investors.[45]

These "opportunity zones" (OZs) can be used for a variety of development or redevelopment projects to improve the community. The objective is to create momentum in the economy by incentivizing employers to move into the area and for developers to create housing that wouldn't otherwise exist.

Many opportunity zones are in gentrifying areas in major metropolitan cities, so the area is primed for new or renovated apartment buildings (I personally prefer to buy land over renovating multifamily complexes in opportunity zones—read on to learn why!).

WHAT I LOVE ABOUT OPPORTUNITY ZONES

1. Tax benefits

Literally trillions of dollars of unrealized capital gains are sitting on the sidelines, and one way to deploy those funds is to incentivize investors. Around 2017, the government realized investors were not putting money into lower-income neighborhoods, so they began to offer significant tax breaks and deferrals for investments into these areas. Sometimes, investors even had the opportunity to walk away tax-free as long as they held onto their investments for ten years.

At the time of the writing of this book, this investment currently offers a capital gain tax deferral of seven years. This means you have seven years to defer capital gains on the sale of your business, your stocks, or whatever you had capital gains on so you can put that money to work for you instead of giving it to the government.

Opportunity zones are one of the strongest tax tools ever given to the American public. Think about the potential power of it: if you were to sell a nine-figure business before the advent of OZs, you would be stuck paying millions in taxes, as there was no opportunity to roll those business gains into anything else in a tax-efficient way. NOW, you can sell a nine-figure business, and instead of paying exorbitant capital gains and other taxes, you can defer by investing in designated opportunity zone projects. The taxes are deferred for seven years. By then, the asset you purchased should have produced more than enough cash flow to pay those taxes after seven years. Even more mind-blowing, if you hold the OZ asset for a full ten years, you can sell it and keep all the profits absolutely tax FREE! Is your mind blown? It should be because this is incredible!

THINGS TO CONSIDER WITH OPPORTUNITY ZONES

1. Substantial improvement hurdles

Opportunity zone properties have rules and regulations associated with them. One such rule is the "substantial improvement" hurdle. In layman's terms, the statute specifies that substantial improvement to the property must be done by investing *at least as much or more money* into the improvement as the amount of the basis over a certain amount of time (generally 30 months). The more basis in the property, the more capital you'll need to inject to meet this hurdle. This is a big reason why I choose to invest in land OZ opportunities rather than existing structures that need considerable capital expenditures.

If you buy a multifamily complex in a really bad part of town (where a lot of designated OZs are located), you not only are dealing with likely poor demographics, crime scores, school systems, etc., but you also still need to cough up several million dollars in improvements because the apartment that sits on that land makes up the majority of the basis, and you need to meet the substantial improvement hurdle. If there is vacant land, any improvement (parking lot, access road, small cabin, pole barn, build a lake, etc.) meets the substantial improvement hurdle at a MUCH lower out-of-pocket cost. You also aren't inheriting an apartment complex that likely has tons of deferred maintenance, low occupancy, and is in a less-than-desirable location. Land is definitely the easier path when looking into OZ investments.

2. Matching the capital gain

Opportunity zone investments do not require you to pay for the replacement asset in cash, but the new purchase needs to be of equal or greater value to protect all the earnings from capital gains tax. For example, if you have a $500,000 gain, to protect the gain from immediate taxation, you need to make a $500,000 purchase.

If you took that $500,000 gain and bought a $300,000 farm, this investment would leave $200,000 unprotected. It is similar to a 1031 exchange in that you need to have something of equal or greater value to match the gain. However, you can get a loan on the property you are purchasing. You're not required to buy it with cash. This can allow you sort of a double arbitrage as you can put enough cash into the purchase to secure a loan for the asset you are buying and then take the rest of the cash and go buy more assets that cash flow!

3. Lack of liquidity

A ten-year commitment may make it challenging to access your funds before the specified holding periods expire. It's true, you lose a lot of the tax benefit if you sell before the allotted ten-year hold time, so you don't want to sell too soon. You can harvest equity, though, by developing the OZ purchase into a cash-flowing asset and doing a strategic equity harvesting event like a refinance. Just because you need to hold the property for ten years to realize maximum tax advantages doesn't mean you can't use your other knowledge and expertise to figure out a way to get cash flow in the meantime.

4. Tax law changes

The tax laws and regulations related to opportunity zones could change in the future, and both political and legislative changes may impact the tax incentives associated with these investments.

There is currently serious discussion about extending this program to make it a permanent potential tax-free investment because many people are still unaware of the benefits of opportunity zone investing. I would advise finding a CPA and an attorney who are intimately acquainted with opportunity zone laws and who have their ears to the ground, listening for changing legislation to make you aware of as things unfold.

5. Limited investment choices

Opportunity zones are specified areas designated by the government, and let's just say their acquisition criteria drastically differs from that of most real estate investors. A lot of these properties are in distressed economic locations with below-average income, job opportunities, and schools, and they may be higher in crime and vacancies than most investors like. To be certain, there are several OZs that you should probably stay away from—no matter what the incentives are. The value is finding an OZ opportunity in an area that does check the boxes for you as an investor and then jumping on it quickly.

WHAT A GOOD DEAL LOOKS LIKE IN OPPORTUNITY ZONES

Finding a good deal often begins when the investment hurdles are low. OZs being new and wildly misunderstood can be an advantage once you've armed yourself with the knowledge of how powerful these investments can be. While most are looking outside of OZs, this lowers the hurdle for you to invest in the area of your choice.

Demystifying this new investment option is the best way to find a good deal. The more you understand about the benefits and requirements, the more likely you are to have success investing in OZs.

The best deals I've found are:

- Land deals where the local municipality doesn't participate in planning and zoning
- When the property is located in the path of development
- When the highest and best use of the property is single-family, multifamily, or industrial development
- The area is within forty-five minutes of a major MSA and

- When it is close to a major interstate
- These variables give you endless possibilities of making your purchase cash flow.

I will say that most people who have not found success with opportunity zone investments have faltered because—you guessed it—they didn't do proper due diligence. Or they didn't fill out the required forms to have their fund deemed legal, or they didn't file their taxes correctly with the IRS. With this category of investment vehicle, complete compliance is *crucial.*

HOW TO INVEST IN OPPORTUNITY ZONES

To purchase in an opportunity zone, the investment needs to be made through a Qualified Opportunity Fund (QOF). As defined by the IRS, a QOF is an investment vehicle that is organized as a corporation or partnership for the purpose of investing in Qualified Opportunity Zone property. For the purpose of this type of investment, you can only contribute money that has been generated through prior investments (i.e., capital gains). The other caveat is that the fund must put 90% of its money, time, and effort into the opportunity zone area.[46]

It's relatively simple to become eligible for a qualified opportunity zone fund. It's a process of self-designation and self-certification. You begin by filling out IRS form 8996 and then hire an attorney to complete the paperwork behind the fund. You attach this information to your federal tax return for that year, and in a general sense, that's pretty much it. Obviously, everyone's circumstances are different, and because this is a more advanced strategy that is often misunderstood, please be sure to consult with both your tax and legal team before filing/submitting.

Before choosing to invest, I also caution you to ask the right questions:

Does this property meet my acquisition criteria?

What improvement hurdles do we need to meet? (This is critical.)

How long do we have to make those improvements?

What is the capital we'll need to complete improvements?

What are your metrics and pro forma for projecting future rents?

The bottom line is that you need to become an investigator and really think about the requirements of what you are buying. You need to ask questions and dig deep to ensure the numbers make sense before purchasing.

OPPORTUNITY ZONES CASE STUDY

A Big Opportunity in Opportunity Zones

I had a sale of a business and realized a nice capital gain.

I obviously would have rather kept the money than give it to Uncle Sam, so I found a piece of land that met my acquisition criteria in an opportunity zone at an auction. I was able to secure it at a very good price because the property being in an OZ spooked most other investors.

The substantial improvement hurdle for this particular property was very low as it was simply vacant land. I proceeded to build a cabin with a simple access road, thereby meeting the "substantial improvement" hurdle in the process. I then leased the land for hunting rights and recreational rights, which covered the small mortgage on the property, and I listed the cabin on Airbnb to generate excess cash flow.

I took that cash flow and invested it in other assets that generated more cash flow.

After seven years, I've made more than enough to pay my capital gains from the original sale and have several new assets to show for it. My goal is to hold the investment for ten years, then sell it completely—walking away with millions in tax-free profit.

What a win!

DEBT LENDING AND PRIVATE EQUITY INVESTMENTS

Private Debt Lending - Lending done outside of the traditional channels of bank lending and the public debt markets.[47]

Private Equity Investing - A form of investment that takes place outside of the public stock market through which investors gain an ownership stake in private companies.[48]

Before we get into the details of debt lending and private equity investing, I think it's important to revisit the meaning of "non-correlated assets." The simple definition is that these investments don't move in the same direction as the stock market. Some people go as far as to say these assets move opposite to the market, but I don't think that's entirely true. The assets don't necessarily move when the stock market moves—it's not a linear relationship—it is simply non-correlated. (It's important to note, though, that nothing is *completely* non-correlated—not even debt and equity investments. They *do* react to the stock market. Everybody and everything does. However, they do have greater *potential* to be non-correlated.)

Investing in a debt fund exposes you to more non-correlated markets. It's a type of investment where a fund will loan money to an entity for a defined period of time. This type of investment tends to be less volatile than stocks and can provide a nice steady stream of income. I use it essentially as a high-interest checking account because of the liquidity. If I have over six figures I want to park somewhere, I'll put it in a debt fund. I'll keep it there for at least ninety days so I can take advantage of the higher interest rate. Additionally, transacting too often will accrue costs in transaction fees and potentially sour the fund manager from wanting to work with you because you are constantly moving money.

Equity investing is attractive because it offers a higher return than traditional investments, which can be beneficial to physicians who want to "set it and forget it."

However, I don't want people to think these types of investments are without risk. Debt, after all, *is* still debt. Equity investing involves placing funds with companies that are in a growth phase that may not necessarily pan out. When done correctly and with the right operators, diversifying with non-correlated assets can help mitigate your overall risk, increase the possibility for stable returns, and help weather a few shaky investments.

WHAT I LOVE ABOUT DEBT AND EQUITY INVESTMENTS

1. Diversification - One of the main benefits of debt and equity investments is that your eggs aren't all in one basket. As a physician, you may have a significant portion of your net worth tied up in either your practice, your 401(k), or something else. I'm also guessing that you likely have stock market-based investments. Having assets in your portfolio that don't generally move in the same direction as the market is a great way to reduce your overall risk.

2. Stability - Debt and equity investments typically provide a good source of stable returns. For instance, if I'm investing in a debt instrument, it tends to be less volatile than stock market investments because—generally speaking—people always try to make at least some effort to pay their debts. If you're investing in a solid fund, they will have completed thorough underwriting and due diligence on the group receiving the debt, which helps to mitigate the risk.

3. Inflation resistant - This type of investment is a good hedge against inflation (meaning it's intended to protect the investor against—hedge—a decrease in the purchasing power of money—inflation49). Most of the debt and equity instruments I am involved in have tended to be a strong hedge because the value increases with the cost of living. I invested in a debt fund that lends to real estate operators, for example, which performs very well because rent prices rise during periods of inflation as the cost of living increases. Debt becomes more expensive, and thus our returns are commensurate.

4. Quick exits - This is true mainly for debt investing. It's possible to get in and out of this type of investment with sixty days' notice or less. In fact, the two groups I am involved in can usually return my money within forty-eight hours. Seen as a kind of high-interest checking account, I gain 10% on my money. There may be fund minimums and transaction fees involved with moving money, but the return these investments give me is well worth the fees involved.

5. Higher returns - When investing with the right group, there is potential for higher returns than through the stock market or more traditional investments. Debt funds can give you nice, consistent cash flow. Equity funds—though often less consistent with cash flow—can potentially offer equity multiple returns much greater than traditional stock market investing.

6. Tax benefits - It's not common knowledge, but equity funds can offer really significant tax benefits. The Qualified Small Business Stock (QSBS) is set forth in section 1202 of the U.S. Internal Revenue Code. It states that any investment in a business worth less than $50 million held for a certain period can take advantage of a tax exemption on capital gains at the point of sale. The QSBS allows investors to deduct up to $10 million in taxes or ten times the adjusted cost basis, whichever is greater.50 It's almost like an opportunity zone for business investing.

THINGS TO CONSIDER WITH DEBT AND EQUITY INVESTMENTS

1. Be first

When I look at a debt fund, I want to ensure the lenders are in first position in the debt stack. This means they receive a preferred position and are first in line to be paid or take title to collateral assets if something goes wrong. You also need to make sure you are first in line to be paid if there is any refinance or liquidation event.

2. Know your timeline

Personally, I don't want to be in a debt fund that locks up my money for several years or an equity fund with a ten-year or longer investment horizon. I want to have as specific a timeline as possible that aligns with my investment goals. If it's a fund that has a long lock-up horizon, it's not a deal breaker—but it does need to align with my near-term and long-term investment goals.

3. Legalities

You need to understand what powers the operating agreement gives you as the investor. Deals go south. People change. People get greedy. People are people. Regardless of what the founder has told you, the most important focus must be on the operating agreement and the private placement memorandum—a document that outlines the terms of securities to be offered in a private placement. You want to be protected. At a minimum, you want to ask about the founder's compensation, the vesting schedule, fees, and how everyone gets paid. Ask who is making the decisions, and who the other investors are. Lastly—can the investors take over if the sponsor of the deal is deemed fraudulent or incompetent?

4. Risk

With debt investments, there is always a risk that the borrowing party may default on their interest payments or principal repayment. This can lead to a loss of the invested capital. However, this is mitigated by partnering with known private equity lenders who complete incredible due diligence, know the space they are lending in intimately, and obtain excellent collateral on their loans.

The value of an equity investment can fluctuate with changes in the economy, company performance, or for one of many other reasons. If the market value of the company invested in decreases, so does the value of your equity investment. Once again—partnering with known fund managers in this space with strong track records can mitigate a lot of these risks (but not completely eliminate them).

As a general rule, I usually consider equity investments somewhat riskier than debt investments. With debt investments, you generally have hard collateral, guarantors, and a loan based on a percentage of the value (LTV). Even if you have to take the asset back, you know it's worth more than the loan amount. With equity investing, the value of the company is dependent on performance, and—just like stocks—that number can go to zero. Investors may lose their entire investment if the company fails, no matter what guarantees are in place.

5. Lack of voting rights

Buyer beware: when you invest in these vehicles, you generally will be a passive member, meaning you will have little to no say in the day-to-day operations.

Debt investors are not involved in the management or decision-making of the issuer. The good news is, if you don't like the direction of the investment, you can always pull your money out. Equity investors often have even less involvement or voting rights in the company. This is why it's super important to understand the rights that are given to you in the operating agreement (OA) and private placement memorandum (PPM) in the event the fund manager is not properly administering the fund. Equity investments are usually completely passive with very little, if any, investor involvement. If you are a control freak, this may not be the right area for you.

6. Dilution

If you are in an equity investment, there is always the possibility of being diluted. Dilution occurs when a company issues new shares that result in a decrease in equity ownership for existing shareholders. It may occur for a variety of reasons, but the most common is when the company needs to issue additional shares to raise capital. This can dilute the ownership stake of existing shareholders—including yours.

WHAT A GOOD DEAL LOOKS LIKE IN DEBT AND EQUITY INVESTMENTS

Debt and Equity investments require a certain level of sophistication. It's important to have a grasp of the right questions to ask, parameters to look for, and the due diligence needing to be performed. It's wise to have specific criteria when looking to invest in this asset class and stick to them.

Equity

One thing I had to learn the hard way was not to be an angel investor (investors who provide initial seed money for startup businesses, usually in exchange for ownership equity in the company[51]). The problem is not usually the idea—it's most often the operators. I invested with a friend of mine who was extremely successful in his career in Silicon Valley for years. He knew his industry backwards and forwards, and it seemed like everything he touched turned to gold. The problem was, this new company he was starting was outside his zone of genius. He didn't know what he didn't know. His ideas and thesis were solid, but he didn't have the team to execute. And now here I am, heavily invested in this venture and still waiting on the *potential* return.

What I wish I knew then was that 90% of all startups fail.[52] And even with the most *experienced* operators and a great idea, the statistics are still abysmal, with over half of startups failing. Even "*super angels*"—people who are serial investors—only see successful exits 25% of the time.[53] They are playing a numbers game, and when they get a "unicorn" exit, the risk is worth it. You'd better have the financial wherewithal to be puckering up and kissing a lot of frogs if you want to be an angel investor!

You also need to consider geography in these investments. If you're starting a tech company in Topeka, Kansas, for example, as an investor, I would want to know why. It's really difficult to raise enough capital these days as it is, and it's nearly impossible outside of Silicon Valley. A large reason companies fail is because they run out of investor capital. I look for the company to be located in an area that makes sense related to its value proposition.

I also look for market fit. Does it solve a problem? Do they have a strong value proposition? Are they well-positioned in the market? If the product doesn't fit the market and solve a problem...well...that's a problem! When a product or service is not a market fit, the market simply responds with a resounding "No thanks," and those invested are left trying to solve an even bigger problem: how to recoup their losses.

Having experience and a strong track record is a must. I want to invest with someone who has done it before: they're experienced in the space, and they are experts at scrutinizing deals, are well-capitalized, and had successful exits. I also want the fund managers to have decision-making capabilities with their investments, have a board seat, or the ability to install the CEO if need be. If the fund is investing capital, it needs to have decision-making clout as well.

I also want to make sure who I'm investing with has a working knowledge of regulatory challenges and has a solid understanding of the costs and expenses. I try to find partners who have already passed the seed round of angel, friends, and family investors. Ideally, they have proven the concept and are looking to grow their idea(s) exponentially by four or five times. That's where the large equity growth is.

If you can invest in a fund that has expert advisory capacity, financial capacity, and back-end systems capacity, you can see a very good return in a short amount of time. A colleague of mine once said, "Never invest in an idea. Always invest in the team." When someone comes to me with an idea, my first question is always, "Who do you have on board?"

Funds invest in companies and businesses. But, as we discussed earlier, it's the people who make or break your success. It's important that the fund manager understands the founders of the companies they are investing in.

Characteristics of founders I find important are:

- They can network.
- They can build rapport.
- They can convince others to invest with them.
- They know what the expectations are.
- They have passion and knowledge for what they are doing.
- They know the problem they are trying to solve.
- They have strong teams.
- They have a solid track record.
- They are likable.

In medical school, we were always told we didn't know medicine well enough unless we could explain it to a seventh grader. If you're in cardiology, you should know the ins and outs of open heart surgery so intimately that you could explain it to any audience whatsoever. Your founder should also have this skill. It's likely you'll never meet the founder of the company you're investing in, but your fund manager should be able to flesh out the founder's capabilities before even one dollar heads their way.

It's people who build businesses and companies. People navigate legal hurdles. People solve problems. If I don't know, like, and trust the people involved, then the investment is a non-starter for me.

Debt

Debt deals are numerous, and several funds and operators pool funds with the goal of lending for a profit. A few important parameters make debt investing profitable and a good deal.

First and foremost is the operator you choose to invest with. The longer they've been in the space they are lending in, the better. Have they been in business through several market cycles? Is their team capable and seasoned and historically proven in operating the business? I personally like private equity lenders in the real estate space because I understand that asset class very well. It's customary to be in a first position with collateral on hard assets as well as have a personal guarantee from one or all of the recipients receiving the loan proceeds. Good operators will understand the value of this and position their loans very favorably for any market condition.

Second, good deals provide consistent returns over any type of market cycle. If the fund manager has done proper due diligence, economic winds can blow as they may and you still receive your interest payment consistently and on time. If a debt lender has a history of suspending payments to investors for any reason, that's a huge red flag, because they should have active safeguards against loan recipients missing payments or default. I generally look for an 8-12% annual return on debt investments. However, there are mixed investments where equity kickers (where the lender negotiates an equity position in the borrower's company as well[54]) or warrant coverage (where warrants give the holder the right, but not the obligation, to buy or sell a specific quantity of common stock at a predetermined price before the expiration date[55]) are attached to the debt deal to push those returns much higher.

Good deals will allow me reasonable liquidity options for my capital invested. While I understand the fund makes its income on funds I invest in being loaned to end users, I still want to protect myself. Life happens. If I need to pull some—or all—of my capital out, I want to know that's a possibility and that I can be in possession of my funds in sixty to ninety days. That's reasonable, and when you enter into a deal of this type, I would make sure you get it in writing.

HOW TO INVEST IN DEBT AND EQUITY INVESTMENTS

As you read above, trying to go it alone for me in the angel investing space didn't work out so well. Investing in debt and equity is definitely a team sport. These are highly nuanced asset classes, so I would advise not trying to do it solo. There are private equity funds and debt funds available to private investors, but very few have access to them. A lot of these funds cater to family offices, large institutional investors, and those who can write seven-figure checks. At CashFlowMD, we use the power of our collective to get an opportunity to invest in these vehicles with our fund, so people in my ecosystem have access to these sought-after investment opportunities.

Whether it's debt, equity, or any other investment, you must have the tools to make sound decisions. Even if you partner with a team, you'll still want to make sure you have your own specific criteria and due diligence practices in place so you don't make the same mistakes I did in the past. If you'd like to learn more about my acquisition criteria, due diligence practices in this and other asset classes, and who I invest with, sign up for my "Cash Flow Prescription" course that will offer a deep dive into this and many other areas.

Just like with medicine, you'll have those you trust around you, but you still need to be educated on the matter at hand in your own right, as well. Don't make a decision just because everyone else is on board. It's easy to get caught up in psychological FOMO (fear of missing out) or groupthink because you don't want to lose out on a "hot" opportunity everyone else is talking about. Stick to your due diligence and make sure you know what is the right investment for you.

DEBT AND EQUITY INVESTMENT CASE STUDY

Groupthink Gone Wrong

Years ago, I was involved in an opportunity that was brought to my attention by an investor group I was a part of. This deal was brought to us by the facilitator of the group, and it already had his backing and that of several very high-level investors I knew and respected. It seemed everyone who was anyone in this investor circle was either already in or sending funds imminently to invest.

I listened to the sponsor of the deal's presentation and heard him answer a few questions from investors on the call. Several of the "what a good deal looks like" criteria above were simply absent in this deal. Instead of being consistent with my normal due diligence practices, I fell into the FOMO trap and groupthink mentality, just like most others on the call. I invested…or should I say…I speculated.

Looking back, I can see there were glaring holes in this deal. Overall, there was a lack of leadership, transparency, strategy, and overall competence. If I would have looked at this deal outside the lens of the group I was in, I simply would have passed on the deal. I got caught up in the groupthink and FOMO, slacked on my due diligence, and lost all my capital in that deal. Warren Buffett would not have been pleased with me.

BUSINESSES

I love business investments. It could be a whole book!

If you have less time than money, business provides a great option for you to become an absentee owner. There are a number of different ways to invest in a business: from the ground up, franchising, or mergers and acquisitions, or by investing in a well-established business, which is simply looking for more equity.

I prefer to buy existing businesses that have great bones but need a little nudge to get over the finish line. They may need improved systems, better marketing, or more advertising, but they already have a solid team. Sometimes all that is needed is one general manager who can 10x the business. That person doesn't need to be me—I just have to find them. Once you implement your systems and improvements, or hire someone who can, you can enjoy the cash flow and benefits of being a business owner.

WHAT I LOVE ABOUT BUSINESS INVESTMENTS

You can build a business around literally anything. Manufacturing, technology, retail, healthcare, food service, design, energy, insurance, fashion—starting to get the point?

1. Tax advantages

As a W-2 employee, Uncle Sam has already taken his cut when you get your paycheck, and you get what's left over. From your net paycheck, you have to then pay all your expenses. Hopefully, after paying all your bills, there is still enough to live a comfortable life. As I've said many times, income tax is the thief of generational wealth. You start out getting a 30-50% haircut off your hard-earned money BEFORE you have to pay your bills.

It's the exact opposite with business ownership. When your business takes in revenue, it pays all of its expenses FIRST before any taxes are levied. After all the expenses/bills are paid, THEN taxes are taken out on what's left over. If you structure your expenses correctly, you can mitigate the massive tax burden and keep more of your hard-earned income in your pocket.

2. The known

Some would call them "boring," but I would call them cash cows. Businesses that have been around longer than five years are generally stable, profitable, and a known commodity. They have a solid customer base, have proven solutions to problems or needs, and offer the buyer stability and profit. These businesses will likely be profitable for years to come and are great acquisition targets.

3. Opportunity

Have you heard of the "gray wave"? It's being discussed excitedly in the business community. This is referring to the massive number of retirees currently in the United States. "Baby Boomers" make up the majority of this population, and they account for 40% of all business owners in America. Even more astounding is that there are 10,000 people retiring EVERY DAY.[56] Most of these business owners own service businesses, which can be amazing acquisition targets. Most of these businesses have been around for decades and have very little debt, allowing the buyer and seller the opportunity to be very creative with financing options. This combination can spell excellent opportunities for buyers and sellers alike!

4. Roll-up strategies

A "roll-up strategy" is the process of acquiring and merging multiple smaller companies in the same industry and consolidating them into a large company. Combining small firms into a larger company allows the latter to pull their resources together, cut down on operational costs, increase revenues,[57] and create the all-important economies of scale we've spoken about throughout the book. It basically entails buying similar properties or businesses and continuing to grow and improve them based on each other's systems.

Let's use RV parks as an example. You have one RV park and have learned some things. So you buy another RV park, implement those systems, and even utilize crossover staffing, software, bookkeeping, and insurance.

As you roll the businesses up, you continue to put more layers between you and the investment. You may have started with a general manager, but now that person has been elevated to COO. The more businesses you own, the more margin you have to bring in amazing people. Your role as owner becomes to equip, empower, and enable.

THINGS TO CONSIDER WITH BUSINESS INVESTMENTS

1. SBA programs

There are Small Business Administration (SBA) programs out there that can help you use Other People's Money (OPM) to get you into business investments. They will help you put together your business plan and get financing, but they tend to be onerous and difficult to navigate. Using these programs often means it will take much longer to get through the lending process than with local and regional banks, which can cost you a deal if it's time-sensitive.

2. Startups

Many people have an awesome idea and want to start a business, but starting from scratch is almost a guaranteed recipe for failure. You definitely need a strong team if you are going to succeed. As mentioned earlier, 95% of new businesses don't make it—no matter *how* good the idea is.

3. Shiny pennies

Don't fall into the "shiny pennies" trap. What does this mean? Don't chase fads. Just because it's intriguing doesn't mean you have to open a business in this area. Boutique retail shops were all the rage coming out of the great recession. They popped up in highly desirable locations with super high rents. Several were opened by those who simply found the idea intriguing and had zero experience in retail, nor did they investigate market trends. A lot of these stores were squashed by online giants like Amazon. Do your research and find out what the community not only wants but also *needs*. Due diligence is super important in planning a startup, given the failure rate.

4. Exit strategies

Keep your exit in mind always. If you don't have a map, it's hard to figure out how to find a new destination. If you want to implement a roll-up strategy, make sure your businesses can be acquisition targets for larger investors, or you may be stuck with something you can't sell. If you have children who want to buy you out when you're ready to retire, this becomes less important. But, if not, you need to build your business to make it attractive to buyers.

WHAT A GOOD DEAL LOOKS LIKE INVESTING IN BUSINESSES

Buying a business is both a financial and strategic decision, and identifying a good deal involves careful evaluation of a number of things.

The first seems obvious but is crucial to making a solid investment: is the business profitable? Be sure to examine the company's financial statements—income statements, balance sheets, and cash flow statements. You're looking for a profitable business with consistent revenue and positive cash flow first and foremost.

Then examine their assets and liabilities. Does the company have intellectual property, equipment, and real estate? Is it holding debts? Does it have any outstanding legal issues? You need to be aware of potential hidden liabilities that could impact the deal.

I also like to ask about the reason for sale. Understanding the seller's motivation for selling the business can help inform your decision. If the motivation is reasonable (such as retirement), it may indicate a more transparent and trustworthy transaction. But then you also need to make sure that when the seller retires, it doesn't leave an operational gap you'll need to fill with an expert who may be difficult to find.

Next, I want there to be "meat on the bone." This means there needs to be lots of growth left in the business. Can I add value to drive appreciation? Look for untapped markets, product/service improvements, or cost-saving opportunities.

Part of your due diligence should also be ensuring the business is compliant with all relevant laws and regulations. I want to identify and clarify any potential legal issues that may arise post-acquisition because—as we've talked about repeatedly throughout this book—you don't want to buy someone else's problem.

Lastly, every good investment has an exit strategy. Consider how you will eventually sell or transition the business in the future.

Remember that each business is unique, and what constitutes a good deal may vary based on your specific goals and the characteristics of the business. Consulting with financial advisors, legal experts, and industry professionals can provide valuable insights during the due diligence process.

HOW TO INVEST IN BUSINESSES

We've discussed many things I love about owning businesses, things to look out for, and what a good business looks like. Now, you're ready to buy a business! But how?

First, establish your buyer profile. This is a document that includes your target statement (what you want to buy, and how involved you want to be in the business), value proposition (why you're qualified to buy it), area of expertise, achievements in the industry, and your professional experience. Get this document to Mergers and Acquisitions brokers, as it will give them a clear idea of the type of businesses you are looking for. There are also paid services like ibisworld.com to help you find acquisition targets. You can also access bizbuysell.com for opportunities, or you can always purchase lists of business owners and cold call them as well. Whatever path you choose, having a buyer profile will establish you as a serious buyer.

Next, you want to establish your budget, create your business plan, and get qualified for financing. Nothing will undermine the purchase process or kill your credibility as a buyer faster than failing on the financing end.

Once you have all this in place, you're ready to evaluate deals and move forward with the dream of being a (hopefully absentee) business owner!

BUSINESS INVESTMENT CASE STUDY

Leveraging Synergies

What I love the most is when I can combine real estate with business. I always look for synergies between the real estate I own and the businesses that fill needs.

I bought an RV park and implemented my value-add plan in the park by adding amenities, more sites, short-term vacation rental options, expanding merchandise sales, and several other initiatives.

We constantly reach out to customers asking how we can make their experience better. It's a nice touch that lets our patrons know we value their opinion, and it gives us ideas for new amenities we could add at the park or businesses that would fill a gap we are missing.

One of our continuing improvement campaigns revealed our campers wanted more food options. I've owned restaurants, and while they can be profitable, they can also be very labor-intensive.

I didn't want to create another job for myself, so I reached out to another excellent restaurateur in the local area to see if they would like to partner. I proposed that I would provide the capital for the build-out and fit-up, and they would run all the operations, drawing from the labor pool they already had in place.

We came to terms on the partnership and built the restaurant onsite at the RV park. It was an immediate and resounding success. We exceeded EBITDA projections by 30% in the first year it was open, and it continues to provide consistent cash flow every month.

This worked out amazing as we now have happier campers and a new excellent source of income for the park, and it takes absolutely zero of my time.

A 30,000-FOOT VIEW OF ADDITIONAL INVESTMENT OPTIONS

This book could very easily be 1,000 pages long if I were to cover all of the infinite possibilities that exist in the Investable Universe. When you've been an investor for as long as I have, the number of opportunities you see out there is astounding. That's great for creating a diverse profile, but untenable when writing a book.

For that reason, this chapter will take a 30,000-foot view of a variety of additional investment options. Think of it as an appetizer platter, designed to whet your appetite. If something tastes appealing and you want more, a ton of information exists to increase your education—including my website at cashflowmd.com.

If you want to dive deeper into one of these investment options, schedule some time to talk with me or one of my team members to see how we can help you on that journey. You can also join our Facebook group called "Physician Investor Network: Beyond the Stock Market" that is designed to help everyone elevate our investing game together. Or—if you're ready to dive really deep—you can enroll in my "Cash Flow Prescription" course to bring your investing acumen to the next level.

RESIDENTIAL ASSISTED-LIVING FACILITIES

A residential assisted-living facility is housed in a local neighborhood setting and feels very much like a home, with a small number of residents who have their own bedrooms but share common areas. These facilities offer a number of services including meals, laundry, recreational activities, and support with medications and personal care. They do not, however, provide medical care as a nursing home would.[58]

Residential assisted living is an excellent option for the "silver tsunami" of aging folks in the United States. Residential assisted living provides an amazing quality of life for residents, so it is a fulfilling business to be in since you are helping our elder community in a truly meaningful way.

I have found that residential assisted-living facilities can produce extremely good cash flow and have the ability to drive appreciation using a "roll-up strategy" to acquire more and more locations.

Key points:

- You will need three important ingredients to set yourself up for success: a knowledgeable general manager, a caring nursing staff, and a talented professional chef who can offer really good curated food.
- Adding a service such as memory care can raise the monthly rent by as much as $2,000/month.
- The most attractive models are beneficial to workers and residents alike because the caregiver ratio is 1:4 (whereas in larger facilities it can be as high as 1:20). These smaller residences seem to have a much higher rate of patient and employee satisfaction.
- The average age of residents entering assisted living is upper seventies or low eighties. This means they are nearing the end of their life expectancy. For that reason, you will want to ensure you create a waiting list of residents who can fill vacancies quickly.

- In my experience, there can be some pushback from neighbors in the area. HOAs will fight against you, but according to federal fair housing laws, communities have to allow these facilities. However, this means you may find yourself in a legal battle.

MARITIME SHIPPING

Maritime shipping is the act of carrying cargo from Point A to Point B using carrier ships.

The pandemic shone a spotlight on this industry because it quickly revealed our global dependency on shipping. When this industry came to a halt, our world erupted in the chaos of true scarcity.

This is an industry with very high demand, and the U.S. is shipping more goods worldwide than ever. As more countries become developed, shipping will become even more intertwined with the global economy.

Key points:

- I typically invest with groups who own the products being shipped (or who at least have contracts to carry them) and own the ships as well. The pinch point for these companies is getting the right ships at the right time when we need them. The solution to this problem became buying the ships to move the cargo. Now, we have guaranteed contracts that generate consistent cash flow for our ships.
- I don't recommend you walk into a shipyard and try to take on this type of investment on your own. It takes years of experience to know shipping customs, the rules and regulations, where the most profitable centers are, and the

rhythms of this industry. This is an investment vehicle where a proven partnership makes sense. You want to make sure you are doing your due diligence—checking out and finding an operator with a track record you can verify, and making sure they have decades of maritime shipping experience behind them.

HEAVY AND LIGHT INDUSTRY

Heavy industry (a.k.a. "heavy industrial") refers to large-scale businesses that utilize big equipment and large areas of land—steel companies and mining projects, for example. Light industry, by contrast, is a smaller-scale business that can operate in factories or small facilities. In these, production generally costs less and has lower barriers to entry.[59]

This is a fast-evolving asset class that, ten years ago, no one was talking about. Once again, the pandemic exposed the world's dependency on imports and exports. Even when COVID-19 subsided, the shipping backlog continued, and that drove prices to absurd levels, creating a massive issue with our supply-and-demand chain.

In 2022, The Bureau of Labor Statistics described COVID-19's impact as the largest manufacturing decline since World War II, stating that output across many industries, both heavy and light (metals, food and beverage, chemicals), fell anywhere from 38-43% in 2020.[60]

With such global dependency on the manufacturing industry, there is certainly potential for money to be made in investments.

Key points:

- While heavy industry allows for all types of products—including petroleum—light industry is more warehousing and non-flammable materials. For this reason, heavy industry is subject to more stringent regulations. For example, you generally will be denied putting heavy industrial facilities near an airport because they don't want flammable products in runway protection zones.
- As I write this book, the United States is experiencing a nationalist sentiment and is heading into an election cycle. People want American-made products because they are nervous about dependency on foreign goods after supply-chain failures caused by COVID-19. Consequently, at the current moment, our country is grossly underbuilt in the industrial space as the repatriation of manufacturing to the U.S. is happening. Therefore, it is a great time to jump into this asset class. If you combine the development of industrial space with an opportunity zone, you can really hit an exit multiple. It can be game-changing!
- This investment category is capital-intensive. This is not a place to jump in by yourself. You want to find a good operator, hitch your wagon to that horse, let it pull you through, and learn along the way. And—of course (say it with me, now!): *"Always do your due diligence!"*

LAND ENTITLEMENTS

Land entitlement refers to the legal process of a landowner gaining approval for the development of their property.[61] Real estate development has several steps. Entitlement is one of the first, and most important, in the journey.

Key points:

- Personally, I don't want to get into a development deal at the beginning of this process. I'd rather be involved once the entitlements are complete, zoning has been approved, and the developer has secured funding from a lender. These are typically the biggest hurdles. Once complete, the project is significantly de-risked.
- This is a potentially lucrative asset for a person who knows what they are doing and purchases with a distinct goal in mind. It's imperative you do your research: demographics, population metrics, economy studies, etc. You need to be able to accurately forecast what the community needs from the land: be it industrial, multifamily housing, or self-storage. If everything is properly zoned and entitled, the land can be sold to a developer, who is usually willing to pay a premium for shovel-ready land.
- Land entitlement is an advanced investment strategy. You need to be careful who you partner with, and—you guessed it—do your due diligence.

LAND FLIPPING

Something you *can* go out and start doing on your own is land flipping. Essentially, you buy a piece of land at a discount and sell it for a higher price. It's basically like house flipping…but without the house.

Land flipping can be a side hustle, or it can be a full-time career. Thousands of parcels per year exchange hands for pennies on the dollar. Most of the time, the land belongs to people who inherited it unwillingly. They are tired of the upkeep, or they get behind on property taxes. Either way, they simply do not want the responsibility of owning the land.

Key points:

- If you don't have a clear exit strategy for the land purchase, it will become a burden to you—and a liability, too. Even if you own the land free and clear, you still need to pay property taxes, and you will likely need to pay to have someone cut the grass, etc. This is simply another job for you. Buy with the exit in mind.
- There is potential for you to see a return on this asset's investment within months, not years. As soon as I purchase a parcel of land, it goes right into the marketing machine, and my team is blasting it out to a bunch of folks who like to buy land. For the most part, my typical buy/sell cycle is sixty to ninety days.
- One thing to consider is short-term capital gains (STCGs). STCGs are taxed as ordinary income. You could acquire a bunch of parcels and hold them for twelve months and one day in order for the sale to be taxed as long-term capital gains, which is generally better than the ordinary income rate. However, even though I love mitigating tax burden, *don't let the tax tail wag the dog.* 70% of something is better than 100% of nothing. If you can make money, make money. You just need to understand the tax ramifications of your activities.

- IMPORTANT: Buying land, selling it in three months, and using a 1031 exchange is frowned upon by the IRS. You can maybe do it once, but if it becomes a pattern, they will disallow the exchange, causing a potential tax headache for you.

ART

The reason I want to include art as an investment opportunity is that it has a long history of being a transactable asset. Art transcends time, economies, wars, and disease. It speaks to the human soul on different levels, so it will always have intrinsic value.

Art auctions have been around for hundreds of years. You don't stay in business that long unless there is substance to the offering. There is potential for profit in the buying and selling of art, but you need to understand the value of art is highly subjective. Unless you have a background in this space, it's definitely not an investment I recommend for beginners.

Key points:

- Art offers diversity to your portfolio.
- For every $100,000 I have to invest, I put $1,000-$5,000 into art—just to give you a sense of the (small) ratio I personally carry as a part of my own investment portfolio.
- Art isn't generally something you can flip quickly. You usually need to hold an art piece for years, and it steadily appreciates over time.
- It is non-correlated with the stock market and holds intrinsic value.

If you don't necessarily have an eye for masterpieces and—like me—may not know the difference between a Picasso and a painting your child brings home, *get help*. Do your due diligence as you would with any other investment. You want to know what the expert's returns have been, their history, how they've exited, and who is involved in choosing the art. Several reputable art syndications have years of experience in this space.

CARBON CREDITS, MINE RECLAMATION, AND CONSERVATION EASEMENTS, AND PIPELINE INVESTMENTS

Carbon credits: A permit that allows a country or organization to produce a certain amount of carbon emissions that can be traded if the full allowance is not used.62

Mine reclamation: Mine reclamation is the combined process by which adverse environmental effects of surface mining are minimized and mined lands are returned to a beneficial end use.63

Conservation easement: A legal agreement that permanently limits uses of the land in order to protect its conservation values.64

I grouped these assets together because I consider them all to be what I call "flypaper" investments: they try to catch physicians by dangling the attractiveness of sweet returns that can get them in a sticky situation with government entities like the EPA or the IRS.

It's not that they're scams necessarily. All of these options can, in truth, be potentially legitimate investments. But I caution new investors when dealing in these realms, because there is a ton of industry jargon and intimidating reports that go along with this territory.

This is where my favorite test comes into play. I've already said it (and I'll say it again): if you can explain something to a seventh grader in a way they understand, then you know what you are talking about and are capable of making a sound investment decision. If you don't understand the investment to that depth, you are treading on thin ice, and it's best just to look for another investment option. It's just not worth it. Plenty of sound investments are out there for you in the investable universe!

Most times I step into something I don't fully understand, I end up losing.

Key points:

- I looked into a conservation easement deal a private equity business was offering years ago. I didn't fully understand the business model or the fact that the IRS heavily scrutinizes these deals. I was told, "This is a rock-solid deal, and you will get tons of tax benefits." I wasn't aware how the IRS could make life very difficult for everyone involved in these deals, even if they are legitimate. The investment was tied up in audits for two years while my money was sitting there doing nothing. When you don't know what you don't know, the bottom line is *don't do it*!
- The IRS will be looking over your shoulder with carbon credits, mining reclamation, and pipeline investments as well. For me, the cost and headache of audits just aren't worth it. I'm not afraid of an audit, but what I *am* afraid of is not being able to justify my deductions. There are just too many other areas to place my capital that offer better returns and less headaches.
- If I have land that I want to utilize for potential greenhouse gas (GHG) incentive programs, I'll evaluate each of the

programs individually and see if it fits my strategy for the land. I generally don't purchase land *because* of GHG programs, but I will utilize them if it makes sense.

STOCKS, BONDS, MUTUAL FUNDS, AND ETFS

Stock: Also known as equity, a stock is a security that represents the ownership of a fraction of the issuing corporation, which entitles the owner to a proportion of the corporation's assets and profits equal to how much stock [an investor] owns.[65]

Bonds: Bonds are issued by governments and corporations when they want to raise money. By buying a bond, you are giving the issuer a loan, and they agree to pay you back the face value of the loan on a specific date, and to pay you periodic interest payments along the way.

Mutual Fund: An investment option where money from many people is pooled together to buy a variety of stocks, bonds, or other securities—overseen by a professional money manager.[66]

Exchange-Traded Funds (ETFs): Exchange-Traded Funds (ETFs) are investments that are similar to mutual funds, but trade like stocks.[67]

For such a smart guy, Warren Buffett led a lot of people into the stock market who really shouldn't have been there. He famously shared his two rules of investing:

- Never lose principle
- Don't forget rule number one

It doesn't make a lot of sense to me for someone to say that and then invest in stocks, as they are notorious for volatility and exacting losses on unsuspecting investors. They've proven this many times in the past and will continue to do so in the future.

What people don't understand is that Buffett's company, Berkshire Hathaway, doesn't just own company stocks. They often own the companies as well. If they don't own the company, they gain control by inserting key players into the C-suites of companies or on their boards. Mr. Buffett has a LOT more control than the average Joe.

If I controlled as many variables as he does, I would probably subscribe to Mr. Buffet's line of thinking as well. But not all investors have the experience, control, and big swinging mallet that Warren Buffett does. In fact, no one on the planet does.

Key points:

- We know from the prior sections and statistics that businesses fail all the time. While it's true that stocks probably won't fall to zero, they can. I saw my dad lose everything in the stock market—twice. Would you rather own a bunch of stocks that have the potential to be wiped out because of economic factors out of your control, or own a hard asset like real estate that is steady and produces consistent cash flow?
- Stocks are simply speculation. They are someone's best guess. Thinking it is safe to invest in a company stock is naïve. Speculating on your principal is not safe practice.
- I have active influence over the fate of the businesses and real estate I invest in. I can make choices based on whether the property manager is doing a good job, whether my sponsor is upholding the operating agreement, or whether we bring in new systems. There are actionable steps I can take to improve our chances of success.
- The only thing you can do to control the fate of stocks, bonds, and mutual funds is to sell them. If you are lucky

> enough to be in Warren Buffet's circle, then congratulations. Most of us, though, are basically giving our money and power away to someone else when we invest in these vehicles, saying, "Please go and make me some more money." Then we sit back and pray it is going to happen. That's not investing—that's speculating. And if it does happen and makes you money, that's luck. Your fate is in someone else's hands, and it's far better off where it belongs—in your own.

Self-directed investments

In recent years, the pendulum has been swinging toward self-directed investments. Compared to stocks, bonds, mutual funds, and ETFs, self-directed investing opens up a world of alternatives.

I love self-directed options because it moves control back where it belongs: to us. With the U.S. debt continuing to rise toward insolvency (some would say we are already there), my fear is that the government will nationalize traditional retirement plans in an effort to garner more tax revenue and kick the austerity can down the road. Self-directed options may go away if this were to happen, so I self-direct as much as possible currently.

This is one of the reasons I personally don't feel safe with my money being in a 401(k) or a 403(b).

That said, if your company matches your investments in your 401(k) s and 403(b)s, it's free money. I would contribute as much as they match (and that's where it would stop for me personally; I wouldn't overcontribute). Most of us don't stay with the same employer our entire careers as physicians. If you ever do leave your employer, you will have the opportunity to roll those proceeds into an IRA that you can then self-direct.

- If you do have a 401(k) or 403(b), try to get a custodian with low fees and a good reputation.
- If I had a choice, I would say the best vehicle is a strong ETF. The problem is, many custodians won't allow an ETF because they usually have their own preferred funds.
- If you're a solo practitioner and don't have any employees, you can do a Solo 401(k). If you are in a private practice with employees, it's possible to set up other types of deferred-benefit plans. There are also many plans where you can self-direct and don't have to invest in the stock market—you can put your money into hard assets or debt/private equity investments.
- There are ways to set up your practice where you are an employee as well as an owner. If you are an employee of your own business, you can have a Simplified Employee Pension Plan (SEP-IRA), where you can invest over $60,000 pre-tax into this vehicle annually.
- If you use a self-directed IRA to invest, try to invest in assets that are not tax-advantaged. I often use my SDIRA to invest in active business pursuits because that money will flow back to the SDIRA tax deferred. If I invest in a rental property, for example, I won't be maximizing the tax advantages of real estate. Instead, choose to invest in options such as mineral rights, which generate less tax-advantaged cash flow. Or, I'll flip properties inside my SDIRA because those proceeds are taxed as short-term gains. We go into many more tax strategies like this in my "Cash Flow Prescription" course.

REITs

Real estate investment trusts (REITs) are basically glorified stocks. They are based on the appeal of owning hard assets, so they're selling the idea that you own a piece of an apartment building, as an example.

The problem is, REITs can be aggregated, securitized, and sold just like stocks. You don't have ownership of any real property. It's really no different than owning stock. This is not property ownership: it's a stock packaged and marketed as a real estate asset.

ADVANCED OPTION STRATEGY

This is a system where I sell coupons to hedge fund managers and other large fund managers who have to buy the insurance to stay within the risk parameters of funds they manage. I get paid immediately, and I set a high-limit trade along with a low-limit trade. After that, I don't care what the stock market does as long as it doesn't go over or under those limits. 95% of the time, the "coupons" I sell expire worthless, and I keep the income generated and do it again. On the outside chance something has to be done, I simply repair the trade or roll it out until the next month. My maximum loss is set no matter what, so I always know what I'm getting into.

I spend about ten minutes every few days on this investment strategy, and it's yielded me a six-figure supplemental income annually. It's based on years of data, and is constantly being tweaked and honed. It truly is one of the best forms of passive income I have ever come across.

It's just one of the tools in my toolbelt of diversified income streams I like to share with my network. If you are interested in diving deeper into this strategy, this is one of the topics we cover in depth in my "Cash Flow Prescription" course.

THE PLAN B STRATEGY

Many investors use a diversification play referred to as "citizen by investment" (CBI). I like to call it Plan B.

This strategy allows individuals to obtain citizenship or residence rights through local investments, or for a flat fee/donation to other government-designated entities.[68]

The main reasons people choose dual citizenship are to diversify outside the U.S., protect their wealth, leverage tax reduction strategies, and have a true Plan B strategy in place in case of domestic unrest.

Spreading wealth across different jurisdictions offers many benefits:

- This strategy can provide protection against economic and political risks in a single country.
- If there is a downturn in the market, you have wealth in other markets generating cash flow.
- Some countries offering CBI have very favorable tax advantages, including no income nor corporate or inheritance taxes.

This is great for investors looking to optimize their tax planning and reduce their overall tax burden both now and for the next generation. Many countries with stable political, economic, and social environments offer these citizenship tracts.

CONCLUSION

Doctors are some of the hardest-working people I know. While most wear this "busy-ness" as a badge of honor, it can also be a one-way street to burnout. I wrote this book to give you the keys to unlock the Investable Universe, and to show you that freedom of time and money *is* possible. You *can* obtain a more balanced lifestyle by creating financial freedom outside of medicine. I know—because I've done it.

My adventure began as a real estate investor and has grown into a diverse and profitable portfolio containing many different investment vehicles. My success comes as a direct result of utilizing my Five Pillars of Financial Freedom:

- Mindset
- Learning
- Network
- Deal Flow
- Action

As physicians, what's great about our medical school training is that it has already given us the foundation to be strategic, logical, and successful. We've developed strong and determined mindsets, dedicated our lives to learning, nurtured beneficial relationships with mentors and colleagues, and created a professional pathway. We are ready to jump into action when necessary. We simply need to harness our skill set and use it in a new way.

Investing in real estate and other cash-flowing assets has afforded me financial freedom that my medical career could not while I was stuck in the debt cycle and trading time for money. It has allowed me to be truly present with those I love in my life and be generous—with both money and time—beyond what I ever could have imagined. I am unbelievably grateful to be building this type of legacy, and I want to open those doors for you as well.

Throughout this book, we've discussed many of my favorite opportunities available to physicians in the world of real estate and other investment avenues in the Investable Universe. One of the key takeaways from our exploration is the recognition of real estate as a powerful wealth-building tool for physicians who want to escape a broken system. Real estate, with its potential for passive income, tax advantages, and ability to drive appreciation, emerges as one of the most compelling options doctors have to secure their financial future. However, it is crucial to strategically diversify your income streams and investments.

We've discussed how important your mindset is in preparation for this new chapter of your life. We have learned, in-depth, about the critical role of due diligence in your success. We have explored ways to make informed decisions, and mitigate the risks associated with investing. We have investigated the incredible variety of investment and financing options available.

The book also emphasized the importance of aligning your investments with individual financial goals and risk tolerance. Whether it's generating additional income to offset student loan debt, to pay for your children's education, or to replace your income as a physician, alternative investing in hard assets is an excellent option to meet your specific objectives. Through careful planning, strategic decision-making, and beneficial relationships, doctors can harness the potential of real estate and other forms of investing to fulfill both short-term and long-term financial goals. It can help you live a life of gratitude, generosity, and purpose.

Another component of this book discussed the significance of leveraging professional networks and seeking mentorship within the real estate community. By tapping into the collective wisdom of expert investors, partners, brokers, and mentors, doctors can accelerate their learning curve and avoid common mistakes. Alternative investing is not just about transactions; it's about relationships, and the book underscores the value of creating a network that extends well beyond the medical field.

As we conclude this book, please know this is not necessarily the end of our journey together. It is essential for doctors to recognize that all investments exist in a dynamic and evolving landscape. Staying current on market trends, regulatory changes, and emerging opportunities is vital for sustained success. My website offers a variety of educational tools such as blogs, free ebooks, videos, trusted affiliates, and access to my online course—embark on a journey beyond the pages of this book with "Cash Flow Prescription," a course meticulously crafted for physicians seeking to navigate the ever-evolving world of investments. Elevate your financial acumen, stay ahead of market trends, and seize emerging opportunities with exclusive resources tailored to your professional and financial growth. Join "Cash Flow Prescription," and let's continue to cultivate your path to freedom together, armed with the tools, knowledge, and support designed for the unique financial landscape of healthcare professionals. Whatever path you choose, I'm here to support you along your path to freedom.

In essence, this book serves as a prescription for financial well-being. As doctors, we know that writing a prescription is only the first step. The ownership then falls to the patient to proceed with the advised action plan. They are the ones who need to take their medication, see the specialists, and follow through with recommendations for care.

I've written you the prescription. Now it is your responsibility to go forth and take action. What's the next step you are going to take to create the future you truly desire?

GLOSSARY OF KEY TERMS & CONCEPTS

1031 Exchange: A strategic tool for deferring the capital gains tax on the sale of real property. Popular with real estate investors, it allows one to sell a property and purchase another like-kind property of equal or greater value while deferring any tax liability.

Accredited Investor: Someone who has satisfied the specific requirements surrounding income and net worth and thus has the privilege of investing in securities that may not be registered with financial authorities.

Acquisition criteria: A set of specific parameters that the acquiring company or investor desires in the company/investment it hopes to acquire.

Advanced options: The ability to buy or sell options contracts based on market outlook. A trader has the right (but not the obligation) to buy or sell an asset at the options' first strike price within a specified time frame.

American Petroleum Institute numbers (API numbers): A specific number given to every oil and gas well for the purpose of tracking.

Appreciation: The increase in value based on market shifts or improvements made to an investment.

Arbitrage: Taking advantage of price differences in different markets or timing to make a profit.

Asset: An investment that puts money into your pocket.

Asset classes: Categories of investments that share similar traits and are subject to the same regulations.

Balance Sheet: A statement of the assets, liabilities, and equity of a company (what the company owns and owes, as well as information about investors/shareholders).

Bonds: A loan granted to a corporation or government by an investor(s).

Bridge debt: Also called a bridge loan, this is a form of short-term financing to carry an investor until more permanent financing options can be obtained.

Broker dealers: Professionals who find potential investors for a percentage of capital raised on the investment.

Buy and hold: Investing in a property and holding it long-term with the goal of appreciation and cash flow.

Capital call: When an investment firm demands a percentage of the money promised by an investor. Also, it can be when a sponsor of an investment requires more capital from investors in order to maintain ownership of the investment.

Capitalization (cap) rate: Calculates the rate of return expected on a real estate investment. Calculated by dividing the property's annual net operating income (NOI) by the sales price, the cap rate is used to estimate an investor's potential return on investment on that particular purchase in cash.

Carbon credits: A credit that allows an organization to produce a specific amount of carbon emissions. Credits can be traded if the full allowance is not used.

Carbon sequestration: A process that removes carbon dioxide from the earth's atmosphere and retains it in solid or liquid form.

Cash-flowing asset: An asset that generates a profit or income.

Cash-on-Cash (CoC) return: The amount of annualized income earned on cash invested.

"Citizen by investment" (CBI): An investment strategy that allows someone to gain citizenship or residence rights by making investments in the local economy or government.

Conservation easement: Legalities that protect the land for future generations by limiting and conserving the way it is used.

Consolidation: Well-funded buyers purchase large amounts of an asset and gain a massive percentage of the market share.

Cost-segregation/Cost-seg analysis: A study that categorizes elements of a property with the intention of accelerating depreciation deductions and minimizing tax burdens.

Debt financing: Borrowing money with interest to purchase an investment.

Debt service coverage ratio (DSCR): Measures the amount of cash flow one has available to pay debt obligations. The DSCR shows lenders whether the recipient of the loan has enough income to pay its debts.

Deferred maintenance: Repairs that are delayed due to budgetary constraints.

Depletion allowance: In mineral rights, this is the allowance available through the IRS code allowing an owner to account for the reduction of reserves as oil and gas are extracted.

Depreciation: A reduction of value in an asset over time secondary to normal wear and tear. This is what most refer to as a "paper loss."

Depreciation benefit: A strategy where businesses choose to leverage depreciation to realize significant tax advantages.

Depreciation recapture: Income gained from the sale of a depreciated asset, which must be reported as ordinary income for tax purposes.

Destination parks: RV parks usually found in or around desirable locations—national parks, state parks, or anywhere people want to go on vacation.

Diversification: An investment strategy that advocates for the inclusion of various different asset classes in one's portfolio.

Dollar-cost averaging: An investment strategy that invests the same amount of money in an asset at regular intervals, regardless of price.

Double net lease: In this agreement, the tenant takes responsibility for many of the expenses normally allocated to the owner, such as property taxes and insurance. However, the landlord still retains responsibility for some of the expenses.

Dual interest banking: Using the chassis of Whole or Index Universal Life policies, you are able to borrow money from yourself, pay interest to yourself, and put the borrowed funds to work in your investments.

Dynamic pricing: Adjusting the price of a product or service in conjunction with fluctuating market conditions.

EBITDA: Stands for earnings before interest, taxes, depreciation, and amortization. This is a popular metric used for measuring a company's financial performance.

Equity financing: Selling equity in an investment in return for capital.

Equity multiple: In real estate, the equity multiple is defined as the total income received from an investment, divided by the total equity invested. Essentially, it is how much money an investor made on their investment.

Exchange-traded funds (ETFs): A type of soft asset that resembles a mutual fund, but can be traded like a stock.

Express tunnels: A type of automatic car wash where the vehicle moves on a conveyor belt through a series of different wash cycles depending on the product chosen.

Fix and flip: Buying a property, renovating it, and then selling it at a higher price.

Guarantor: A person who legally agrees to pay the borrower's debt if they are unable to meet the financial obligations.

Hard assets: Tangible, physical resources or assets you can own that possess value.

Hard money lenders: A loan from an individual or entity that is secured by real property or another hard asset.

Heavy industry: Large-scale businesses that need massive space in order to utilize big equipment (for example, steel companies and mining projects).

Housing and Urban Development (HUD) code: Legislation stating that manufactured homes must be built upon a permanent chassis.

In-bay automatic car wash: This is a non-conveyor type of car wash where the vehicle is stationary and the machinery moves around it.

Installment sale: Rather than paying in a lump sum, the buyer makes several payments to the seller over an agreed-upon period of time.

Investment-grade tenant: The tenant or renter has earned a strong credit rating, which lenders find appealing.

IRR (Internal Rate of Return): A calculation of potential annual growth of an investment, considering the amount of time and money that has been invested.

Land entitlement: The legal process of a landowner gaining approval for the development of their property.

Land reclamation: Reclamation is the process by which adverse environmental effects of surface mining are mitigated by returning the land to some form of beneficial end use.

Leverage: The act of using other people's money (like a bank's) to buy an asset that cash flows.

Liability: Any attempted investment activity that takes money out of your pocket.

Light industry: Businesses that can operate in smaller-scale facilities (such as factories).

Liquidity: The ease with which an asset can be converted into cash.

Long-term rental: Stays of more than thirty days.

Manufactured home: A residence that is pre-built in a factory and can then be transported onto a piece of land. These homes were built after 1976.

Maritime shipping: The act of carrying cargo from Point A to Point B using large ships.

Mineral rights investments: The acquisition of the rights to extract and/or sell minerals that are found beneath a particular tract of land.

Mitigation planning: The assessment of natural hazards, in an effort to reduce the potential impact on land, community, and environment.

Mobile home: Similar to a manufactured home, these structures are prefabricated homes built prior to 1976.

Money on Invested Capital (MOIC): Similar to equity multiple, this is a measurement of the profit made from your initial investment.

Metropolitan Statistical Area (MSA): Statistics providing information about a defined geographic area including population growth, unemployment rates, median household income, etc.

Multifamily housing: A single building divided into separate housing units to accommodate more than one family.

Multifamily development investing: The construction of multifamily housing facilities.

Multitenant: A single property that has multiple units, each with their own rental agreement.

Mutual funds: Money from multiple investors is pooled to buy stocks and bonds and is overseen by a professional money manager.

The National Association of Real Estate Investment Trusts (NAREIT): Based in Washington, D.C., this association monitors entities such as REITs and real estate investment trusts.

Net operating losses (NOLs): When the allowable deductions are greater than the taxable income.

Net operating income (NOI): A formula that determines the profitability of an investment by subtracting the operating expenses from the income.

Nonrecourse option/nonrecourse debt: A loan that is secured by the property as collateral rather than a guarantor.

Opportunity zone: Designated areas in the United States where tax benefits are given to investors who choose to develop in these lower income, under-developed, or distressed areas.

Pass-through parks: A low-amenity, overnight stop for RV travelers.

Private equity lenders: A financing option in which pooled funds of high-net worth individuals or institutions are used to invest in assets that can offer the lender a stake in the equity.

Private Placement Memorandum (PPM): A legal document given to potential investors that describes the terms and conditions of the investment deal.

Qualified opportunity fund: Offers partnership to investors looking to invest in an opportunity zone.

Recreational Vehicle (RV): A category of motor vehicles that include living quarters.

Real Estate Investment Trust (REIT): A publicly traded company that finances, owns, or operates real estate properties.

Repair credits: When the seller agrees to pay for some of the necessary repairs to a property by crediting the buyer the amount it would take to fix those issues.

Real Estate Professional Status (REPS): The tax designation given to anyone who meets criteria established by the IRS to be a full-time real estate professional.

Residential assisted living facility: A housing facility where a small number of residents live in separate apartments but have shared common areas. These facilities offer a number of services including meals, laundry, recreational activities, and support with medications and personal care.

Return on investment (ROI): Calculates how much can be made (or lost) on an investment or project after accounting for its costs.

Self-directed Individual Retirement Account (SDIRA): Investments that, though monitored by a professional, are directly managed by the account holder.

Self-service car wash: A car wash where the driver pulls their vehicle into a bay in order to use the sprayers and equipment to manually wash their car.

Seller carryback: A financing option that involves the owner providing some or all of the financing.

Short-term rental: A rental of a property for a short period of time, usually 7 days or less and generally no more than 30 days. Vacation rentals are an example.

Single-family housing: A housing facility built to accommodate one family only.

Single net lease: A commercial lease agreement that requires the tenant to pay property taxes in addition to rent. The landlord is responsible for all other operating expenses associated with the property.

Single-tenant net lease: An agreement between a sole renter of the property and the owner.

Site lock fees: An additional charge to RV park guests who want to choose a specific site to stay in.

Soft asset: An asset that does not have a tangible, physical form (such as stocks and bonds).

Stocks: An investment option where the buyer purchases a fraction of a publicly traded company and is entitled to a percentage of that company's profits.

Stumpage value: The amount of money a timber harvesting company is willing to pay the landowner for the right to harvest and remove timber from the property.

Syndication: The partnership between a group of investors who pool their money to make a single investment.

Syndication sponsor: In a syndication, the person or company who has strategic relationships, may be raising investment capital, and/or has experience in structuring real estate deals. May also be known as the syndicator.

T12: A financial statement showing annual income and expenses.

Tax avoidance: The act of mitigating tax liabilities and maximizing income.

Timberland: Land primarily used for growing and harvesting trees for timber production.

Timber Stand Improvement (TSI): Intended to nurture the growth of desirable trees by removing poor quality trees and maintaining optimum growth conditions.

Transient parks: RV parks that accommodate seasonal workers.

Triple net lease: An agreement where the tenant pays all the expenses of the property above and beyond their rent and utilities.

Turn time: The time from when a current renter vacates the property until a new renter occupies the property.

Underwriting: This refers to the criteria and research a financial lender uses to determine the creditworthiness of a borrower.

Value-add: Improvements made to an asset that are intended to increase the value and cash flow.

W2: This is a tax document used to record and report annual wages and taxes paid to the government.

Wholesaler: Professionals who obtain deals under an assignable contract below market value and then sell that contract to investors or end users.

Working interest: An active investment that offers a proportionate share of income along with the costs, rewards, and risks associated with the exploration, development, and production of oil and gas.

Yield maintenance: When a borrower prepays a loan before maturity, they often have to pay a yield payment to the lender as compensation of lost interest.

ENDNOTES

1. Ally, Daniel. "7 Reasons to Become a Millionaire." LinkedIn, February 5, 2021. https://www.linkedin.com/pulse/7-reasons-become-millionaire-daniel-ally-2#:~:text=Inspire%20Others%3A%20When%20you%20have,to%20work%20on%20charitable%20ventures.

2. "Why You Should Be Rich (3 Big Reasons)." Healthpreneur, April 28, 2017. https://healthpreneurgroup.com/why-you-should-be-rich/.

3."Decades of Scientific Research That Started a Growth Mindset Revolution." The Growth Mindset - What is Growth Mindset - Mindset Works. Accessed January 31, 2024. https://www.mindsetworks.com/science/.

4. The Difference between Tax Avoidance and Tax Evasion - IRS." irs.gov. Accessed January 31, 2024. https://apps.irs.gov/app/understandingTaxes/whys/thm01/les03/media/ws_ans_thm01_les03.pdf.

5. Rogers, John. "Chapters of Think and Grow Rich." Wealth Creation Mastermind, December 1, 2019. https://wealthcreationmastermind.com/blog/chapters-of-think-and-grow-rich/#:~:text=Think%20

and%20Grow%20Rich%20Chapter%2010%20Summary%20%E2%80%93%20Power%20of%20The,Mastermind%20alliance%20amplifies%20power%20exponentially.

6. Fernando, Jason. "Return on Investment (ROI): How to Calculate It and What It Means." Investopedia, December 22, 2023. https://www.investopedia.com/terms/r/returnoninvestment.asp.

7. "How Far Up, How Far To The Right, And When? A Real Estate Return Metric Glossary." https://www.birgo.com/blog/real-estate-return-metric-glossary#:~:text=The%20Multiple%20of%20Invested%20Capital,of%20your%20investment%20is%2010x.

8. Kenton, Will. "Cash-on-Cash Return in Real Estate: Definition, Calculation." Investopedia. Accessed February 22, 2024. https://www.investopedia.com/terms/c/cashoncashreturn.asp.

9. Fernando, Jason. "Internal Rate of Return (IRR): Formula and Examples." Investopedia. Accessed February 22, 2024. https://www.investopedia.com/terms/i/irr.asp.

10. Segal, Troy. "Hard Money Loan Definition." Investopedia. Accessed February 22, 2024. https://www.investopedia.com/terms/h/hard_money_loan.asp#:~:text=A%20hard%20money%20loan%20is,or%20companies%20and%20not%20banks.

11. "Benefits of Leverage in Real Estate: Definition & Tips." Buttonwood Property Management, February 10, 2023. https://buttonwood.ca/benefits-of-leverage-in-real-estate/.

12. Chen, James, "Capitalization Rate: Cap Rate Defined With Formula and Examples." Investopedia, December 22, 2023. https://www.investopedia.com/terms/c/capitalizationrate.asp.

13. Kagan, Julia, "Seller Financing: Definition and How It's Used in Real Estate." Investopedia, April 8, 2022. https://www.investopedia.com/terms/s/seller-financing.asp.

14. Hanson, Melanie. "U.S. Public Education Spending Statistics [2023]: Per Pupil + Total." Education Data Initiative, September 8, 2023. https://educationdata.org/public-education-spending-statistics#:~:text=Federal%2C%20state%2C%20and%20local%20governments,billion%20or%20%241%2C935%20per%20pupil.

15. Clark, Ken, "Recourse Vs. Non-Recourse Loan: What's the Difference?" Investopedia, May 11, 2023. https://www.investopedia.com/ask/answers/08/nonrecourse-loan-vs-recourse-loan.asp.

16. Dillingham, Scott, "Real Estate Syndication - a Strong Investing Choice in 2023: Finance Corner." Canadian Real Estate Network - Real Estate Investing in Canada, April 28, 2023. https://canadianrealestatenetwork.com/real-estate-syndications/#:~:text=Real%20estate%20syndication%20pools%20the,to%20manage%20on%20their%20own.

17. Williams, Bradley, "43+ Latest RV Industry Statistics (2023)." May 2, 2023. https://www.dreambigtravelfarblog.com/blog/rv-industry-statistics.

18. Wikipedia contributors, "RV Park," Wikipedia, November 6, 2023. https://en.wikipedia.org/wiki/RV_park#:~:text=There%20are%20over%2013%2C000%20privately,included%20in%20the%20campsite%20fee.

19. Di Cerbo, Daniel. "What Is T3 in Real Estate? &Amp; What Is T12 in Real Estate?" Willowdale Equity, December 11, 2023. https://willowdaleequity.com/blog/what-is-t3-in-real-estate/#:~:text=in%20Real%20Estate%3F-,A%20T%2D12%20in%20real%20

estate%20investing%20refers%20to%20the,expenses%20at%20 a%20particular%20property.

20. Chen, James, "Net Lease Definition and Types—Single, Double, Triple." Investopedia, March 1, 2021. https://www.investopedia.com/terms/n/net-lease.asp.

21. Investopedia Team, "Single Net Lease: What It Is, How It Works." Investopedia, July 4, 2021. https://www.investopedia.com/terms/s/single-net-lease.asp.

22. Chen, James, "Double Net Lease: Definition, How It Works, Vs. Triple Net Lease." Investopedia, August 31, 2022. https://www.investopedia.com/terms/d/double-net-lease.asp.

23. Kagan, Julia. "Non-Recourse Debt: Definition, Example, Vs. Recourse Debt." Investopedia, December 22, 2022. https://www.investopedia.com/terms/n/nonrecoursedebt.asp.

24. https://www.lawshelf.com/videocoursesmoduleview/mineral-rights-leases-form-and-function-module-3-of-5.

25. Fernando, Jason. "What Is an LLC? Limited Liability Company Structure and Benefits Defined." Investopedia, October 1, 2023. https://www.investopedia.com/terms/l/llc.asp.

26. "Britannica Money," n.d. https://www.britannica.com/money/depletion-allowance.

27. "Britannica Money," n.d. https://www.britannica.com/money/depletion-allowance.

28. Wikipedia contributors. "Big Oil." Wikipedia, February 15, 2024. https://en.wikipedia.org/wiki/Big_Oil.

29. Hayes, Adam. "Dollar-Cost Averaging (DCA) Explained With Examples and Considerations." Investopedia, February 6, 2024. https://www.investopedia.com/terms/d/dollarcostaveraging.asp.

30. Tuovila, Alicia. "Depreciation Recapture: Definition, Calculation, and Examples." Investopedia, July 20, 2023. https://www.investopedia.com/terms/d/depreciationrecapture.asp.

31. Federal Insurance and Mitigation Administration. "Local Hazard Mitigation Planning." https://www.nh.gov/safety/divisions/hsem/HazardMitigation/documents/local-hazard-mitigation-planning-factsheet.pdf.

32. Forest Service, U.S. Department of Agriculture. "Timber Stand Improvement." https://www.fs.usda.gov/, n.d. https://www.fs.usda.gov/Internet/FSE_DOCUMENTS/fseprd622035.pdf.

33. Wikipedia contributors, "Site Index." Wikipedia, February 3, 2023. https://en.wikipedia.org/wiki/Site_index.

34. "Types of Car Washes." n.d., https://www.carwashadvisory.com/learning/types-of-car-washes#:~:text=Tunnel-,IN%2DBAY,as%20%E2%80%9Cnon%2Dconveyor%E2%80%9D.

35. Professional Carwashing & Detailing, "Driving Forward: The Growth and Opportunities in the Evolving Carwash Market." Professional Carwashing & Detailing, October 3, 2023. https://www.carwash.com/growth-carwash-market/.

36. Peter Jones, "Car Wash Demographics: 65 User Facts & Numbers [2023]." Motor & Wheels, October 19, 2023. https://motorandwheels.com/car-wash-demographics/.

37. Reis, Matthews. "Update on the Car Wash Market." Matthews, June 5, 2023. https://www.matthews.com/

thought-leadership-update-on-the-car-wash-market/#:~:text=The%20 car%20wash%20market%20is,and%20in%202022%2C%20 %2438.4%20billion.

38. "U.S. Car Wash Services Market Size, Share & Trends Analysis Report by Type (Tunnels, Roll-over/In-bay, Self-service), by Mode of Payment (Cash Payment, Cashless Payment), by Region, And Segment Forecasts, 2023 - 2030." August 7, 2023. https://www.grandviewresearch.com/industry-analysis/us-car-wash-services-market#:~:text=According%20to%20a%20blog%20 by,handwashing%20in%20the%20last%20decade.

39. Mid-America Regional Council. "Wash Your Car the Right Way." https://cfpub.epa.gov/, n.d. https://cfpub.epa.gov/npstbx/files/KSMO_CarWashing.pdf.

40. Tardi, Carla. "Syndicate: Definition, How It Works, and Types of Syndicates." Investopedia, April 8, 2020. https://www.investopedia.com/terms/s/syndicate.asp#:~:text=Key%20Takeaways,the%20 potential%20for%20attractive%20returns.

41. First National Realty Partners. "What Is a Private Placement Memorandum (PPM) in Commercial Real Estate?" January 24, 2023. https://fnrpusa.com/blog/private-placement-memorandum-real-estate/.

42. Nareit. "Public Storage's 50-year Evolution Into the Self-storage Giant." February 21, 2024. https://www.reit.com/news/reit-magazine/november-december-2022/public-storages-50-year-evolution-self-storage-giant.

43. Nareit. "Public Storage's 50-year Evolution Into the Self-storage Giant." February 21, 2024. https://www.

reit.com/news/reit-magazine/november-december-2022/public-storages-50-year-evolution-self-storage-giant.

44. Nareit. "Public Storage's 50-year Evolution Into the Self-storage Giant." February 21, 2024. https://www.reit.com/news/reit-magazine/november-december-2022/public-storages-50-year-evolution-self-storage-giant.

45. "Opportunity Zones | Internal Revenue Service." n.d. https://www.irs.gov/credits-deductions/businesses/opportunity-zones.

46. "Certify and Maintain a Qualified Opportunity Fund | Internal Revenue Service." n.d. https://www.irs.gov/credits-deductions/businesses/certify-and-maintain-a-qualified-opportunity-fund#:~:text=A%20Qualified%20Opportunity%20Fund%20is,than%20another%20Qualified%20Opportunity%20Fund).

47. BlackRock. "Private Debt Primer - Institutional | BlackRock." n.d. https://www.blackrock.com/institutions/en-us/insights/private-debt-primer.

48. Davis, Chris, and Connor Emmert. "Private Equity Investing: What It Is and How You Can Invest." NerdWallet, October 18, 2023. https://www.nerdwallet.com/article/investing/private-equity-investments.

49. Wikipedia contributors, "Inflation Hedge." Wikipedia, October 6, 2023. https://en.wikipedia.org/wiki/Inflation_hedge.

50. "Qualified Small Business Stock (QSBS) Tax Rules - SmartAsset | SmartAsset." May 9, 2023. https://smartasset.com/taxes/qsbs.

51. Ganti, Akhilesh. "Angel Investor Definition and How It Works." Investopedia, September 29, 2023. https://www.investopedia.com/terms/a/angelinvestor.asp.

52. Howarth, Josh. "Startup Failure Rate Statistics (2024)." Exploding Topics (blog), November 3, 2023. https://explodingtopics.com/blog/startup-failure-stats.

53. Hudson, Marianne. "Studies Find Angels Significantly Impact Success of Funded Companies." Forbes, May 27, 2015. https://www.forbes.com/sites/mariannehudson/2015/05/27/studies-find-angels-significantly-impact-success-of-funded-companies/?sh=5af832912ca8.

54. CFI Team, "Equity Kicker." Corporate Finance Institute, October 19, 2023. https://corporatefinanceinstitute.com/resources/valuation/equity-kicker/.

55. Scott, Gordon. "Warrant Coverage: What It Is, Examples, and FAQs." Investopedia, May 20, 2022. https://www.investopedia.com/terms/w/warrantcoverage.asp#:~:text=A%20warrant%20coverage%20is%20simply,a%20company%2C%20not%20from%20traders.

56. Hall, Mark. "Unsexy but Thriving Businesses: The Hidden Opportunity Gifted to Us by Baby Boomers." Forbes, January 25, 2022. https://www.forbes.com/sites/markhall/2022/01/25/unsexy-but-thriving-businesses-the-hidden-opportunity-gifted-to-us-by-baby-boomers/?sh=614108334620.

57. CFI Team, "Roll up Strategy." Corporate Finance Institute, December 19, 2022. https://corporatefinanceinstitute.com/resources/valuation/roll-up-strategy/.

58. National Institute on Aging. "Long-Term Care Facilities: Assisted Living, Nursing Homes, and Other Residential Care." n.d. https://www.nia.nih.gov/health/assisted-living-and-nursing-homes/long-term-care-facilities-assisted-living-nursing-homes#nursing.

59. Kenton, Will. "Heavy Industry: Considerations for Large Scale Businesses." Investopedia, February 25, 2021. https://www.investopedia.com/terms/h/heavy_industry.asp#:~:text=

Heavy%20industry%20is%20a%20type,has%20lower%20barriers%20to%20entry.

60. U.S. Bureau of Labor Statistics. "U.S. Manufacturing Output, Hours Worked, and Productivity Recover From COVID-19." https://www.bls.gov/, October 27, 2022. https://www.bls.gov/opub/ted/2022/u-s-manufacturing-output-hours-worked-and-productivity-recover-from-covid-19.htm#:~:text=After%20the%20COVID%2D19%20pandemic,declines%20since%20World%20War%20II.

61. Marshall, Mike. "What Is Land Entitlement? | REtipster.com." REtipster, n.d. https://retipster.com/terms/land-entitlement/.

62. https://www.oxfordlearnersdictionaries.com/us/definition/english/carbon-credit.

63. Department of Conservation. "What Is Mine Reclamation?" https://www.conservation.ca.gov. Accessed February 22, 2024. https://www.conservation.ca.gov/dmr/SMARA%20Mines/reclamation/Pages/index.aspx.

64. "What Is a Conservation Easement? – National Conservation Easement Database | NCED." n.d. https://www.conservationeasement.us/what-is-a-conservation-easement/.

65. Hayes, Adam, "Stocks: What They Are, Main Types, How They Differ From Bonds." Investopedia, December 15, 2023. https://www.investopedia.com/terms/s/stock.asp.

66. Hayes, Adam, "Mutual Funds: Different Types and How They Are Priced." Investopedia, February 18, 2024. https://www.investopedia.com/terms/m/mutualfund.asp.

67. Beers, Brian. "Introduction to Exchange-Traded Funds (ETFs)." Investopedia, January 18, 2024. https://www.investopedia.com/articles/01/082901.asp#:~:text=Exchange%2Dtraded%20funds%20are%20investments,financial%20needs%20and%20investment%20goals.

68. The Organisation for Economic Co-operation and Development (OECD). "Residence/Citizenship by Investment Schemes." https://www.oecd.org/, n.d. https://www.oecd.org/tax/automatic-exchange/crs-implementation-and-assistance/residence-citizenship-by-investment/#:~:text=While%20residence%20and%20citizenship%20by,under%20the%20OECD%2FG20%20Common.

Find all the resources provided throughout the book in one easy to access place at cashflowmd.com. Discover tips, tricks, and actionable advice when it comes to making real-life investment decisions.

ABOUT THE AUTHOR

Dr. Daniel Bramer is both a physician and a successful serial entrepreneur. Since using real estate to help fund his way through medical school, he has been the principal on over $250 million of real estate and business transactions generating both active and passive income.

He graduated medical school with top honors and was inducted into the Alpha Omega Alpha Medical Honor Society during this time. He then went on to become board certified in Anesthesiology and received his post graduate certificate in Global Health from the London School of Hygiene and Tropical Medicine. His passion for the underserved leads him to work alongside non-governmental organizations (NGOs) and Ministries of Health worldwide to improve surgical and healthcare delivery in developing countries through training and education.

Since backing away from clinical medicine in 2013 after a life-changing medical diagnosis, he now devotes his time to helping other physicians and entrepreneurs achieve financial freedom, take back their time, and pursue a life of purpose.

He is blessed with a wonderful family including Jeanne, his wife of 22 years, and their four children Elizabeth, Max, Sam, and Isabella.

Printed in the USA
CPSIA information can be obtained
at www.ICGtesting.com
LVHW041346200924
791552LV00004B/887

9 781949 635324